BERNIE

Bill Aitken

Mondegreen Books

Mondegreen Books

Acknowledgements

Sincere thanks to all who helped me with this project - including, but not limited to Lindsay Aitken, Pat Aitken, Bill Bebb, John Beecher, John Cavanagh, Alexis Church, Bob Conduct, Jimmy Grant, Jeff Griffin, Nick Gomm, Paddy Kingsland, Annie Nightingale, Andy Peebles, Bev Phillips, Pete Ritzema and Julian Spear.

Author's Notes

I met Bernie Andrews in the 1970s, when I was a recording engineer and producer.

This book is not a biography, and it is not a historical document. This book tells a story based on the life of Bernie Andrews. This story is based on my own recollections, those of Bernie's friends and colleagues and recorded interviews with Bernie himself.

Many characters are non-fictional. The better known ones are obvious. Some characters are fictional. They are stereotypes which I have created to illustrate institutional attitudes and prejudices which were prevalent at the time. Any resemblance between these fictional characters and anyone living or dead is co-incidental.

In order to tell the most interesting story, I have sometimes taken minor liberties with location and chronology. However, if any parts of the story strike you as interesting, amusing or tragic, I have no doubt they are based in fact.

Bill Aitken – 2023

Mondegreen Books

Contents

Once In A Lifetime   1

Meet the Beatles   1

The Rolling Stones   54

Keep Your Head Down   76

The Turn of the Year   115

The British Invasion   137

A Frank Exchange   162

Into Top Gear   184

What's Going On?   202

Salvation   222

Rising Tensions   245

Floyd, Hendrix, Zeppelin, T Rex, Bowie et al   255

On Top of the World   265

Apocalypse   270

The Big If   285

A Band Called Queen   288

The Long Goodbye   297

Early Retirement   316

OBITUARY   328

Langham Place

BBC Broadcasting House and All Souls Langham Place
as viewed from The Langham – circa 1960s

Once In A Lifetime

Author's note: *I wanted to set the scene by quoting the first verse of **Once In A Lifetime** by **Talking Heads**. However, I wasn't able to get permission from the publisher. If you can Google it, please do. Then skip to the beginning of the story. Hopefully, this context will make the opening line of the story seem a bit less prosaic.*

*If you don't have access to Google, the first verse of **Once In A Lifetime** by **Talking Heads** alludes, in an expressive way, to those memorable moments in our lives when we become conscious of the fact that we are where we are, not because we planned it that way, but because that's just the way it turned out. And then, on reflection, we might ask ourselves how these things have come to pass. Hopefully, this explanation will make what comes next a bit more meaningful.*

Meet the Beatles

"How the fuck did I get here?" Bernie mused to himself.

"I beg your pardon!"

Startled, Bernie spun round on his heel and found himself staring a stern looking gentleman in the face. Wrong side of middle age. Dark trilby. Black horn-rimmed spectacles. Grey overcoat and trousers. Well-polished pair of black brogues and carrying a briefcase. Unremarkable. In a word.

This unremarkable gentleman had just exited the hallowed portal of All Souls Church in Langham Place, London W1, where he had encountered Bernie on the front steps. Stock still. Staring across the road at the monolithic facade of BBC Broadcasting House. Muttering. It suddenly dawned on Bernie that, rather than musing to himself, he had mused out loud.

Oh dear! He had already made his appraisal of the stern looking gentleman. *'Officer class,'* he had swiftly concluded, making sure that this time, he was keeping his musings to himself.

Instinctively, he dealt with the situation in the way he had always done when dealing with those in authority, whether at school, in the RAF during National Service, or at the General Post Office, his last place of employment prior to joining the BBC. And the gentleman looked as if he considered himself to be in a position of authority.

"Oh… Sorry…" said Bernie, adopting his most reasonable demeanour, smiling engagingly and behaving in an oblivious manner. "I must have been talking to myself," he remarked amiably.

He had learned from experience that on committing a faux pas, the best chance of recovering the situation was to convince those on the receiving end that they were mistaken, and that the faux pas had never happened. And he would do this simply by acting, often surprisingly successfully, as if the faux pas had never happened.

It was difficult for Bernie to read his inquisitor's reaction to his anodyne response. The older generation had endured a great deal during the last war, only twenty year's prior, and quite a few had bitter memories of the previous one as well - closely followed by the Wall Street Crash and the Great Depression. The first half of the Twentieth Century had not been a barrel of laughs. Those who had lived through it had learned to be stoic, and to keep their emotions to themselves.

His eyes fixed Bernie's through his horn-rimmed glasses until, concluding that he would receive no further utterance, he averted his gaze and, without another word, strode down the steps and across the road towards the front door of Broadcasting House.

As he watched him go, Bernie wondered who he was. Head of Religious Broadcasting? He knew the BBC had a Head of Religious Broadcasting, but he had never seen him. Not his line of territory. He chuckled at the thought. It was plausible that the Head of Religious Broadcasting would drop in to have a chat with his other boss before setting off for work, even at this ungodly hour. At least it was ungodly to Bernie. He'd dragged himself out of bed half an hour early to make sure he had plenty of time to savour this moment.

Bernie had no degree of any kind - never mind Oxbridge. He couldn't read music and had no knowledge of how to play any kind of musical instrument. He had no *'old boy'* contacts in show business in general, and the music business in particular. And he had never been a BBC Radio Studio Manager - the recognised and, until now, necessary step before progressing into production. So, he asked himself, again, how on earth it was that he had managed to secure his new position, at the age of 29, as the youngest ever radio producer in the history of the BBC Light Programme Popular Music Department?

The surreal nature of the occasion was heightened by the fact that today, he would take charge of his very first recording session. That session was for *Saturday Club* - the only programme on BBC Radio which offered younger listeners a regular and reliable opportunity to hear the kind of music they craved. A programme which Bernie had listened to avidly long before he joined the BBC. A whole two hours of skiffle, rock'n'roll, trad jazz and top twenty favourites starting every Saturday morning at 10 o'clock.

Today, he was producing a new beat group called the Beatles. He'd heard them a few times during the previous year, broadcasting from the BBC Manchester Playhouse. One of the producers up there, Peter Pilbeam, had put them on a programme called *Teenagers' Turn*, and Bernie had immediately taken notice.

3

They were different. Definitely not one of the army of Elvis impersonators who would turn up with depressing regularity at the local Palais de Danse. They didn't seem to have a front man at all and took it in turns on lead vocals. Very egalitarian. When they started on *Teenagers' Turn*, they had no recording contract. They were just one of many aspiring local groups lucky enough to be given some national airtime courtesy of the BBC Northern Regional Service.

Since then, they'd managed to get a record deal with Parlophone. Not the most glamorous of labels. Their first record, *Love Me Do*, had scraped into the lower end of the top twenty, but as soon as Bernie heard their follow up, *Please Please Me*, he knew it was a smash. So it was that, in the early days of 1963, *Please Please Me* was already shooting up the charts and Bernie was really looking forward to hearing what else this new group had to offer.

He set off with purpose across the road, following the footsteps of the *(possibly)* Head of Religious Broadcasting, towards the monumental art deco edifice in Portland Place, London W1 - and then on through the very doors that the great and the good, from King George V to Charlie Chaplin, from Elizabeth Taylor to the Dalai Lama, had passed at one time or another on their way into Broadcasting House.

But today, it was he, Bernard Oliver Andrews, a working class bloke from Eltham, who would choose what was to be broadcast. Or at least approximately fifteen minutes worth of what the listeners would hear during *Saturday Club* on the BBC Light Programme in a few days' time.

Bernie pushed open one side of the massive pair of bronzed doors and stepped through into the marbled reception area. He had walked across this space so many times before when he was a humble engineer working in the Tape Recording Unit that he had come to take the palatial surroundings for granted.

But this was his first time as a producer. Someone with editorial control over the BBC's output. Or at least a small part of it. So he took the opportunity to view his surroundings afresh. He even smiled at the prominent inscription, high on the opposite wall, which hit every visitor, first time, right between the eyes. Bernie didn't read Latin, but he had been told that it said something like *'This temple of the Arts and Muses is dedicated to Almighty God... blah, blah, blah...'*

He nodded to the commissionaire, the World War II veteran whose job it was to keep the building secure. The commissionaire - military bearing, clad in smart black serge, white shirt, black tie, white topped cap with a black peak - nodded back. He knew Bernie's face well. No need to check Bernie's BBC ID card. The unwritten protocol was that when the commissionaire got to know your face, he would let you pass without bothering.

This ambiguity had led to some questionable admissions over the years. Bernie was convinced that if a Russian spy turned up with a bomb in his briefcase, he would just as easily sail through what passed for security at the entrance to BH - the iconic headquarters of our beloved national broadcasting service - so long as he was dressed in a similar *'senior management'* style as the stern gentleman he had encountered earlier on the steps of All Souls, and he displayed a similar air of superiority as he swept past.

But front door security was the last thing on Bernie's mind as he made for the lift at the rear of the foyer. He pressed SB - another BBC abbreviation. Broadcasting House boasted no less than three floors below ground floor level: the lower ground floor (LG), the basement (B), and the last stop was SB - the sub-basement. The doors closed behind him. He turned round to face them once more, waiting patiently for the lift to descend gracefully and bottom out with a slight jolt.

When the doors finally drew apart, Bernie found himself stepping onto another planet.

Gone were the high ceilings, the marble, the statuary and the Latin inscription, to be replaced by the close proximity of the opposite wall of a claustrophobic corridor rendered in the drabbest of institutional, matt grey-green paintwork. A prosaic sign on the wall read, *'In Case Of Fire, Break Glass'*. The sign was positioned beside a bright red cast iron box mounted on the wall. In the box, behind glass, was an emergency plunger. At the end of a stout piece of string attached to the box dangled a little brass hammer, forlorn. If BH reception was palatial, the sub-basement was the antithesis.

Bernie hurried out of the lift, oblivious to the industrial surroundings. He trod a well-used path, following the air ducts, the water pipes and the various electrical cables mounted on brackets high on both sides of the corridor walls.

The sub-basement was home to the heating and ventilation control plant for the whole building, whose footprint spanned an entire block. The technical facilities were of the same early 1930s vintage as the rest of the establishment and were as robust as the reception area was palatial, but while the foyer was still relatively pristine, the boiler room facilities, some thirty odd years on, were not standing up quite so well to the test of time.

As he rounded the corner, he saw a striking, dark haired figure in a fashionably cut suit, in the process of marshalling a heavy and awkward Vox AC 30 bass guitar amplifier through the door of Studio S2.

"Let me hold the door for you," said Bernie, "It's a fire door and the springs are pretty vicious".

"Ta very much." said the smart young man with the full mop of dark hair.

Having negotiated the doorway, he put the amplifier down carefully and held out his hand.

"I'm Paul," he said, a broad smile on his face. Bernie smiled back and shook his hand.

"I'm Bernie Andrews, and I'm producing the session today."

"Right. So who's the other guy?" Paul motioned over his shoulder towards a short, balding, bespectacled gentleman wearing a white shirt with a dark tie. He was connecting a long, thick, grey cable to a large, heavy, brown microphone. This diminutive figure also wore a pair of light grey flannels with finely engineered creases which would have won the heart of a drill sergeant. Bernie's heart sank.

"That's Dave. The studio manager."

Dave Bisley. Big band aficionado - preferably American big bands: Ellington, Basie... Ted Heath or John Dankworth at a push... Tolerated vocalists, so long as they were accompanied by what he considered to be a sophisticated big band accompaniment: Ella Fitzgerald, Frank Sinatra... Cleo Laine at a push... Nothing wrong with that. Except that, if a musical performance of any description didn't meet Dave Bisley's highly selective parameters, it was crap. At least according to one D. Bisley Esquire. Nothing wrong with that, either, so long as he kept his opinions to himself and did the job he was paid for, to the best of his abilities - even though the material he was working on might not happen to be exactly to his taste. But he didn't. And what was worse, he was quite likely to telegraph his attitude to anyone he came in contact with - including the artists.

The other boys in the group were already setting up their kit as directed by Bisley. Paul walked over.

"This is Bernie Andrews, the producer," he announced. "Bernie, this is John. John plays guitar. This is George, lead guitar, and the drummer over there is Ringo".

Bernie pressed the flesh, and explained,

"We'd like to record four numbers today. You've done a BBC Radio session before?"

"Only live radio broadcasts in front of an audience - until now,' said the one called John, "Can we mime like on the telly?" he joshed.

Everyone in the business knew that *Saturday Club* sessions were specially recorded at the BBC. Groups who had been heavily supported by session musicians on their records could often find BBC sessions difficult, and might try to persuade the production staff to copy the record onto tape, pretending it was a proper BBC session. That was a no-no.

The BBC was strictly bound by a commercial agreement with the Musicians Union which insisted on limiting the number of records the BBC could play every day. If you were a big star, you had a better chance of getting your new record played as part of the BBC's quota of *'needletime'*. Otherwise, if you wanted to promote your new record on the BBC, you would have to come in to a BBC studio and recreate it.

This arrangement was a job creation scheme intended to generate work for session musicians - almost exclusively those who worked in orchestras and dance bands. Lesser known groups like the Beatles didn't give a toss about job-creation schemes, but they were obliged to re-record their latest releases at the BBC in order to get them heard on the radio - and they were obliged to do it all in a fraction of the time they spent making the actual record. However, there were benefits for the listeners.

The youthful *Saturday Club* audience was very switched on, and would recognise straight away if what they were hearing was a record, or a special BBC session which had been done without the aid of all the tricks that record producers and engineers got up to in commercial recording studios. Part of the fascination of turning on the radio on a Saturday morning was to hear how the latest bands might sound - off the record so to speak - like at a gig. Some artists did better than others. BBC sessions tended to sort out the wheat from the chaff.

The one called John also had a mop of dark hair. In fact, they all did. The prevailing music business cliché at that time was that a pop group would have a lead singer sporting a pompadour hairstyle in reverence to the undisputed King of Rock'n'Roll, Elvis Presley. But this lot didn't even have a lead singer, and the uniformity of their conspicuously unconventional haircuts was something of a surprise. To the uncharitable, descriptors like *'fringe'* and *'bowl haircut'* might come to mind. Bernie could see that their hairstyles were well cut and nicely groomed - but very different. He quite liked this new look. It was innovative. Fun, even.

John, now with a more earnest air about him, asked,

"This is our first proper session recording at the BBC. Can we do overdubs?"

"No problem," said Bernie.

"Time permitting," Dave Bisley chipped in, as he busied himself adjusting a mic over the drum kit.

"Good morning Dave," said Bernie, sighing inwardly.

"Morning," said Bisley, brusquely, without looking round.

"Everything will be fine," continued Bernie, ignoring the interruption. "We'll sort it out as we go along. So what numbers do you want to record?"

John looked around. *"Love Me Do* and *Please Please Me*?.."

The others nodded.

"What else?.."

"Some Other Guy?.." suggested Paul.

A murmur of approval.

"Keep Your Hands Off My Baby?..". chipped in George.

No dissent.

"Great." said Bernie, thinking to himself *'that was easy.'* He flipped open the cover of his spiral bound BBC notebook, and wrote down the titles.

"Both your A-sides are Lennon-McCartney compositions. *'Keep Your Hands Off My Baby'* is Little Eva, so I guess that's Goffin and King. *'Some Other Guy'* is Richie Barrett?.. Isn't it?.. But I don't know who wrote that one."

John approached and held out his hand once more to shake Bernie's. Hesitantly, Bernie reciprocated, somewhat mystified.

"Congratulations Bernie!" he said with a broad, good natured grin on his face, placing his left hand, in affirmation, on Bernie's shoulder. "You have passed."

Bernie was none the wiser. In his unmistakable, but well-articulated Liverpool accent John continued expansively,

"You have proved beyond all reasonable doubt that there is at least one person in the BBC who actually knows something about today's popular music repertoire."

He released Bernie's hand. Dave Bisley scoffed, audibly. No one noticed.

"'*Some Other Guy*' was written by Richie Barrett in collaboration with Jerry Leiber and Mike Stoller. So, Bernie, please write that down in your BBC notebook before you forget."

'*Cheeky bastard,*' thought Bernie. '*This John Lennon is supercilious, sarcastic, impertinent...*'

Bernie took an immediate liking to him. He grinned back.

"Well, thank you very much Mr Lennon. Now if you don't mind, I will leave you gentlemen to finish setting up here in the studio, while I retire to the control room in order to prepare myself for your imminent performance."

Bernie needed the names of the writers of the songs as well as the names of the artists performing them, so that everyone who was entitled got the royalty payments they were due from the BBC when the recordings eventually went out on the radio. Having got what he needed, he turned and made for the control room door with a smile on his face, pleased that he had established a rapport of sorts with the band.

Inside the control room, Nick Crossland was already setting up the tape recorders.

"Hi Bernie," he chirped.

"Hello Nick," replied Bernie. "How's it going?"

"Fine. Soon be ready to go."

Bernie flopped down in his chair, put his notebook and pen on the mixing desk and retrieved his stopwatch from his pocket.

"Did you see the Beverly Hillbillies on the box last night?" he asked.

"Must have missed that."

"That Granny cracks me up."

"ITV, isn't it?"

"Yes," said Bernie, wondering why that was germane to the discussion.

He was very happy to watch anything on the *'other side'*, whether people considered it lowbrow or not. And he was also very happy to put up with the adverts in order to enjoy the very welcome variety in programming that ITV - the BBC's only domestic competitor - had to offer. In radio, the BBC still held a monopoly.

Bursts of high pitched tone emanated from the tape recorders as Nick twiddled knobs and calibrated the tape machines. He was too preoccupied for a conversation. Bernie doodled on the notebook with his pen and gazed out into the vast expanse of sub-basement studio S2. What a dump! Ceiling too high. Proportions way too big. Not at all suitable for a beat group.

And the decor? There wasn't any. It was an industrial shell. Walls completely covered from ceiling to floor in relentless geometrically aligned columns of acoustic enclosures of some indeterminate lightish colour. If asked what colour they actually were, he would probably have said something like *'dull.'*

High up on one wall, an air vent had been taped over. Presumably, the noise from the extraction fan had caused an acoustic problem on a session at some time or other. However, it must have been a while ago, because part of the tape had come away, and the loose end flapped, gently, in the breeze. Clearly, no one could be bothered to do anything about it. Not surprising, since the operation would involve a precarious trip up a tall ladder. Better left well alone.

The floor was constructed of best quality wooden boards. Acoustically very reflective. Great if you're recording the Palm Court Orchestra or the Big Ben Banjo Band, but fashions had changed. The studio had been constructed within the same subterranean complex as the boiler room - and to the modern ear the studio also sounded like a boiler room. Ideas relating to acoustic design had changed a bit since the 1930s. By the 1960s, the studio manager mixing the sound in sub-basement studio S2 had to be very careful.

Bernie shifted his attention back to the band. They had a guy helping them in with the equipment, but that hadn't stopped them all getting stuck in, moving their amplifiers and instruments from place to place. Bernie fretted that their physical exertion might cause undue wear and tear to their clothing. They were dressed in identical stage suits. Nicely tailored. Mid-grey. Italian cut. Looked like mohair. Expensive. He looked at his own suit. Black. Crimplene. Cheap. Ill fitting. He'd have to do something about that. But what? He couldn't afford a made-to-measure mohair suit. He quite fancied a sports jacket, or a blazer.

Something a bit more casual. But when he first joined the engineering department of the BBC he had been left in no doubt that a suit was the thing.

His fellow engineers on the initial training course at Evesham would soon disperse to all corners of the United Kingdom. Many of them would go to regional network centres in big cities like Birmingham and Belfast, while others would end up in the sticks, working on transmitter sites in places like Wenvoe or Kirk o'Shotts. Bernie had set his sights on London. So when they were told that their course included a day trip to Broadcasting House in the capital itself, he was very excited.

Then they were warned. They were advised that they should be on the lookout for staff wearing suede shoes or corduroy trousers. These would be production staff, and they were told to stay well clear. Bernie quite liked the idea of suede shoes and corduroys.

He had been disappointed when he eventually joined the production staff in the Popular Music Department. The dress code didn't seem much different to how the engineers dressed in the main switching centre. There were some members of staff who seemed to get away with unconventional garb. As it turned out, those who sported conspicuously flamboyant clothing often seemed to hail from the drama department. Although, there were one or two in the classical music department who might wear a brightly coloured cravat from time to time. That looked a bit poncy to Bernie. Trying too hard to emulate the upper classes, he thought.

Eventually, his sartorial reverie was interrupted. All was ready and after a brief run through, Dave Bisley pronounced himself ready to do a take. Bernie wasn't at all happy with the sound balance. But he thought they should put one down and get some feedback from the band.

After the red light was turned off at the end of the take, he put the talkback key down,

"Come and have a listen."

"Since when do we have time for playbacks?" objected Bisley.

"I always give the artists a chance for feedback," said Bernie.

"Not a good idea," came the laconic reply.

As the Beatles carefully put down their instruments, Bernie reflected on the ethos of BBC Radio production methods as practiced by Messrs. D. Bisley & Co.

Most of what was produced in BBC studios at that time could be classed as *'wallpaper music'.* A *(sometimes)* pleasant background noise played by in-house BBC orchestras and dance-bands, designed to relieve the tedium for millions of radio listeners across the nation. A familiar tune to hum or whistle along with as they performed their otherwise mind-numbing daily routines.

Like any other product, success depended on an efficient production line. Professional session musicians were hired to read the music that was put in front of them, reproduce the notes as instructed in the musical code, and then move on, as quickly as possible, to the next session.

The last thing on their minds was the opportunity to listen to a playback. What a waste of time! These musicians had no emotional investment in what they had just performed. What was front and centre of their minds was how quickly they could get out of one studio, and move on to the next studio where they could earn their next session fee.

And it was the task of Studio Managers like Dave Bisley to ensure that nothing interfered with production. So long as all the right notes were played in the right order, and everything was *(more or less)* audible to the listener, scant regard was paid to the subtleties of acoustic balance, never mind the nuances of musical performance and interpretation.

However, the advent of the electric guitar was in the process of radically changing the sonic landscape of popular music - as were the production techniques employed by the more switched on class of record producer. But BBC staffers saw no reason why these upstarts should behave any differently to the average, disinterested participant on a BBC recording session.

Bernie had long since ceased to be shocked by the insensitivity of the BBC system. During his days in the Tape Recording Unit, he had watched countless young hopefuls nervously conform to orders barked by staff producers and studio managers. These newcomers were routinely rushed into the studio. Then, after they had duly performed as directed, as promptly as they had been rushed in, they were rushed out again. They wouldn't have any idea what the recording sounded like until their session went out on the radio. By that stage, if they weren't happy with the results, well... that ship had long since sailed.

With listening audiences measured in the millions, the BBC enjoyed immense power, so, if emerging artists were given the opportunity to promote themselves on the radio, the BBC production regime was the regime up with which they were obliged to put. Would-be pop stars knew only too well that this might be their one and only chance to impress and advance their career. On the other hand, if the session failed, their career might fail with it. Not that the likes of Dave Bisley gave a moment's thought to anyone's career other than their own.

Bernie was determined that things were going to change.

By this time, the group were trooping into the control room. Bernie nodded to Nick to start the playback. Everyone listened intently and at the final chord, the room fell deadly silent.

"Any comments boys?" Bernie asked.

"Well, on the record, the bass and bass drum are really punchy," said Paul, looking at the others for some support. They nodded.

Then John pitched in, "Yeah, and the whole sound isn't as tight as the record."

"How long did you take to make the record?" Bisley enquired.

Bernie could sense an argument coming on. He interrupted, hastily,

"Look, I'm sure we can have another go, and tweak the sound a bit." He turned to Bisley, "OK Dave?"

Bisley sat, arms folded, in sullen silence.

The band mumbled their acquiescence and started out to the studio once more. John was the last to leave. Just before he disappeared, he turned and delivered his parting shot.

"Our amps are all lined up facing against the wall in a line, and we usually play facing each other so we can hear everything better. Maybe you could have a look at that too?"

Then he was gone.

"How about it Dave?"

"How about what?"

"Taking account of their comments and having another go?"

"If you want four numbers recorded during this session we don't have time for all this prima donna stuff."

"I'm happy to take the risk, Dave. All the risks are on me."

"But what do these musical illiterates know about sound production? Anyway, the material is rubbish. I'm amazed you think it's worth broadcasting."

Bernie had expected difficulties, especially with one Dave Bisley, but this unwarranted bullshit was wearing his patience thin.

"Look Dave, I am politely requesting that you act on the feedback from the band and try changing the layout along the lines they have requested. And while you're at it, can you please do anything you can to mitigate the effects of the boomy acoustics in this studio?"

Bisley's face reddened. He sat for a moment before speaking in an unnaturally controlled manner.

"I have been an audio professional for over ten years, and I am also a seasoned musician. I know my job, and if you want this session to reach a satisfactory conclusion within the time available, I advise you, very strongly, to accept the sound mix I am offering and get on with the recording without any further interruptions."

'What a wanker.' thought Bernie.

"I hear what you're saying Dave, but I've decided to try something different today. So, please. Can we get on with it?"

"This is outrageous." spluttered Bisley. "You clearly don't have any use for my experience and skills - never mind my advice... I might as well go back to the office and let Nick here use this shambles as a training session."

Bernie chose his words very carefully.

"If that's how you feel about it Dave, I respect your decision. Please, feel free to have the morning off." Then, after a judicious pause, he added, "If you want to..."

"Right!" Bisley exploded.

He gathered up his professional belongings, dumping them into his briefcase, while Bernie looked on, detached, and Nick looked on, aghast.

As he made for the door, Bernie noticed that his pace gradually slowed until, on reaching the door, he paused. Clearly, the wanker was having second thoughts.

"If that's your last word then?.." he offered.

"I think the last word was yours," Bernie retorted. The door swung shut.

*****

"What are we going to do now?" asked Nick, looking worried.

"We're going to do exactly as Dave suggested. You're going to rearrange the layout in the studio so it's how the band wants it and then you're going to sit down and mix the sound."

"Hadn't we better phone the office first, and clear it with them?"

The idea of any kind of communication between himself and the Programme Operations Manager hadn't occurred to Bernie. He judiciously slipped the phone off the hook.

19

"No need for that Nick. You may be a junior, but they gave you a go on the Jack Bentley Trio last week. Sounded OK to me."

"How did you know about that?"

"I was passing on my way to Maida Vale 5, and when I saw it was somebody new twiddling the knobs in 4, I sneaked in to the back of the control room and had a listen."

"Yes, but piano, double bass and drums is a bit different to this lot. I've never done a beat group before."

"There's always a first time, Nick. And I know you've got those gadgets in your bag. Those tobacco tins with home-made electronic filters in them? You can put them to good use too."

"I got carpeted for that Bernie. I was told not to use them again. They're not authorised BBC technical equipment."

"Well, I'm the producer, and if the BBC is not prepared to give us the kind of equipment which is now in everyday use in commercial recording studios, then we have a duty to the licence payer to do everything possible to provide for ourselves what the Luddites in the Capital Projects Department are inappropriately withholding from us. That's how we'll get the job done properly. Even if it means using your tobacco tins. I'll take the flak. And I'll operate the tape machines too. I haven't forgotten how to do that. So, if you want to take this opportunity, what are you waiting for?"

Nick needed no further encouragement. He flew into the studio and was transformed into a veritable whirlwind as he helped the band rearrange themselves and their instruments in the way they wanted. Bernie saw him talking to Ringo, and after a brief discussion the front skin of the bass drum was whipped off and the folded up bass drum cover was stuffed up against the remaining rear skin. When everyone was tucked in, Nick pulled out all the acoustic screens available and placed them to best effect.

Once back in the control room, he retrieved various home-made electronic filters from his bag and hastily plugged them in. Time was running short, but Bernie didn't put any pressure on Nick. He was getting things done as fast as he could and Bernie was very interested to hear what difference Nick's efforts would make. After a couple of runs through, the band seemed more relaxed. To Bernie's ear, the sound was much improved.

"Let's go for a take then."

"OK."

Just then, Bernie noticed some horsing around in the studio. The antics seemed to involve some sort of variant of pass the parcel. He immediately sussed what was going on.

"Hang on a minute!" he said, getting up and making for the studio.

When he got there, Ringo, who had just retrieved the parcel from the floor, lobbed it back to John with the warning,

"BBC bombs away!"

A BBC toilet roll, fresh in its wrapper, hit John square on the head. Laughs all round.

All toilet rolls purchased by the BBC bore the proprietary insignia of our esteemed national institution on every single sheet. For an outsider, this was truly remarkable - if not ridiculous. It wasn't every day you got to wipe your arse on the BBC. Bernie assumed the branding was to discourage pilfering, although he wondered why on earth anyone would want to steal them. Just a year or two later, Martha, the lead singer of the Tamla Motown girl group, the Vandellas, would publicly cite two major dislikes she had about British culture: one was warm beer, and the other was BBC toilet rolls - which she said were *'what we Americans would call wax paper.'* Yuk!

As Bernie approached, John quietened down, like a schoolboy caught in the act. Bernie, grim faced, held out his hand. John, looking contrite, placed the toilet roll in Bernie's hand.

"I'll have to report this, you know."

Silence reigned. Bernie stared intently at John. Then he could bear it no longer, and burst out laughing. Great hilarity ensued.

Bernie turned to go and, as he went, lobbed the toilet roll back over his head. It was a well-judged throw as John was able to catch it, one-handed, accompanied by a round of sarcastic cheers.

"There's only one thing I've got to say to you, Bernie Andrews..." John shouted, waving the bog roll in the air as Bernie departed.

"Yer a swine!.."

More whoops and laughter.

The atmosphere in the control room was quite different when the band came in to hear the next playback. Bernie had never heard so many Liverpool accents in a single room at any one time. He had encountered a few Scousers during his time in the Air Force, but Liverpool accents were not common down South, and definitely not familiar within the confines of Broadcasting House. If northern English accents were heard at all on the BBC they usually emanated from stereotypical characters in a *'trouble at t'mill'* melodrama, or to a northern radio comedian like the Clitheroe Kid.

While the accents were unfamiliar, the voices around Bernie were clear and articulate. They were also a lot more forthcoming than the first time around. All agreed that things had improved, and Ringo pronounced himself happy with the bass drum sound. The general consensus was that, while the overall result wasn't as polished as the record, it *'felt good'* and was ok to go out a couple of times on *Saturday Club.*

Then Bernie asked, as they were short of time, if it would be possible to run through the remaining tracks back-to-back, without the band checking each playback. He accompanied this request with a promise that they would get the chance to check all the tracks after the final vocal overdubs, and, if they didn't like any of them, he wouldn't broadcast them. To his relief, all was agreed.

Before they restarted, Bernie asked Nick, "Do you think we've got enough time on the clock to record all the tracks and overdubs? I'd rather cut a number in order to get quality rather than quantity."

"You're in luck." said Nick. "There are no other sessions booked in here today, and I have a long break after this until an edit suite at 4 o'clock, so I can work into lunchtime if you want?"

"Good man. You'll join me afterwards in the club where I'll treat you to lunch and a pint?"

"Definitely!"

*****

After a late lunch in the Langham consisting of ham and cheese in the Salad Bar, Bernie and Nick made their way along the corridor to the BBC Club.

From some viewing points, the Langham, situated just across Langham Place from All Souls Church and Broadcasting House, resembles a baroque wedding cake. It was constructed in Victorian times and has a colourful history.

Opened by Prince Edward in 1865, the Langham Hotel was the most advanced of its time, boasting a hundred water closets, thirty six bathrooms and the first hydraulic lifts in London. It was one of the first establishments to install electric lighting and, at the time, was highly fashionable. Clientele included Mark Twain, Napoleon III and Oscar Wilde. In two of Conan Doyle's Sherlock Holmes novels, some scenes were set in the Langham, and during its Belle Epoch days, it earned something of a reputation as a high-class knocking shop.

After the First World War, the hotel was hit hard by the Great Depression and during World War II, after suffering bomb damage, it went out of business. Then, the BBC took it over, turning much of it into offices and training facilities along with an operational studio on the ground floor.

Some of the hotel rooms were retained as overnight accommodation for production staff who were scheduled for early starts or late finishes. *'Farming Today'* went out at 6:00 am in the morning. If your name was down for that particular broadcast, you were glad of a basic, but comfortable bedroom in the Langham the night before, in order to avoid a barbaric early rise and a bleary-eyed commute into work the next day.

The only downsides were the grunts and groans of the original - now antique - central heating system, and, if you were superstitious, you might worry about the unpredictable attentions of the Langham ghost.

This semi-transparent lady was said to wander around the mezzanine floor without any feet. The favourite explanation being that when the BBC took over the building, one of the few renovations involved raising the floor level of the mezzanine about twelve inches or so, thus cutting off from view the lady's no doubt shapely ankles.

Bernie wasn't superstitious, but he had occasionally wasted a few moments wondering about the philosophical conundrums posed by those reported sightings. If supernatural forces were powerful enough for the lady to manifest herself during the small hours, why weren't they powerful enough for her to be manifested in her entirety, and not be partially obscured by a mere man-made obstacle. It seemed a highly contradictory contradiction of the laws of physics to Bernie.

He and Nick ambled along the corridor towards that most popular wing of the Langham which was home to the BBC Club.

Under BBC ownership, the building had become dowdy, and the various departmental sign boards along the way contributed to a character that was functional rather than aesthetic.

The suite of rooms that housed the club itself bordered on the shabby and Bernie wouldn't have been at all surprised if many of the architectural features - dark brown mahogany panelling, skirting boards, dados and window frames, together with the faded flock wallpaper - dated back to the original. But he liked the place. It was like a comfortable pair of old slippers.

He scanned the room for faces. One of the things he enjoyed was that it wasn't just BBC staff who frequented the club. You were just as likely to see a film star, or a politician, or a captain of industry rubbing shoulders with the hoi polloi. And the celebrities enjoyed the fact that they were safe from unwanted attention in these unprepossessing surroundings.

Of course everyone had a good look around to see who happened to be in on any particular day. But no member of staff would dream of accosting a public figure just for the sake of it. Unless you were working on a programme with a well-known personality, once you recognised their presence, you would leave them well alone and you would refrain from staring. Even if you were working with someone famous, there was a strict *'no autographs, no photographs'* policy. In all his time at the BBC, Bernie had never known anyone transgress those unwritten laws.

On that particular day, Bernie was not disappointed. Propped up at the bar, sipping his pint, was Rupert Davies, the middle aged actor who was best known for playing the lead in the hugely popular television series, Maigret. The opening titles featured a shadowy Maigret in a moody, nocturnal, Parisian street scene, striking a match against the wall in order to light his pipe.

What did disappoint Bernie was that Rupert wasn't smoking his pipe. But he could see that, in any case, he would have had trouble trying to strike a match on the papered wall.

Having collected a pint of lager for Nick, and a gin and tonic with ice and a slice of lemon for himself, they retired to a quiet table in the corner.

"Well that was all a bit weird this morning, wasn't it?" said Nick after they had settled down.

"In what way?" asked Bernie.

Nick didn't know how to answer that. He thought for a bit, trying to frame things as diplomatically as he could.

"Well... The way Dave got upset... and left the way he did."

"Didn't do you any harm, did it?"

"What do you mean?"

"I thought you did a great job. So did the band."

"Yes... but..."

"What else matters Nick? We're here to make sure that the licence payers get their money's worth. And we do that by booking the bands they want to hear, and recording them, not just to our own satisfaction, but also to the band's satisfaction. So that they feel they are being presented to the listeners in the best possible way."

Nick nodded.

"I think the way you handled this morning's session is a huge feather in your cap, and I'll make sure everybody knows about it."

This cheered Nick up considerably. Then he asked Bernie, "How did you find the selection process for your job?"

"You mean how did a lowly engineer from Eltham manage to wangle a job in production?" said Bernie.

"I didn't mean it like that," said Nick, a bit miffed. Bernie chuckled.

"Tape recorders."

"Tape recorders?"

Nick's brow furrowed.

"Yes. Tape recorders are machines and machines are looked after by engineers. So when the BBC got tape recorders, the engineering department claimed ownership of this new-fangled apparatus. But when production saw all the clever things you could do with tape recorders, the dividing lines between engineering and production got very hazy. So engineers like me got the chance to work much more closely with producers like Jimmy Grant."

"When I was working with him on *Saturday Club*, he found my knowledge of skiffle, jazz, blues and rock'n'roll very useful - particularly if American artists like Little Richard or Gene Vincent happened to be on a UK tour."

"But how come you know so much about all that stuff?"

"Well the BBC doesn't run courses on it," Bernie laughed.

"When I was in the Air Force I was a radio engineer and I used to rig up my own radio receivers. I could pick up stuff from all round the world. I got particularly hooked on the American Forces Network - you know, the radio station for US troops stationed in Europe. Loads of jazz, rhythm and blues, country, gospel... The music's just so different. New and exciting. You can feel it. So different to what we have here in the UK."

"And you just asked personnel about a job?"

"Wouldn't have dreamt of it. Jimmy Grant was on holiday for a couple of weeks, and John Kingdon was standing in for him on *Saturday Club*. He doesn't know much about current pop music, so I helped him out. He was very grateful. It was John who told me there was a job going in the Pop Music Department and he said I should apply for it. I thought he was kidding. But he kept nagging me. So I applied, and to my amazement I got it. I suspect John, Jimmy and a few others must have put in a good word for me."

Bernie paused a while. "The Dave Bisleys of the world will never forgive me... As far as they're concerned, I'm a Johnny come lately."

Just then, Lesley's dulcet tones resonated on the club's public address system. Lesley - short, grey-haired, and with a bit of a stoop - had been the BBC Club commissionaire as long as Bernie could remember. He was regarded affectionately by the regulars and was never shy of an opportunity to pick up his microphone, which he guarded jealously. Those of a mischievous nature had been known to phone up the club on a regular basis to request Lesley to page *'Mr Hugh Janus to the phone, please. Mr Hugh Janus.'* just so they could hear these absurd announcements on the PA in a voice that was as nasal as it was pompous.

"Bernard Andrews to the phone, please. Bernard Andrews."

Bernie was not surprised to hear the summons. He guessed who was phoning him and why. He didn't rush to answer the call.

If staff were taking a break, but were urgently required back in their place of work for whatever reason, the club phone was the most efficient way to call them back across the road. Bernie couldn't see any reason why he should need to be contacted urgently, and if the call was from the source he suspected... Well... They could wait.

Bernie retrieved a packet of Players and a lighter from his trouser pocket, pulled out a cigarette and lit up, taking a long drag.

"Aren't you going to answer that?" asked Nick.

Bernie shrugged,

"I suppose so."

He strolled over to the phone booth, cigarette in hand, and picked up the large, black, Bakelite telephone receiver.

"Bernie Andrews," he announced.

"Ah... You *are* there." said an unfamiliar voice.

"Who am I talking to?" enquired Bernie.

"It's the A. P. O. M. here," said an officious voice.

"That spells Apom," said Bernie, "Which doesn't help much. What I meant was what's your name?"

Slightly flummoxed, the voice replied, "Er.. Its Jeremy Cooke here. I'm the Assistant Prog Ops Manager."

Bernie loathed BBC abbreviations and avoided them at every opportunity.

"Nice to talk to you Jeremy. What can I do for you?"

"The P.O.M. would like to see you straight away," said the voice, trying to reassert some sense of authority.

"I assume you mean the Programme Operations Manager wants to talk to me? And that would be Ray Etheridge?"

"Er... Yes..."

"Well why didn't you say that? Please tell Ray I've received his message, and as soon as it's convenient I'll drop by."

He dropped the receiver back on its cradle without waiting for a response.

'Wanker.' muttered Bernie as he put down the phone. The studio operations people were still having great difficulty in accepting him as a *'proper'* producer. Many who were recruited as studio managers had strong ambitions to move into production. Those who didn't make it might reluctantly have to settle for a position as a departmental manager in operations. Bernie's career path did not conform to the established conventions, and while many of his new colleagues were welcoming, there were a few whose resentment simmered. Dave Bisley being a case in point. Bernie suspected that Ray Etheridge wasn't exactly enthusiastic about Bernie's career progression either.

"Who was that?" enquired Nick as Bernie returned to the table.

"It was your office. We should drop by and have a chat with Ray."

"What does he want? Is it about this morning?" Nick was looking anxious.

"No, nothing to do with that," lied Bernie. "I need to have a word with him about something else entirely."

When Bernie and Nick finally got to the open plan expanse of the Programme Operations office, lunchtime was long gone and Jeremy Cooke was poring over the following week's work schedule. It was his job to look at the requests for studio facilities from production and match those requests with the studios and studio managers most suited to that type of work. At least, that was the theory. Bernie knew it didn't quite work like that.

The current week's allocations were pinned to the wall so that the management could see at a glance which staff should be in which studio at any particular time.

Ray Etheridge's secretary was a friendly middle aged lady with glasses called Audrey. Bernie smiled and nodded to her as he invited himself into Ray's partitioned off space in the corner. Nick wasn't quite sure what was going to happen, so he decided to hover for a while outside his boss's office, so that he could either go in, if invited, or, preferably, bugger off if it turned out to be a one-to-one.

As Bernie walked into the office, Ray looked up, surprised. Bernie took the initiative.

"Hello Ray, I'm glad you invited me over. I have a special request."

"And what is that?" asked Ray, looking puzzled.

"I would like Nick here…" he motioned to the figure hovering just outside the office door, "…to mix all my *Saturday Club* sessions from now on."

Ray did not like to be ambushed. He took stock of the situation, stood up, walked round the desk and pulled out a chair.

"Take a seat please, Bernie."

As Bernie followed his invitation, he deftly closed the door while explaining to an equally confused Nick, "We'll talk later." He returned behind his desk and, placing both elbows on the desktop and forming his fingertips into a pyramid beneath his chin, he continued,

"We'll come to that, but first I'd like to talk to you about this morning."

It seemed to Bernie that Ray was doing his best to strike a pose that appeared open and forthright. However, the broad, toothy grin spread wide across Ray's broad, ruddy face suggested to Bernie a completely different adjective. Smarmy. Bernie sat and listened.

"I am told there was a bit of a situation in the studio this morning?"

"A situation?" said Bernie, "Now where did you hear that?"

"From Dave Bisley," Ray continued.

"Really?.. And what exactly did Dave Bisley tell you?"

"He said that you said that his services were not required on the session."

"He said that I said?.. It's all a bit *'he said, she said...'* Isn't it?" Bernie responded.

Ray's expression grew a bit less smarmy.

Bernie continued, "As a matter of fact, it was Dave Bisley who voted himself surplus to requirements this morning. He was not happy about the way I wanted to run the session - not that production decisions are anything to do with him - and he suggested that we might as well use the studio time as a training session for young Nick Crossland. So I took him up on his helpful suggestion, and here we are."

It was Bernie's turn to offer a smarmy smile.

"Nick did a marvellous job. Hence my request for his services on all my future *Saturday Club* sessions."

"Look Bernie," Ray was now completely devoid of smarm, "I'm sure you understand my difficulty here. I only have your word against his. Dave is an experienced member of our team and is a very talented sound mixer. I need to keep staff like him on side."

"Well he's been around for a while, I'll give you that," said Bernie. "As regards his word against mine, you can also get Nick Crossland's word about what actually happened and, if you need more, I can give you Brian Epstein's phone number if you want to talk to him?"

"Who the hell is Brian Epstein?"

"He's the group's manager. I'm sure they'll be happy to give you their side of it."

Bernie paused. "I could always lodge a formal complaint about Bisley's behaviour?" he suggested helpfully.

Etheridge blanched. This was not how things were done in the BBC.

"That won't be necessary," he retorted. Then he thought long and hard.

"I hear what you say Bernie," he finally offered. "I can't make you any promises, but I'll see what I can do."

*****

Despite the non-committal response, when Programme Ops released their next set of work schedules, Bernie was delighted to see Nick Crossland's name listed against his *Saturday Club* commitments.

So far so good.

It wasn't just the Beatles who appreciated Bernie's efforts to make BBC sessions go as smoothly as possible. Artists who had been *Saturday Club* regulars long before Bernie's arrival were pleasantly surprised when this new producer with his new ideas started looking after their sessions. Soon expectations were raised in relation to other productions, and gradually, Bernie's artist-friendly approach was adopted more widely.

By the time the Beatles came in for their next session, Bernie's way of doing things was taken for granted - on *Saturday Club* at least. Their third single, *From Me To You*, had rocketed to the top of the UK charts and demand for personal appearances was on the same trajectory - a trajectory that the UK music business had never witnessed before.

On this particular occasion, the Beatles had a chap called Terry Doran in tow. Terry was an attractive young man who sported a well-tailored suit and a shock of curly brown hair.

He had an easy way with him. He was cheeky, witty and charming; a close associate of the band, and particularly of John Lennon. During breaks, Bernie and Terry chatted and found they had a lot in common. They shared similar views of the world, and enjoyed the same dry sense of humour.

After the session, the boys hurried off to their next commitment. Terry was still hanging around as Bernie and Nick were clearing up. He sidled up to Bernie and asked him, sotto voce,

"Any chance of getting a copy of the tape? The boys were very pleased with the session, and they did a couple of numbers they've never recorded before."

With a discreet movement of his head, Bernie motioned him out of the door and into the corridor.

"You're asking the wrong guy Terry," he explained. "You should be talking to Nick's assistant, the tape operator."

"Billy? Isn't it?"

"Yes. But when you ask him, please do it quietly, and when I'm well out of earshot."

Terry, being a bit of an entrepreneur, caught on straight away. "What's the going rate?" he asked with a twinkle in his eye.

"Usually a couple of quid," said Bernie. "Although with inflation, that might have gone up a bit. You'll have to haggle."

"Of course," Terry grinned, enjoying the subterfuge. "Thanks for the tip. Can I treat you to a drink after?"

"Well, I haven't got much time, but if you fancy a quick one in the BBC Club across the road, I'm up for it."

"Great! Why don't you nip off to the khazi while I do some business?"

Bernie smirked and sloped off for a totally unnecessary visit to the toilet.

A few minutes later, he returned to the control room. Billy had a pair of headphones on studiously tending a pair of tape recorders which were both running. Terry, who had been lounging in Bernie's chair, got up, walked over to Bernie with a straight face, and winked,

"Are we off to the club then?"

*****

Terry insisted on buying the drinks. A G&T with ice and a slice for Bernie and a bottle of Mackeson stout for himself. He carried them over from the bar.

"Thanks for the tip Bernie," toasted Terry.

"You're welcome."

They clinked glasses and took a sip.

"How did you get involved with the Beatles then?"

"Oh, Brian and I were friends long before he started managing the Beatles." Terry explained. "I was working for a car dealer at the time. Whenever Brian or the lads needed anything on wheels, I was always there to help them out. I sold George his first car, a Ford Anglia. And I sold them a Ford Thames van after they sacked their first drummer, Pete Best. He owned the transport. Of course, I did them a really good deal, and in return, they agreed to pose in an advert for the dealership."

"So, you're literally, a wheeler-dealer?"

"Absolutely," said Terry, grinning. "So tell me Bernie, about the session tapes, why all this under the counter stuff? Why don't the BBC just sell

37

copies of the tapes from their archives?"

"What archives?" asked Bernie.

Terry looked puzzled, his eyebrows raised.

"All the brilliant programmes they've broadcast over the years," he said questioningly. "I've heard loads of stuff - which I'd be willing to pay for if I knew where to find it. There must be loads of Lonnie Donegan in there, and I remember a brilliant version of *Blues For Jimmy* by Acker Bilk's Jazz Band a couple of years ago. Jonathan Mortimer did some great trombone slides on that one. Much better than the record."

"Well, I'm sorry to disappoint you Terry, but there are no BBC archives."

Terry looked blank.

"Well… that's not strictly true," Bernie backtracked. "There's an organisation called the Archives Unit. But they concentrate mainly on saving speeches broadcast by our leading statesmen at critical points in our history. You must have heard the recording of Neville Chamberlain announcing the start of the Second World War?"

"But isn't there anything saved apart from political stuff?"

Bernie laughed. "Well, before I became a producer, I did some tape copying for Archives. I remember a recording of an old geezer, a shepherd, I think. He had a very broad Norfolk country accent which some boffin in Archives thought was endangered. Unforeseen consequences of education, and all that… So, he thought that the old guy's phonetic proclivities should be saved for a grateful nation. I often get that one out of an evening, and put it on while I'm having my cocoa."

Terry looked at Bernie. Only when Bernie couldn't resist a smirk did they both burst out laughing.

"That's not to say there's nothing in there about popular culture," he continued. "Once I heard a recording by that French film actor... what's his name?.."

"Yves Montand?"

"No."

"Louis Jourdan?"

"No. Much older than that."

"You've got me," said Terry.

"You know!.. The old guy who was in that film with Leslie Caron?"

"Gigi?.."

"That's the one.."

"Maurice Chevalier!" they both said together.

"Wow!" said Terry, a little deflated. "So the BBC Archives haven't got any British jazz or skiffle, but they've got an entire catalogue of songs recorded by an old French guy called Maurice Chevalier."

Bernie laughed once more. "I'm afraid not. The only recording of Maurice Chevalier the Archive Unit has is an interview done in the 1950s. In the course of this interview, Maurice recounts his time in the trenches during the First World War.

According to him, the only thing that kept the infantry going was..."

Bernie looked at Terry, mischievously,

"Well... Have a guess!"

Terry thought for a bit.

"Letters from home?"

"No."

"Dirty pictures?"

"No"

"I give in."

"Cocaine," said Bernie.

"Cocaine!" exclaimed Terry. "Well, they were a bit ahead of their time then... Christ! How do you do a line in a mud-filled trench?"

They paused, silently for a while. Then, deciding that they had spent quite enough time reflecting on the horrors of war, they turned back to the present.

"But where do all the BBC tapes go?" asked Terry.

"Which tapes?"

"The ones of the lads that I just bought over the road, for example? What happens to the master tapes after the recording session?"

"They'll get played out on Saturday, and then they'll get a repeat broadcast in a few weeks' time. Then they'll be sent to the Tape Recovery Unit to be erased and used again on another session. Saves at least the price of a sausage roll or two."

Terry was dumbfounded.

"But that's fucking stupid!"

Bernie sat silent.

"Do you mean to tell me that anything that I've ever heard on the radio that I thought was really exciting just doesn't exist any more?"

Terry looked really upset.

"Not unless you go to the AA."

"The Automobile Association?"

"No. The Andrews Archives."

Terry shook his head. Uncomprehending.

"The only person I know who saves session tapes is me," said Bernie. "I am the Andrews Archives. I've got copies of every single *Saturday Club* broadcast since I started working in the Tape Recording Unit. And I've got a few more besides."

"I have lots of Lonnie Donegan from *Saturday Club, Jazz Club*, and a few other radio programmes. I've got some Acker Bilk, and some Ken Colyer, Chris Barber and a few others. But the archives that I'm really proud of are the rock'n'roll recordings in my collection: Little Richard, Gene

Vincent, Jerry Lee Lewis, Eddie Cochran... That sort of stuff."

"Wow!" said Terry, suddenly excited. "The last *Saturday Club* that Eddie Cochran ever did... Not long before he died in that car crash with Gene Vincent... *Hallelujah I Just Love Her So*... You've got that on tape?"

"I've got the whole programme on tape,"

"Brilliant!" said Terry. "Can I buy a copy off you?"

"Got a tape recorder?"

"Yes."

"What make?"

"It's a Grundig."

"3¾ inches per second. I'll run you off a copy," said Bernie.

"How much do you want?"

"Forget it. It won't cost me anything except my time. And I'll enjoy listening to it again."

"But this must be totally illegal?" said Terry.

"Absolutely!" said Bernie. "But it's the only way the good stuff is ever going to be saved. I'm bloody sure I'm not wiping anything that I think is important."

"Good for you!" said Terry. "I'm sure that, one day, the BBC will come to their senses, and realise what a massive favour you're doing them."

"I wouldn't hold your breath," replied Bernie. "As far as the BBC is concerned, all pop music is crap!"

Just then, across the room, Billy the tape operator caught Bernie's eye as he walked through the door.

"I'd best be off," said Bernie, not wanting to be around when the consignment was delivered.

"How will I get the Eddie Cochran tape?" Terry asked, hurriedly, as Bernie departed.

"Give me a ring next week, and we can meet up for a drink or whatever."

On his way out, Bernie helpfully pointed Billy in the right direction.

*****

Now that Bernie was involved in the production of a radio show reaching around ten million listeners every week, he found himself on the A-List for invitations to all manner of record biz PR events. Naturally, the purpose of these events was to promote record sales. They could be lavish affairs. To Bernie, it was surreal.

He had moved from a job where his daily work schedule was accounted by the minute, to one where it was perfectly acceptable to swan off for an early, boozy lunch, and then return later - at some indeterminate time of his own choosing, inebriated to some indeterminate degree of his own choosing.

In the course of these junkets, Bernie would often run into Terry, particularly during those events which involved the Beatles. Sometimes, they would lunch together, or join each other for drinks after work.

One day, Terry phoned his office.

"Bernie!.."

Bernie immediately recognised the broad, Scouse, hail-fellow-well-met greeting.

"Hello Terry. What can I do for you?"

He was expecting some sort of business proposal of a good-natured, wide-boy variety.

"How would you like to live in a Mayfair flat?"

Bernie didn't know how to answer that.

"You told me that you wanted to move into town, but all the places you liked were far too expensive?.."

That was true. Bernie hated early starts, and was fed up with the long, daily commute from the suburbs each day. But London was expensive. The cost of even the grottiest bedsit was guaranteed to inspire a resentment barrier which Bernie found so insurmountable he could never bring himself to move into town.

"And a flat in Mayfair is the solution?" Bernie laughed, wondering where this was going.

Terry didn't miss a beat and breezed on with his sales patter.

"You're in luck. Things are going so well with the lads that Brian's decided to move the management down to London. Not just the Beatles, but the entire NEMS operation. The interest in Liverpool acts is rocketing, and he thinks he'll be able to exploit the artists on his books much more effectively down here."

Bernie was intrigued, but still confused.

"And what's a flat in Mayfair got to do with it?"

"Well, I've been helping the lads, not just with the nice motor cars they can afford now, but with a lot of other business - personal and professional - and Brian wants me down in London too. We're in the process of setting up a luxury car dealership aimed at the trendier end of the business."

Bernie still didn't get it.

"So Brian's giving me a bit of help setting up, and he's been offered a good deal on this flat in Mayfair. The thing is, it's got two good sized bedrooms, and I only need one. I could do with some company, and we get on well. We're on the same wavelength. So if you're interested, I could let you have the other bedroom for eleven quid a week. What do you think?"

BBC wages were not bountiful, even for a radio producer, but Bernie didn't need to do any arithmetic to know that Terry's proposition was affordable - and attractive. Bloody hell! A flat in Mayfair!

"What about bills?"

"Eleven quid a week, all found. No other expenses. You'll have to provide your own food, mind," said Terry, with a laugh.

Bernie moved in within a week. OK, the flat wasn't exactly modern. The furniture was heavy, dark mahogany, probably from the 1930s, and the fixtures and fittings were a match. Someone had spent a lot of money a long time ago, but nothing had been done to tart it up since, and it all looked a bit tired and dated.

None of that mattered to Bernie. Terry was a considerate flatmate. The flat was clean and warm. The big double bed was comfortable and it was a twenty minute walk to BH, or, if it was raining you could jump on the tube at Green Park.

Luxury!

*****

Some weeks later, Bernie was pottering around the flat, cooking up a late breakfast on a bright Saturday morning. After eating heartily, washing up, and stowing away the dishes, he made himself a coffee. Then he made for the front room to lounge on the sofa and pick up *Catch 22* from where he had left off. He was finding Joseph Heller's satirical novel heart-warmingly reminiscent of the BBC. If not the BBC as whole, then at least the Popular Music Department of BBC Radio.

Terry wandered in, bleary eyed, having just surfaced from what seemed to have been a not very restful sleep after a long night out.

"Hi," he mumbled, clad in his pyjamas, slumping down in an armchair."

"You look bright-eyed and bushy-tailed this morning," said Bernie, chuckling. "Shall I prepare some drugs for you?"

"What'you on about?" slurred Terry.

"Coffee?"

"Oh!.. Yeah!.. That would be great... Thanks."

Bernie soon returned with a brew. He picked up his book and started reading again. Terry carefully consumed the coffee, warming his hands on the cup while meditating on the meagre froth on the surface. After a few minutes, the caffeine was beginning to take effect.

"How's your restructuring of the BBC going?"

"Sarcasm is the lowest form of wit," said Bernie, grinning.

"Actually, I can't complain."

"They seem to have got the message that, at least as far as I'm concerned, beat music is not a load of crap, and younger audiences are entitled to be taken as seriously as the most avid 1940s big-band fan."

Bernie paused.

"Perhaps I'm succeeding in coaxing them out of the rut of post-war austerity and repression? At least that's the way some guy described the state of the nation on a tv documentary I saw last night."

Terry nodded his head.

"Very interesting," he said, unconvincingly, taking another mouthful of the rejuvenating brown stuff.

To Bernie's surprise, Terry picked up the theme, elaborating, leading Bernie to believe that the caffeine must indeed be kicking in.

"It's not just the BBC that needs to be dragged into the 1960s you know," said Terry.

"The record business likes to tout itself as a progressive bunch of 'hepcats' - not that they have the faintest idea of what a 'hepcat' is. And neither would most of the white, anglo-saxon, beatnik crowd who love to flaunt 'cool' patois which was conceived, like a love-child, in the back streets of Harlem or Detroit. People like Dick Rowe, Mike Smith and Tony Meehan wouldn't be able to distinguish a 'hepcat' from a drowned rat!"

The imagery tickled Bernie.

"Why are you picking on those guys?"

"Because they're the geniuses at Decca who turned down the Beatles. Not that the boys are complaining any more. But at the time, they were gutted when Brian got a letter from Decca saying, *'guitar groups are on the way out... the Beatles have no future in show business.'* "

Bernie cackled, and Terry, suddenly bursting into full flow, joined him in the cackling. After the jollity had died down a bit, Bernie reflected,

"That sort of brushoff is hardly in keeping with Decca's carefully cultivated image of *'having a finger on the pulse of the latest trends in pop music.'* Is it?"

More cackling.

"Let's face it Terry, despite how the record companies like to present themselves to the public, they are just a disparate bunch of capitalist corporations striving to do what capitalist enterprises do best. Make money. People who run these companies like predictability, not risk. They want each record release to sound as much as possible like the previous one. On the basis that they have found a successful formula which will continue to generate money - forever."

"And as a result," said Terry, "they just lurch from one monumentally stupid decision to the next. You have to wonder how any artist with anything new to offer could ever make it past a record company's so-called talent scouts."

Bernie nodded. "The public love the novel. The unpredictable. The record companies don't get it! Unless they get it by mistake." Then, turning to Terry, "How _did_ the boys eventually manage to get a deal?"

"You've got to hand it to Brian. He didn't give up. That was the key."

Terry finished off the coffee in his mug.

"When the approaches to the record companies failed, Brian started pushing John and Paul as songwriters. He was doing the rounds of the publishing companies when one of his contacts, a guy from Ardmore and Beechwood... Sid Colman, I think?.. Anyway, he liked the songs, and thought he could exploit them."

"And?" said Bernie.

"Well Ardmore and Beechwood, like Parlophone, are subsidiaries of EMI, so when Colman pressured the Board of EMI to sign John and Paul as songwriters, the Chairman started asking why his record companies had decided to turn down the Beatles if they wrote such good songs."

"But how did they end up on Parlophone? Why not the main EMI label alongside all the other EMI pop stars?"

"Ah!... You think it's just the BBC who make nonsensical decisions then?"

"Go on! Thrill me!" said Bernie.

"When they took another look, the Parlophone boss, Len Wood, was particularly taken with one of the songs John and Paul wrote - *Like Dreamers Do*. But this is where the lunacy starts. One of Wood's producers is George Martin. Wood didn't like George Martin. In fact, Len Wood must be a very upstanding sort of a guy because what he didn't like about George Martin was that he was having an affair with his secretary."

"What the hell does that have to do with anything?" asked Bernie, bemused.

Terry chuckled.

"At that point, no-one at EMI was taking the Beatles seriously as recording artists. But Len Wood wanted to sign *Like Dreamers Do*, so he could get the song covered by a *'proper'* singer."

Bernie started grinning.

"And Wood thought he could kill two birds with one stone. In order to get his hands on *Like Dreamers Do*, he agreed to sign the Beatles to Parlophone as recording artists. But he did a package deal. He secured the publishing rights to Lennon & McCartney's songs - which is what he was really after - bundled in with the recording contract."

"He'd been told that the Beatles would be a complete flop on disc. But this suited him fine, because he dumped the thankless task of producing records by these no-hopers onto his public enemy #1 - the degenerate George Martin - in the juicy anticipation of George scoring a very public and humiliating failure."

Bernie burst out laughing.

"That is too stupid for words!.. So, the best thing that EMI have ever done resulted from the actions of a sanctimonious prick who assigned, out of spite, a group who he thought were a bunch of losers, to George Martin - a record producer who didn't want to have anything to do with them in the first place?"

By this stage, Terry and Bernie were beside themselves.

"Oh! That's really cheered me up, Terry. Even the BBC Radio Popular Music Department hasn't done anything as daft as that for at least a week or two."

"Mind you," Terry continued, "the lads weren't exactly thrilled at the prospect of releasing records on a label best known to the public for promoting comedy and novelty acts. Parlophone is not a serious pop music label. So, the whole thing was a bit of a fiasco, if you see what I mean."

"I see exactly what you mean," said Bernie. "Out of the crap, came forth sweetness... Or something like that?.."

"Where's that from?" said Terry, giggling like a schoolboy.

"Book of Judges?.. " mused Bernie. "Or maybe Tate & Lyle?.. Somewhere of mystical significance anyway. So significant that I can't remember..."

More hilarity.

There was a momentary pause while they regained their composure.

"That's a hell of a story. But where next for the Brian Epstein Empire?"

"It's already happening," said Terry. "As you know, Brian's signed more top talent from Liverpool. Gerry and the Pacemakers... Billy J Kramer and the Dakotas... the Fourmost... the Big Three... And he's after everything he can lay his hands on. They can't get enough of the Mersey Sound down here. Times have changed."

"They certainly have," said Bernie. "Not just Liverpool either. The patronising southern English attitude to all things Northern seems to have gone right out of fashion. The record labels are signing up anything that moves up North. Manchester bands like The Hollies and Freddie and the Dreamers are the latest. Who knows where it'll stop? The old chestnut that *'if it's not London-centric, it can't be taken seriously'* has surely gone forever?"

"You must be well-pleased. All this upheaval is right up your street. You thrive on it."

"I love it," said Bernie, "But I've got to be careful. *Saturday Club* is Jimmy Grant's baby. His initial vision - which was spot on at the time - was for a programme featuring a mixture of skiffle, jazz, folk, rock'n'roll and middle-of-the-road pop. New-fangled beat groups are considered rubbish, at best, by many of my elders and betters, and I can't push too hard."

"Well, it seems to us - Brian, the boys and me - that you're doing a great job. We've heard big changes on *Saturday Club*. I'm sure Jimmy has too. Times are changing. You're changing with them. And from what you say, the audience figures are going up all the time. So Jimmy can't be finding much to object to. He's letting you get on with it because, unlike some of the captains of industry who run the record business Bernie, you do, in fact, have your finger on the pulse."

The Rolling Stones

It all started in the kitchen, over lunch.

Terry and Bernie's flat was something of a meeting hub and it wasn't only the Beatles who were regular visitors. Brian Epstein and any number of his rapidly expanding stable of artists - at various stages of career development - were liable to drop in at any time.

George Harrison had called by in the hope of persuading Bernie to rustle up his favourite meal - egg and chips - a request which Bernie was most happy to oblige.

While buttering a slice of toast, Bernie commented on the ease with which a stream of beat groups from the North of England had been signed by the major record companies in the wake of that unexpected phenomenon - the Beatles.

"It was very difficult to get anyone to take us seriously to begin with," said George. "I don't know whether they didn't like it because we weren't based in London, or whether they thought we were all a bit backward up there, but they take their bandwagons very seriously down here, and nowadays, it's the Northerners who get first pick. It must be tough for a London band to get a look in these days."

"I haven't heard anything that's really grabbed me coming out of London for a while," said Bernie. "I wonder if that's because there isn't anything new, or whether new bands are being overlooked because they're not from up North?"

"The Rolling Stones'll grab you." said George.

"Oh really?.. " Bernie's interest was immediate. "I've seen them advertised at the Marquee, but I've never heard them play."

"You should check them out. We were at the television studios in Teddington doing *Thank Your Lucky Stars*, and we heard there was this band on at a club called the Crawdaddy in Richmond. It was only about fifteen minutes away. We'd finished recording and we had nothing else that day, so we thought we'd go and have a look. They were stomping around, doing R&B tunes. Kind of stuff we'd been doing before we got out of our leather suits to try and get on record labels and television. But the beat they laid down was solid. Shook the walls. They make a great sound."

Bernie took George at his word. He found out when the Rolling Stones next gig was and went to have a look for himself.

*****

Bernie had never been to the Crawdaddy. The name was exotic. The venue was not. It was located in the back room of the Station Hotel in Richmond. It had been a jazz club in a previous incarnation, but interest in jazz had been fading, and younger audiences were more attracted to bands featuring electric guitars. Audiences could be intensely tribal. The jazz crowd despised rock and roll, so if you tried walking in to a jazz club carrying an electric guitar, you'd better have a good back story.

Fortunately, for bands like the Rolling Stones, respected '50s jazzers like Chris Barber had already introduced jazz audiences to a variety of guitar based music - first of all to skiffle, in the days when Chris himself jammed on double bass with Lonnie Donegan, and then to electric blues artists like Muddy Waters, who he brought over, specially, from the United States, to perform in British jazz clubs.

So, in the early '60s, if you touted your electric guitar band as a rhythm & blues outfit, that gave you all the respectability you needed to play in a jazz club.

An enthusiast by the name of Giorgio Gomelsky had seen the way things were going, so he thought he would try his luck by re-opening what had been the Station Hotel Jazz Club as a rhythm and blues venue called the Crawdaddy - after a song by American R&B artist, Bo Diddley.

When Bernie arrived, it seemed as if the plan was working. The crowd was youthful. Smart but casual. The place was packed, and a recording of *Baby What You Want Me To Do* by Jimmy Reed was belting out on the PA system. The band were not yet on stage, but Bernie could sense a frisson of anticipation.

He asked for the manager. Giorgio was tall, with a beard, and wore a tie with his casual jacket and trousers. In keeping with the informal nature of his surroundings he had loosened his Windsor knot a few notches. When Bernie explained who he was, he was immediately ushered into a back room. The music and hubbub from club was still audible but it was comfortable enough for a reasonable conversation.

Gomelsky had been born in the 1930s in Georgia. Not in the Southern States of the USA - as in *Georgia On My Mind* - but in the Georgian Soviet Socialist Republic - as in *Back in the USSR*. It was the birthplace of Joseph Stalin, in the Caucasus Mountains located somewhere between Armenia and Russia. This particular Georgia was one of the republics which, at that time, made up the Soviet Union.

Gomelsky's family had come to England via Syria, Egypt, Italy and Switzerland. A colourful, cosmopolitan character, he earned a living as a filmmaker, but he had become obsessed with jazz and blues at an early age.

Like many other émigrés, he applied himself industriously to his ambitions in ways that many of the natives might not.

He pulled out a rickety chair for Bernie, then took his place behind a desk that looked as though it had been retrieved from a junk shop. He tried to strike as business-like a pose as he could.

"Welcome Bernie. I'm a big fan of *Saturday Club*. What can I do for you?"

Bernie thought a bit of name dropping wouldn't go amiss.

"I was talking to George Harrison, and he suggested I should come and have a listen to the Rolling Stones."

Giorgio tried his best to play it cool, but Bernie got the distinct impression that if he was considering offering some sort of proposition, not only would both of his hands be bitten off, but Mr Gomelsky might be looking for a third.

"The boys are just bringing their gear in now. When they've set up, I'll ask them to come and introduce themselves."

"Will they play their set straight through, or will they be having a break?"

"They play for forty-five minutes, then a twenty minute break, and then it's the final forty-five."

"Well, why don't we wait until the break? I wouldn't want to distract them. Just let them do what comes naturally."

"No problem," said Giorgio. "Just one thing I should mention. They've just failed a BBC audition for BBC *Jazz Club*. Does that matter if you want them on *Saturday Club*?"

Bernie was taken aback. Yes it did matter. It mattered very much. He knew nothing about this, but he passed it off with a few nods of the head, some pursed lips and an indeterminate remark of an inconclusive nature. However, Bernie knew in his heart that this was a real problem.

The BBC in Manchester had an informal attitude to auditions. After each batch of prospective artists had made their recordings, the tapes were played to all producers looking for new acts. They would listen together, casually, and if any of them liked the sound of a particular band or singer, they would take them on. It only needed one producer to take a liking to something new to get it on the air. Peter Pilbeam had chosen the Beatles.

Down in London, it was a different matter. Audition tapes were reviewed by a nominated committee who had to put down their thoughts, formally, in writing. This led to very conservative reviews, since the reviewers knew their comments would be on record, and if subsequent broadcasts were considered to be below par, their judgement might be questioned. It was smarter and safer to avoid risks.

Added to that, young hopefuls would need a significant majority of the audition committee behind them in order to be successful. Therefore, in London, the dice was loaded - and not in favour of emerging talent. Not only that, in London, audition panel decisions were final.

Having sidestepped the issue of the audition, Bernie followed Giorgio out of the office. They parked themselves at the side of the hall to watch the proceedings. Eventually, the Stones sorted their gear out on the small stage.

After a lengthy tune-up, followed by a brief sound check, the music on the PA was faded out and they launched into *Round and Round* - the B side of a Chuck Berry classic, *Johnny B Goode*.

Chuck was one of the original rock'n'rollers, who scored his first hits in 1955, in the heyday of Fats Domino, Little Richard, Jerry Lee Lewis and, of course, Elvis Presley. Bernie smiled to himself while recalling a press release he had seen publicising the debut of the Rolling Stones at the Marquee Jazz Club in Wardour Street.

'I hope they don't think we're a rock and roll outfit,' their lead singer was quoted as saying. *'We're an R&B band.'* he insisted.

Bernie reflected that in the space of eight years or so, Chuck Berry had been classified, firstly, as a rock'n'roller, and then as a convicted sex offender. Now, after spending a couple of years in jail and a couple more in the artistic doldrums, he was enjoying a golden period of rehabilitation.

This miraculous resurrection was due in no small measure to the massive interest generated by the Beatles who, from their earliest days on stage, had included lots of Chuck Berry numbers in their repertoire. And now Chuck was being redefined by the Rolling Stones as an R&B artist, so they could get away with playing his stuff in jazz clubs. It was a strange world. But Bernie really wasn't bothered about classification. It was the music he was interested in. And the sound was impressive.

As George Harrison had predicted, the beat was heavy and the walls shook. On the downbeat of their first number, the mass of bodies on the dance floor - who, up until then had been quite inert - spontaneously erupted, intoxicated by the hypnotic rhythm. Bernie was blown away by the raw exuberance of the atmosphere. It was loud. It was tight. It was brutally exciting. And the first forty-five minute set passed in the blink of an eye.

'This is what the kids want.' thought Bernie. *'Not just the kids here in the Crawdaddy. Kids everywhere.'*

Giorgio spoke to the band as they came off stage. The bass player and drummer headed for the bar, and the other three came over to the back room. Giorgio made the introductions. He motioned to a well-built young man of average height with a blonde, page-boy haircut.

"Bernie, this is Brian Jones, the leader."

Before Bernie could put out his hand, Brian demanded,

"What do you want?"

"How would feel about appearing on *Saturday Club*?"

"Well they didn't want us on *Jazz Club*, did they?"

Then a pause.

"Said we sounded too black."

The other two sniggered quietly. One was slouching on a filing cabinet, while the other was leaning back against the wall, arms folded.

"Bernie, what are the audience figures for *Jazz Club*?" Giorgio interjected.

"Oh, I don't know…" said Bernie, knowing full well where this was going.

"Maybe in the hundreds of thousands?…" he guessed, not having a clue.

"And what about *Saturday Club*?"

Bernie was much more confident on this point.

"Ten million plus," he replied, "and going up every week."

During the ensuing silence, Bernie observed quietly. These guys were far too cool to display any outward signs of emotion, but he felt the atmosphere thaw a little, until, eventually, the one who was leaning back against the wall unfolded his arms and pushed himself up straight, asking,

"So, what did you have in mind?"

He was taller. He wore a stripy, crew neck sweater and his lanky hair curled down over his ears. Bernie was fascinated by his generously endowed lips.

"I'm very interested in having you on *Saturday Club*," said Bernie, "but I'll be honest, I knew nothing about your failed audition until Giorgio told me earlier."

Giorgio raised his eyebrows a little.

"I'm here about *Saturday Club*, not *Jazz Club*, and I've no idea what happened on your audition. It does complicate things. But I think I can work round it, and I would like you to record a session for *Saturday Club*... If you want to?.."

Once more, the cool demeanour was maintained. Nothing was said, looks were exchanged, heads nodded, and then Brian turned to Bernie,

"All right... If you can fix it, we'll do it."

He turned to his band mates and motioned to the one with the lanky hair and lips, "This is Mick Jagger, lead singer and harp, and this is Keith Richards, guitar."

"Yeah... And that's Richards wiv' an 's'." Then, labouring the point... "Not like Cliff Richard."

Bernie suppressed a smile. After that, it was handshakes all round and the boys repaired to the bar to enjoy whatever period of relaxation was available before the second half.

"So, is that a done deal?" hustled Giorgio, when they had the back room to themselves once more.

"Not quite." said Bernie. "The audition business is a bit of a headache, but I will do my best," he reassured.

Bernie decided to split. He had seen enough. Now he had to figure out how to get them on the show. On his way back home, he reflected on the differences between the Beatles and the Stones. Not so much musically. In that respect, they had quite a lot in common, particularly in their fondness for covering what appeared to be *The Complete Works of Chuck Berry*. What fascinated him were their very different personalities.

The Beatles had no leader, no front man, were eclectic in their musical influences and seemed like a unit, even off stage. In marked contrast, the Rolling Stones had a leader as well as a front man, and seemed more like a group of individuals - albeit individuals who really got it together on stage.

The biggest difference was that the Beatles wrote their own material, while the Stones emulated black American R&B artists to the exclusion of everything else.

*****

When Bernie arrived at his office the next day, the first thing he did was call up the Auditions Department.

"Mary Cotgrove," came the cheery response from the other end of the phone.

"Hi Mary. It's Bernie here. You had a band in for an audition recently called the Rolling Stones?.."

"Yes, that was the week before last."

"Do you have the tape?"

"It's here in the office."

"Could I come round and listen to it? And have a look at the audition report?"

"Of course you can."

Bernie hung up and headed round. When he got there, Mary had the tape on her desk, together with a brown cardboard file containing a few sheets of paper.

The first sheet was a proforma on which she had handwritten the name of the band, their contact details, the names of each band member, details of who played what, who sang what, who wrote what, and a list of the songs recorded on the audition tape.

The second piece of paper was a carbon copy of the BBC's rejection letter to the Rolling Stones:

The recording has now been played to our production panel with a view to general broadcasting, but we regret to inform you that the performance was not considered suitable for our purposes. However, this is an instance when it would seem likely that it might be of help to you to know our opinion in a little more detail.

It was unsigned.

"Brian Jones phoned up to get some feedback, and he was told their singer sounded too black?" queried Bernie.

"Oh, I don't know anything about that," said Mary. "I think he was put on to Rhys Williams."

'Sounds about right', thought Bernie.

Rhys Williams! Head of Music Production, or HOMP, if you liked BBC acronyms. He controlled all live music production in the Popular Music Department and, as a result, was one of Bernie's many overlords - but a particularly influential one. As his musical tastes were at least two decades behind the times, Rhys Williams was also a big fan of the BBC's in-house dance-bands and light music orchestras. The BBC employed hundreds of musicians to perform in these musical ensembles, the costs of which were, naturally, funded by the listeners - those who paid the BBC an annual fee for their radio licences. The vocalists who fronted these in-house bands were invariably middle-of-the-road types. Crooners who were more comfortable covering songs made famous by the likes of Frank Sinatra or Johnny Mathis. Regrettably, these session singers were ill-equipped to perform convincing cover versions of real belters like Little Richard's *Long Tall Sally*, or Jerry Lee Lewis's *Great Balls of Fire*. When these shortcomings were pointed out to Williams he, would dismiss them out of hand.

"What matters is the tune!" he would insist in his precise Welsh brogue.

"You people are far too concerned about fly-by-night recording artists who are here today and gone tomorrow. What lasts is the tune! If a good tune stands the test of time, it really doesn't matter who is singing it. With a professional musical accompaniment, most competent singers can carry a good tune and will soon have the audience singing along."

Having heard Williams hold forth on the latest record releases on more than one occasion, Bernie could well imagine the thoughts which would have passed through his head when reviewing the Rolling Stones audition tape. *'Accompaniment? - Hardly professional! Singer? - Hardly competent! Tune? - Hardly!'* But Williams was no mug. He rarely put his opinions in writing.

Some people, however, were obliged to put their opinions in writing.

Bernie flipped through the comments, also handwritten, taking note of who had been appointed to *the 'production panel'* - a nomination which bestowed upon the chosen, the weighty responsibility of passing judgement on that particular day. *'The usual suspects'*, he thought, as he scanned through the documentation. Then his eyes alighted on one particular name. "Margo bloody Benson?" scoffed Bernie. "The world's greatest living expert on Rhythm and Blues?"

Margo Benson was a middle aged producer in the Gramophone Department. The likes of Alma Cogan and Max Bygraves were more her cup of tea.

Mary smiled to herself and got on with her correspondence. Better to leave Bernie alone when he was in a mood. When he had read enough of the production panel's inane comments, he enquired,

"What did you think of them?"

"Not bad." said Mary. "Nervous... They didn't have much time, as we had a lot of acts to get through. And I overheard some chat while they were setting up. I got the impression that some of them weren't regular members of the band. It was all a bit of a rush, really..."

Bernie looked at the session sheet. Mary was right. He knew the names of the band members he had seen at the Crawdaddy - including Charlie Watts on drums and Bill Wyman on bass guitar. On this audition, a guy called Carlo Little had depped for Charlie and instead of Bill Wyman, it was Ricky Fenson on bass.

"Can I hear the tape please?" asked Bernie.

"Sure, the office machine's over there." Mary replied. "Do you know how to work one of those?"

Bernie enjoyed the sarcasm.

He picked up the tape from Mary's desk, walked over to the machine and laced it up. Then he turned up the volume and hit the start button. The bass drum and bass guitar were barely audible and the rest of it sounded unbalanced. It was really quite tinny. This recording was a very poor representation of what he had witnessed on stage the other night.

"Who did the sound balance?"

"Dave Bisley."

Bernie said nothing. There was already a lot of bad blood on record, and he was circumspect enough not to pour any more fuel on that fire - even indirectly. News travelled fast on the BBC grapevine. He didn't want to give anyone any reason to accuse him of conducting some sort of vendetta. Life was difficult enough.

Bernie went back to the office, agitated, wondering how on earth he could surmount this obstacle. As it happened, he didn't have to wait long to see an opportunity and hatch a plan.

*****

A few days later, Bernie heard that Bo Diddley was planning a tour in the UK. He was very keen to book Bo, and, given the current upsurge of interest in R&B he was doubly keen. But Bo Diddley was an American artist. That was a problem because the British Musicians Union had no reciprocal arrangement with the US equivalent. The regulations meant that, as British musicians were not allowed to perform on the radio in the US, American musicians could not perform on BBC Radio.

However, there was a loophole. There was no problem in the BBC employing American *'Variety Artists'*: comedians, crooners, jugglers, magicians, ventriloquists and the like. (There wasn't much call for jugglers and magicians on the radio, although, unlikely as it seems, the BBC Light Programme had often broadcast a ventriloquist called Peter Brough and his imaginary friend, Archie Andrews).

Those were the kind of acts that were common in *'Vaudeville'*, as they referred to it in the US, or *'Music Hall'* as we knew it in the UK. So, if Bernie booked Bo Diddley as a *Variety Artist*, he could bring him in as a *'self-accompanying musician'*, and the Musicians Union could not object.

The rest of Bo's band was another matter. They were all Americans too, so Bernie would have to find a suitable bunch of British session musicians to back Bo instead. This sort of thing had been done before. For example, when Jimmy Grant booked Gene Vincent and Eddie Cochran some years previously, he had hired Marty Wilde's backing group, the Wilde Cats, to accompany them.

It was when he was mulling this over that it occurred to Bernie that the Rolling Stones were a perfect match. They could be hired as individual session musicians to back Bo on *Saturday Club*. They were big fans, and included a lot of Bo's material in their act.

So, if he got them in the door that way, maybe they could record a few of their own tracks on the same session?

Then, he found out that the Rolling Stones were scheduled on the same package tour as Bo. That was the clincher. The tour was headlined by the Everly Brothers and Little Richard. The Stones were bottom of the bill, but it would be good exposure for them. Although how the audiences who came to see a tour headlined by a couple of rock'n'roll acts would react to seeing an R&B band on the same bill - or vice versa - how the Stones diehard R&B fans might react them playing on such a tour rather than in a jazz club?.. Well... There were risks involved.

As far as Bernie was concerned, those were someone else's tribal problems. Once he got the idea in his head, he was not to be deterred. He asked Shirley, his secretary, to place a call to the Stones' manager, and was duly put through.

He found himself talking to a guy called Eric Easton. Giorgio Gomelsky's position seemed to have been usurped in the meantime. Bernie had no interest in the Machiavellian manoeuvres being conducted behind the scenes by those vying for the position as manager of the Rolling Stones, so he took Eric at his word when he assured Bernie he was the man. After a brief discussion, all was agreed and a session date was fixed.

*****

When the day rolled around, another chap turned up along with the Stones. His name was Andrew Loog Oldham. Nineteen years old. Boyish good looks. Perfectly tailored mid-grey, three piece suit. Broadcloth-blue tab-collar shirt. Jet black knitted woollen tie. Ostentatiously complemented by a shiny, black walking cane with a silver ball handle. Very chic.

Given Andrew's appearance, Bernie was well pleased with his chosen attire. He was wearing a casual jacket along with his suit trousers. Under the jacket he had an open-neck shirt with a button down collar. He hadn't got as far as corduroy trousers yet, and he made sure that he left his suit jacket and tie back in the office so that, when he got back from the session, he could do a quick change if he was called to a meeting.

They shook hands. Andrew told Bernie he managed the Stones - along with Eric. Bernie made no attempt to keep abreast of the vicissitudes. He just wanted a good session on tape. He had warned Nick they had a lot of work to get through - practically double the usual amount of material, assuming everything worked out ok - so Nick applied himself to the task of organising the session like a greyhound out of the traps.

Sound checks were completed and tracks were laid at a hell of a pace. Thankfully - as far as Bernie was concerned - Bo Diddley showed absolutely no interest whatsoever in checking the playbacks. He seemed much more keen to get things done as quickly as possible so that he could scarper back to his hotel. He did, however, obsess over one point.

Bo Diddley is, of course, famous for the *'Bo Diddley Beat'*, a distinctive rhythm pattern that features in many of his and other people's songs. So, when Bo saw that Charlie Watts wasn't performing it quite the way Bo had conceived it, he wasn't slow in offering advice, along the lines of,

"No man, it's *'Dum, de dum dum, de dum dum.'* "

Then Charlie would respond with a drum lick that wasn't quite *'Dum, de dum dum, de dum dum.'*

And then Bo would stop him and say again,

"No man, it's *'Dum, de dum dum, de dum dum.'* "

69

And so on… Until…. Bo got so frustrated, he put his guitar down, walked over, positioned himself behind Charlie at his drum-kit, and grabbed Charlie's hands - still holding the drumsticks - in his own.

When he was in control, he repeatedly growled, *'Dum, de dum dum, de dum dum.'* in Charlie's ear while moving Charlie's hands up and down in time with the chant, and beating out the rhythm on the floor tom-tom. This process continued until Bo finally released Charlie's hands from his grip and, hey presto, Charlie continued to thump out the Bo Diddley beat - to perfection.

That particular lesson would come in very handy when the Rolling Stones released their third single the following year - a cover of an old hit by the already deceased rock'n'roller, Buddy Holly, called *Not Fade Away*. On the original, Buddy had shamelessly borrowed Bo's unique beat. So, in years to come, each time Bernie heard the Stones version of *Not Fade Away*, he would recall, with some delight, the historic drum lesson which took place before his very eyes at the BBC.

Soon, Bo Diddley's allotted tracks were down on tape and he departed with what Bernie thought was undue haste. On another day, he might have considered this behaviour quite rude. But that day, he was eager to get on with recording the Rolling Stones in their own right. The track list was quickly agreed, including their first single - *Come On* - originally written and recorded by none other than Chuck Berry.

He looked through the control room window. The Stones were making their final adjustments before recording their radio debut. He was as convinced about their potential as he had been about Beatles when he first met them. Here were a bunch of young guys doing what they loved most, and hoping to make something of themselves in the process. Bernie wondered what path lay ahead. Somehow, he thought it might be a very different path to that of the Beatles.

70

Unlike Bo Diddley, Andrew Loog-Oldham and the Stones were very interested in hearing the playbacks. After each one, they would huddle, and then Brian Jones would turn to Bernie and say something like, "Yeah... 's alright." Then they would move on quickly to the next track.

Bernie sensed that they would really like to spend more time trying different things, like they did on their own sessions. But they were realistic enough to understand the time pressure, and were balancing their impractical desire for perfection with the fact that they weren't going to get another chance to play to another ten million plus audience anytime soon.

When it was all over, Bernie didn't think the BBC Club would appeal to those more used to the youthful hustle and bustle of the Crawdaddy. So he suggested sinking a quick pint or two round the local pub, the Crown and Sceptre - or the Hat and Stick, as it was known to those BBC staff who frequented the place.

The boys demurred. Bernie shrugged. Unlike the Beatles, they were London based. No doubt they had girlfriends to hurry off to, or, in the case of Bill Wyman, a wife to go home to.

"I'll keep you company," said Andrew.

So he and Andrew toddled off to the pub while Nick tidied up the studio and then buzzed off home himself.

*****

When they got to the pub, Bernie ordered. Over drinks, he learned that he wasn't the only one who had been pointed in the direction of the Rolling Stones by George Harrison.

71

According to Andrew, George had been judging some talent competition or other sponsored by a national newspaper, and one of the other judges on the panel that day was the boss of Decca Records, the inimitable Dick Rowe. Just a year earlier, Dick had gone down in history by turning the Beatles down flat, famously opining in writing that, *'guitar groups are on the way out.'* and *'the Beatles have no future in show business.'*

Andrew also told Bernie that Dick Rowe would often proclaim to anyone within earshot, *'I don't know the first thing about music. But I know what I like.'* So, when Dick heard George Harrison singing the praises of the Rolling Stones, he instantly realised that, although he didn't like the Beatles, he liked the Rolling Stones - despite the fact that he'd never actually heard them play. Accordingly, he lost interest in the talent competition, immediately jumped on a train to London, and offered the Rolling Stones a very attractive recording contract. Dick Rowe might know what he liked, but what was more important to him at that time was what George Harrison liked. Rejecting the Beatles had turned out to be the most unmitigated fuckup of all time, and Dick was determined to avoid a repeat.

Bernie thought the Stones first record, a cover of Chuck Berry's *Come On*, was ok, but he'd heard much stronger material at the Crawdaddy. And he thought the band had a lot more potential than just slavishly covering other people's material.

"Of course the Beatles write their own stuff," Bernie commented. "It makes them sound much more distinctive."

Andrew agreed. "I've had a go at them about that. I mean, keeping the blues purists happy in London jazz clubs is one thing, but when it comes to business, why spend all that effort making a record to generate song-writing royalties for some middle aged has-been, when we could be coining it in ourselves?"

If Andrew noticed Bernie's raised eyebrows, he showed no sign of it. Bernie's opener had given this brash teenager licence to expound, which he did, at length.

"It's a crowded market out there, and we've got to claim our territory. We're not cuddly, like the Beatles. We've got to develop an atmosphere of menace and danger…. feral machismo that will appeal to girls and boys alike."

Bernie was fascinated by how different Andrew's mindset was. Bernie's first impression of the Beatles was that what you saw was what you got. An opinion he confirmed after getting to know them better in the flat in Mayfair. They were happy go lucky, down to earth, and just as surprised as everyone else was when Beatlemania exploded.

Andrew Loog Oldham came from an entirely different cosmos. The music was important, of course, but what was of paramount importance was image - and money. Everything was calculated.

Despite his cocksure attitude, Bernie found his young guest very interesting. It was clear that they might not see eye to eye on everything, but he thought Andrew was refreshingly frank. Which was more than you could say for most people in the record business. Some of Andrew's observations, while honest to the point of brutality, had the ring of prescience about them, and Bernie was coming to the conclusion that, in the future, it would be the Andrew Loog Oldhams of the world who would be deciding things rather than the Dick Rowes.

"When will the session go out?" asked Andrew as he sipped his cocktail.

"Bo this Saturday… Your boys the week after," replied Bernie, following that up with, "What did you think of it?"

Andrew was way too much of a player to display a visible tell, but the measured pause spoke volumes. Behind the shades that Andrew had donned since leaving the studio, Bernie was sure a lot of things were being weighed up. Maybe he was choosing his words carefully in order to avoid alienating someone who could be of critical use to the Rolling Stones at this point in their career - such as it was. He wondered just how explicit Andrew's reply would be. When it came, he was not surprised.

"Well... looking at the bankrupt technology you are forced to work with, and the extreme time pressure you are forced to work under, I thought you did a fair job under the circumstances."

Bernie had heard a lot worse. Usually behind his back.

"I agree." said Bernie. "I complain about both of those things, constantly. But it's difficult to know who to complain to in the BBC. Often, if the top management get to know what the problems really are, things get done to solve them. Unfortunately, I've never met the Director General, and I'm not likely to get the opportunity to have that kind of a conversation with him. It seems to me that the people I deal with have a vested interest in keeping the same old thing ticking along in the same old way. All I ever achieve in taking my complaints to them is to piss them off. It is very frustrating."

"Well, you have my condolences. I wouldn't be able to sustain any sort of enthusiasm in that sort of working environment."

Andrew sighed, "So, until you can persuade the powers that be to take the future seriously, from our side of the fence, we'll continue to see BBC sessions as a grating necessity, a ludicrous opportunity to prove that records are manufactured and not real."

Bernie nodded. Not in the least surprised by either the candour, or the cynicism.

"Believe me Andrew, I'm working on it. I just want to see the younger audience get the airtime they deserve, and give the groups who will connect with that audience the best chance to show them what they've got. Like you, I think the sooner the better."

"I wish you well in your endeavours," said the smart teenager with the old head on his shoulders.

After which they finished their drinks, said their goodbyes and went their separate ways.

Keep Your Head Down

It was only after the Rolling Stones made their first ever broadcast - on *Saturday Club* - and there was positive reaction in the music press that Bernie got the summons.

"Rhys Williams wants to see you," said Shirley, as he arrived for work.

When she saw Bernie shrug and ignore, she reluctantly added,

"Straight away... he said."

"What the bloody hell does he want?" growled Bernie.

He put on the tie he had just extracted from his desk drawer and donned the suit jacket hanging on a hook on the back of his office door. Then he stomped off down the corridor.

Bernie found Williams particularly distasteful. His office door was guarded by a sentinel by the name of Prunella Butcher. Some thought the surname was apt, while others relished calling her Prunella de Ville - behind her back, of course.

"He's expecting you," she proclaimed, before turning her attention back to her typewriter.

Bernie knocked firmly, then waited until he heard an assertive *'Come!'* from within. He stood in front of Williams, waiting for him to finish studying a document which was placed squarely in the middle of his neat and tidy desk.

Williams was ex-army. Bernie was ex-RAF. Bernie had been conscripted as a Junior Tech on National Service in the 1950s.

Williams had served his time for King and Country during the Second World War - as an officer. He was not slow to tell people about this. He was also not slow in moving the conversation on afterwards, in order to avoid follow up questions like,

"What did you do in the war?"

If obliged, Rhys Williams would explain that, among other duties, he had been responsible for ensuring critical logistical support during the D-Day Landings - the largest invasion force in history. What he rarely disclosed was that he was in command of an operation responsible for delivering truckloads of tinned food to the Royal Navy in Felixstowe, and destined for onward shipment to our brave boys who were fighting and dying in their thousands in France. It was an important job.

Williams had been a Captain in the RASC. Bernie had befriended a few squaddies during his time in the RAF, mostly paratroopers. In more sober exchanges he had learned that the Royal Army Service Corps was responsible for the supply of food, water, fuel and other essential materials. Over a pint or two, his para friends would delight in telling Bernie that the abbreviation RASC could be more descriptively expanded to spell out 'Rissoles, Arseholes, Sausages and Chips' and that while some members of that distinguished regiment might describe their regimental shoulder flashes as brown lettering on a yellow background, drunken squaddies would be more likely to describe the colour scheme as *'shit and custard'*.

Eventually, Williams looked up at Bernie and then told him to,

"Sit down!"

This was an order rather than an invitation.

Bernie surmised that Williams would probably feel more at home if he was required to remain standing, like he was up on a charge or something.

Williams was short in stature. Thin face. Small, bright, alert eyes. Like a ferret. He wore a dark blue gabardine suit and a tie decorated with insignia - probably regimental - although Bernie wasn't interested in finding out the details. His hair was greying, as was his thin, black moustache. Both of these features looked as if half-baked attempts had been made to touch them up with Grecian Formula 16 - an amazing new hair dye for aging locks. The 'tache looked much too Hitleresque for Bernie's liking, and he wondered if Williams was aware of the connotations? Probably not. Even he couldn't aspire to such nastiness. Could he? He looked at Bernie for a moment and then, with a steely stare, demanded,

"Can you explain how a group of musicians who recently failed a BBC audition, managed to appear on *Saturday Club* last week?"

"It was a trial broadcast," said Bernie, deadpan.

There was a silence. Williams was not expecting such a manoeuvre. Bernie and Williams sat for a while, looking at each other, while Williams' brain whizzed around.

In the RAF, Bernie and his mates knew the best way to avoid being told not to do something dubious was to do it without asking, and then, when your actions were questioned, you politely explained that you were using your initiative. The officer class were always cracking on about using your initiative - until they didn't like you using your initiative.

After a long pause, Williams spoke, as if to a child.

"Yes, Bernie…"

He managed some sort of unctuous smile for a moment or two. Bernie had no doubt that Williams would rather have referred to him as *'Andrews'* rather than *'Bernie'*, but it was strictly first name terms in the BBC. In 1963 this was a remarkably progressive custom for such a conservative organisation. It was a custom which Bernie greatly appreciated.

"… but as you know full well, that sort of thing only applies if known faces are putting together a new combo."

What this BBC jargon meant was that in order for a new band to be able to bypass a BBC audition, the players involved had to be known to those producers who regularly hired from a familiar clique of professional dance band musicians. It was all very incestuous.

Labouring the point, Williams continued, "For example, if the piano player from the Ted Heath Band gets together with the bass player and drummer from the Jack Bentley Trio…"

Bernie chortled inwardly. This was starting to sound like a fatherly lesson in sex education.

"Well… They're known quantities. There's little risk involved."

"Were you happy with the Bo Diddley session that went out on *Saturday Club* the week before the Rolling Stones?" enquired Bernie politely.

Williams looked at him, blank.

"Who's Bo?.. whatshisname…"

"Diddley," prompted Bernie."

"What's he... Or she... Or whoever they are... Got to do with anything?"

"Bo Diddley's a well-known American rhythm and blues artist. "

It was Bernie's turn to be patronising.

"And he can't use his own band on UK radio. They're all American. MU rules and all that. So he asked us to book some local session musicians. The session musicians he asked us to book are the members of the band currently touring under the name of the Rolling Stones."

Bernie paused while Rhys Williams took it all in, then added,

"Did you listen to the show last week?" he asked, knowing full well that there was as much chance of that as of the Director General of the BBC being elected Pope.

"That's bye the bye, Bernie. The official position is that the Rolling Stones have failed a BBC audition."

Bernie thought he should make a few points in his defence,

"The Rolling Stones who failed the audition are not the same Rolling Stones who backed Bo Diddley the week before last. The band who failed the audition had a different drummer and bass player from the band who successfully backed Bo Diddley on *Saturday Club*."

"The band who appeared as the Rolling Stones on *Saturday Club* were the same band who performed on the Bo Diddley session the previous week. Both broadcasts were received well by the public and I haven't had a single complaint about either of them."

"I also saw the same Rolling Stones lineup which we broadcast, playing live a few weeks ago. They were sensational, and the Bo Diddley session only confirmed my high opinion of them. Also, they got paid Musicians Union rates for backing Bo Diddley."

"Because we got Bo's numbers recorded so quickly, I was able to let the band use the spare studio time to record a few numbers of their own. They were happy to record their extra tracks without any additional fee and they didn't use any more studio time than that which was already allocated. Among other things, I let them record their debut single which shows signs of moving up the charts as a result of their *Saturday Club* appearance. I can't understand why giving them a trial broadcast is such an issue. There are precedents and the reaction to the broadcast in the music press has been very positive."

While delivering his case for the defence, Bernie had noted, with a mixture of curiosity and apprehension that Williams' face was becoming increasingly flushed. As soon as it was clear that Bernie had finished saying his piece, Williams' cork popped!

"Now look here Bernie! You're not going to weasel your way out of a very serious matter. The BBC has to be beyond reproach when it comes to artist selection. There's absolutely no room for any *'old boy'* network in this organisation."

A great guffawing exploded inside Bernie's head. The unrequited guffaws quickly subsided, as the funny side of the absurdity faded away, and Bernie was left with a most disagreeable feeling. Thankfully, he had enough sense to realise that this was now a matter of damage limitation.

There was no reasoning with Williams. He had decided what the outcome of this meeting was going to be before it had even started.

So Bernie refrained from further comment, trying not to look sullen, while recognising at the same time that he was probably failing in that regard too.

After listening to a lengthy rant while his eyes glazed over, Bernie finally heard Williams closing with,

"So if you ever put any new artists on any radio programme for which I am responsible without clearing it first with the auditions panel, you will find yourself facing a disciplinary procedure. Do I make myself clear?"

"Perfectly."

"You may leave."

*****

Bernie shambled back to the office which he shared with a chap called Jeff Griffin. He took off his jacket and hung it behind the door. He looked downcast.

Jeff, a fresh faced, athletic young man, had moved in with Bernie when he joined the pop music production department some months previously. Like Bernie, Jeff had been an engineer in the Tape Recording Unit, and had followed him through the breach in the wall that previously existed between the engineering and production departments.

Bernie observed that Jeff had overtaken him as the youngest member of the popular music department. *'Or should that be undertaken?..'* he reflected. He loved puns, malapropisms and any other sort of word play - and the more childish the better.

In matters of musical education, Bernie and Jeff had followed different paths.

Bernie had gained his knowledge through listening to AFN - the American Forces Network. This radio station exposed him to the whole spectrum of American music: white country and folk music, black American jazz, gospel, country blues and Chicago R&B - all direct from the USA.

Jeff, on the other hand, had absorbed his influences in London jazz clubs, listening to a similarly wide spectrum of American influenced music performed live by British musicians: traditional jazz, modern jazz, skiffle and rhythm and blues.

He also got the chance to hear visiting black American R&B musicians. These artists often accompanied themselves on guitar, sometimes of the electric variety, and were greatly revered in British jazz clubs.

Between them, Bernie and Jeff had the potential to bring a whole range of fresh ideas to a moribund BBC Radio popular music department. But for Bernie, the key question was whether the bosses were open-minded enough to let these radical new ideas flourish?

He pulled out a cigarette, lit up, and took a long drag. As he exhaled, he felt the tension easing. He sat at his desk, aimlessly shuffling a few papers around.

What's up?" asked Jeff.

"It's that obvious?" Bernie replied dolefully.

He sighed, gathered his thoughts, and then gave Jeff a review of the highlights.

"Might be good to keep your head down for a while then?" Jeff suggested.

"I think you're right," Bernie paused.

"But in my case, that's often easier said than done. When I was in the Air Force, my mouth used to get me into all sorts of trouble. If I see something I think is wrong, I find it very difficult not to point it out.   Used to drive my superiors mad. Though I have to say that some of them were a bit more open to other people's ideas than Rhys bloody Williams. He's fucking impossible."

Bernie sat at his desk, brooding.

"Look on the bright side," said Jeff, "you enjoy your job."

"I love working on *Saturday Club*." said Bernie. "I've never enjoyed anything so much. That's what I'm worried about. If they take me off *Saturday Club* I really don't know what I'll do. I never dreamt of getting that job. The thing is, now I've got it, I care about it so much. I can't stop letting people know how I think things could be improved. Which pisses people off. Which upsets the likes of Rhys bloody Williams. Which only increases my chances of getting into trouble."

"Then you definitely need to keep your head down."

"I suppose you're right," said Bernie, grudgingly. "What really gets me is that it is blindingly obvious to anyone with more than half a brain that things can't stay as they are. It's not just the music. The music is only an outward sign of what's going on out there."

"Take a walk down the street and you'll see the kids are dressing differently, doing their hair differently, thinking differently..."

"They've got a bit of money in their pockets, they spend it how they like, and a lot of it goes on visiting clubs and buying records. The bands in the clubs aren't just a musical accompaniment to afternoon tea, they're a clarion call for the youth to stand up and be what they want to be. These new groups are their heroes."

"They represent liberation from the out-of-date attitudes of the grown-ups: parents, teachers, politicians, church. They're fed up being seen and not heard."

"Wow!.." Jeff laughed. "Why don't you tell us what you really think?"

Bernie joined in the laughter.

"But you agree, don't you?" said Bernie.

"I do," said Jeff, "but maybe I'm a bit more realistic? The BBC is very conservative. At least the Popular Music Department of the Light Programme is. And if you push too fast, I think the barriers might go up."

"Look at the state we're in." Bernie persisted. "The Rhys Williams of the world just want things to continue as they are. *BBC News* while people are their eating their breakfast, *Housewives Choice* for the captive female audience at home doing their chores, *A Story A Hymn and A Pr*ayer for a little bit of daily Christian indoctrination followed by that cultural high point of the day, *Music While You Bloody Work.* "

"I mean *Music While You Work* was concocted during the war, to keep morale and productivity up in the factories. But that was twenty odd years ago. And today, we've still got the same old bunch of musos scraping and blowing and plunking away at the same old repertoire. The whole thing is an exercise in keeping that wartime generation of superannuated session players in work. I mean... "

"I could see the point when a lot of musicians whose careers were interrupted by the war finally came home, and it was politically imperative to keep everybody in full time employment. The BBC had to do its bit, like all other major employers. But that was a long time ago. People like Rhys Williams still think it's the sole reason for the BBC's existence, and all they want to do is perpetuate the tedium."

"The kids want something different. They want something lively... Exotic... Fun... Sexy... And we know where they can get it. We just have to put the kids together with the music that we know is out there."

Bernie dried up, and slumped back in his chair.

"Have you got any more work to finish off?" asked Jeff.

"Nothing I can't put off," said Bernie.

"Look, it's nearly clocking off time. Why don't we take an early exit, and nip round the pub?"

*****

They ordered drinks at the bar in the Coach and Horses and found themselves a quiet table in a corner. Bernie lit up another cigarette, sipped a mouthful of his G&T, savoured the taste and leaned back.

"Better?" asked Jeff.

"Yeah... this was a good idea." They sat for a while, enjoying the moment.

"I'm sorry for sounding off like that." Bernie was more composed.

"My problem is that I've always found it difficult to just let things go. In my school days, I'd often see kids going along with things they didn't really think were a good idea. Even then, I was never one for being persuaded to do things I didn't want to do. Stubborn, bloody minded... I got a reputation for that sort of thing. A reputation for being an outsider, I suppose. Not a team player... I was often described as... I was never keen on herd instinct... Following the pack... You know what I mean?"

Jeff nodded and drank his beer.

"Of course that sort of attitude didn't go down well with the teachers. Or the officer class in the Air Force."

"So how do you deal with it?" asked Jeff.

"Well... Quite often I don't." Bernie chuckled.

"I know I'm my own worst enemy. But when I try to conform, I feel such a fraud. It's like I have to pretend all the time. And I really don't like pretending."

Bernie took another sip. Getting things off his chest had done Bernie the world of good. The conversation turned to other topics and the troubles of the day were, for a while, forgotten.

Then they finished their drinks, and went home.

*****

The following week, Bernie found himself hurrying along Piccadilly and turning up Half Moon Street, dropping in to a corner shop on the way to pick up some provisions: 2lbs of potatoes, 1 doz. eggs and 1 packet of chocolate digestives. John Lennon was partial to chocolate digestives.

87

He was feeling very pleased with himself. He'd just finished another successful session with the lads, and felt very lucky that he had been able build such a good working relationship with them and their manager, Brian Epstein. Bernie could now take it for granted that the Beatles would appear on *Saturday Club* every time they released a new record. Their record sales were only going one way.

Their popularity was heading towards the phenomenal, and that phenomenon even had a name - Beatlemania!

Of course the benefit was symbiotic. Their popularity fed into the popularity of *Saturday Club*. Every time Brian Matthew, the presenter, trailed a Beatles appearance for the coming week, it was guaranteed that the following Saturday, the listening figures would hit a new high.

He made his way through the wide passageway which led to a cloistered area in the heart of Mayfair called Shepherds Market, then he turned immediately left, and there, tucked away at the end of a short alleyway between an art dealer's gallery and a block of flats was an unprepossessing front door, painted black.

Three doorbells were on display. The top floor belonged to a Mr Jarvis, now retired, who apparently had been a tailor of some repute. Bernie and Terry's flat was on the middle floor, and the ground floor flat was taken by a Miss Veronica, who, it seemed to Bernie, was fighting a losing battle in her desperate attempts to fend off middle age. Despite the challenges posed by the passage of time, she too was apparently of some repute, as her front doorbell was busy all day and all night - weekends included.

After the session that morning, the boys had proclaimed that they were starving.

Early starts after late nights on the road didn't leave time to grab much more than a bowl of cornflakes. In the old days, that would be no problem. They would just pop in to the nearest caff to refuel whenever they felt like it. But these days, people would quickly recognise them in the street, and they were likely to get mobbed. So Bernie had come up with a plan.

"How do you fancy egg and chips? I can do you some round at the flat."

Bernie's brainwave was gratefully received, so he outlined the rest of the plan.

"Look, give me half an hour to go and get the stuff, and then get Mal to drop you off at the door. I'll put the front door on the latch, but for God's sake remember to drop the latch when you're inside. The tart downstairs goes ballistic if we leave the door open."

Bernie then departed for Mayfair, leaving the boys exchanging ribald comments about Bernie's enterprising neighbour.

Cradling the groceries in a large, brown paper bag in one arm, Bernie struggled to extract the key from his pocket with his free hand, inserted it in the lock and then turned the key. As he stepped inside, he heard some muttering in the hall. It sounded like female muttering. Who on earth could that be?

He quietly closed the door, crept to the corner and peered round to see a pretty young lady with short red hair, cut to her jawline, in a figure-hugging dress quartered in black and white. It was Cilla Black, the latest of Brian Epstein's fast growing roster of protégés. Terry must have let her in. Bernie regularly got all the inside track from Terry, and he knew that Brian had negotiated a record deal on Cilla's behalf. In fact, he had already heard a white label copy of her, as yet, unreleased first single.

"I 'ate Dusty... I 'ate Dusty..." she intoned in a liturgical manner, as she stood, bent over a large bird-cage on the hall table.

The mynah bird which was the focus of Cilla's attention, responded with a cheerful, melodic warbling sound. She had another go.

"I 'ate Dusty... I 'ate Dusty..."

Bernie must have rustled his paper bag or shifted his weight on a creaky floorboard.

"Oh!.. Blurry hell!.. It's you Bernie. What are you doin' creepin' round like that?.. You scared the blurry life out of me."

"What am *I* doing?" Bernie laughed.

Then the penny dropped. Bernie had overheard everything.

"It's just a bit o' fun Bernie," said Cilla, looking a bit sheepish. "I didn't mean any harm."

"I'm not sure Dusty Springfield will agree when I give her the news," Bernie teased.

"Oh gawd!.. You wouldn't do that? Would you?"

"Go on!" Bernie laughed. "Your secret's safe with me."

"It's just that everybody I speak to in the business…. Well, it's Dusty Springfield this and Dusty Springfield that…. And even the people at the record company are always on about her. It's like I'm expected to be another Dusty Springfield - which I'm not. I'm nothing like her."

"Well I think your record's great," said Bernie.

"You've heard it? They haven't given me a blurry copy." she complained.

"When they finally get around to releasing it, I'll book you on *Saturday Club*. If you want?"

Cilla stretched out her hand and laid it affectionately on Bernie's arm, "Aw... Yer a pal Bernie." Then, switching to nosey parker mode, "What's in the bag then?"

"A little something for the boys Cilla. They haven't had time for a proper breakfast yet. Do you want to join us?"

"Yer all right, thanks. I'm being picked up in a mo' for a lunch meeting with Brian. Some songwriter 'e wants to introduce me to."

"Anyone I'd know?" asked Bernie.

"I forget his name," said Cilla.

"You can sit and keep me company in the kitchen then, until your driver turns up," Bernie suggested to Cilla.

As they walked down the hall, Joey, the Mynah bird suddenly sprang into life.

"Hello Ringo! Fuck off Ringo!.."

It squawked triumphantly.

"Hello Ringo!.. Fuck off Ringo!.."

Bernie and Cilla collapsed in a heap of laughter.

*****

Bernie leafed through the latest copy of the *Melody Maker* to see if he
could find any interesting snippets of music business gossip to keep him
entertained while waiting for the others to arrive for the meeting.
A departmental production meeting. Not that much was discussed in the
way of production. Far too much hot air for that, in Bernie's opinion.

When he was working in the main BH network switching centre, he found
music business papers like *Melody Maker* and *Record Mirror* were the
best way of keeping in touch. But since he started producing *Saturday
Club*, Bernie figured he probably knew more about what the next big thing
was likely to be than most journalists working for the music press.

It sometimes seemed that the entire promotional activity of the UK record
industry was focused on him, via every possible means of communication:
letters, flyers, phone calls and invitations to PR events - not to mention
the constant parade of cheerful (sometimes), persistent (always)
promotion men and women who dumped mountains of new record
releases and accompanying bumph on his desk every day.

Increasingly, he was getting calls from journalists sniffing around to see if
he knew anything they didn't. This was not surprising. One record
producer had admitted to Bernie that getting a new release played on
Saturday Club could result in tens, or even hundreds of thousands in
orders - starting at 9am prompt the following Monday when the record
shops opened. So Bernie was not only a prime target for those whose
living it was to sell records, but also for those who dealt in the rumour and
gossip which accompanied that sort of activity.

BBC Radio still had a monopoly throughout the UK, which gave it immense power. To the constant resentment of the record biz. The record companies would have much preferred the kind of arrangement they had with Radio Luxembourg, which beamed in record shows of dubious technical quality from the continent every evening. There was no *'editorial'* function as such on Radio Luxembourg. Record companies simply paid for their records to be played.

So, *'product'* from the richest record companies got the prime promotional spots, whether their latest releases were any good - or not. The record companies loved that sort of control.

At first, Bernie fretted about the immense power he now wielded. In vulnerable moments, he might ask himself just exactly what qualified him, in particular, to wield this cultural Sword of Damocles? In the eyes of a record or song plugger, he could make or break their careers, not to mention the careers of all the artists and songwriters they represented. But in those vulnerable moments, Bernie would make a conscious effort to remind himself of the preponderance of dickheads who ran the UK record business. Then he would start to worry a lot less.

Only a week before, he had been introduced to the boss of a big record label who, it was said, at a recent board meeting, had asked his subordinates to explain why one of their leading artists, Johnny Kidd and the Pirates, had not achieved any hits for some considerable period of time.

When the said executive was informed that Johnny Kidd had been killed in a car crash some months before, he went quiet. But his expression left all present in no doubt that he thought this sort of excuse to be quite lame.

Another captain of the music industry had recently explained to Bernie, over a long, liquid lunch, why he should relax and cease to worry about the apparent profligacy he witnessed in the record business on a daily basis.

Bernie had observed that the immense number of new releases every week, and the fortunes spent on recording and promoting each of these aspiring acts compared very unfavourably with the incredibly small number of records which actually made it into the charts. Then he voiced the opinion that, based on that sort of experience, the industry might do well to be a bit more selective.

His jovial host's response was that nobody needed to bother with all that. It wasn't as if it was high art or anything, was it? This pop stuff was here today, gone tomorrow. Who knew what the general public might want next? They probably didn't even know themselves. So, he explained, in primary school terms, that the best way of developing new talent was to apply the 100 to 1 strategy. "Look Bernie, if you throw 100 per cent of crap at the wall, at least 1 percent of it has got to stick. Hasn't it?"

Mass-market ladies' fashions - his day job - provided him with more than a luxurious living on a daily basis - thank you very much. So spending surplus cash on making records was his hobby. As long he broke even, it was a very nice pastime. He met lots of nice young boys in the process. And occasionally, he hit the jackpot. Lovely jubbly!

Bernie was sure that if people of that ilk had his job at the BBC, the last thing on their minds would be what was good for the audience, or the artists struggling to connect with them.

*****

Just then, Bernie's thoughts about the motivations of those running the record business were interrupted by the next arrival for the meeting.

Alex Radford. If Bernie thought these meetings ran on hot air, then Alex was a major supplier.

Alex was a frustrated thespian. What he really wanted to be was a film star. If not a film star, then the West End would be good. Of course, he wouldn't say no to a good, meaty part on a gritty TV drama. If he was really desperate, he might reluctantly agree to a role on a radio drama - of any kind. *'You have to start somewhere.'*

But poor old Alex hadn't yet managed to get his foot in any of these doors, and, in the meantime, had to be content with whichever am-dram parts he could drum up in his spare time.

While his life was on hold, he spent his days emulating the classic matinee idol, preening his hair and wearing fashionable suits with flamboyant ties while producing weekend shows for the more mature end of the Light Programme audience.

Interviews with fading actors from the musical theatre were his stock in trade. Lots of retrospection with a few nostalgic songs from yesteryear chucked in for good measure.

What he really enjoyed was a feature about a big star of stage or screen. Something that involved him prerecording a story about one of his heroes and delivering the narrative in his heightened prose, unconsciously (or perhaps consciously?) in the hope of catching some drama producer's ear out there in the ether. What he was not interested in was pop music.

Alex nodded at Bernie. Bernie nodded back.

Next to arrive was Margo Benson. One of those eminent few who had blithely consigned the Rolling Stones to the dustbin of history on reviewing their BBC audition.

Margo had worked her way up. She had been a very efficient production secretary: good shorthand and typing, efficient, if curt, telephone manner, and a deserved reputation for getting things done. Being married to one of the Light Programme's Executive Producers hadn't done her career prospects any harm either.

Now, as the producer of a very popular morning show herself, she seemed the personification of her target audience - the housebound housewife. But beneath that demure exterior of pastel coloured twin set and pearls lurked the steely determination of a skilled political operator. The younger stratum of her favoured demographic might already be showing signs of interest in the more unruly end of the pop music spectrum, but Margo was determined not to give in to them.

It was Margo's duty to maintain standards and stick, not only to what she saw as the middle-of-the-road, but to stick to what she preferred to be the British middle-of-the-road.

If she found that listeners were sending in so many requests for a particular song that it couldn't be ignored, she would, for example, select the British version of *Only Sixteen* performed by our own Craig Douglas in preference to the US original by the peerless black soul singer, Sam Cooke. Even then, she only did so with the greatest of reluctance. She abhorred the increasing Americanisation of the British music industry and really couldn't understand why the general public was so interested in material which she considered to be both primitive and morally subversive.

Margo was fortunate. She was never short of a friend or two in high places for political support in her endeavours to keep the content of her shows on the straight and narrow.

'Straight and narrow?' thought Bernie.

On one occasion, Margo decided to feature Pat Boone's lame version of the rock 'n' roll classic *Tutti Frutti*. Bernie was most inquisitive, and couldn't resist sidling up to Margo's secretary in the canteen a day or two later. He was on good terms with Pam, and she didn't bat an eyelid when he enquired,

"Here, when you played *Tutti Frutti* the other day, was the request really for the Pat Boone version?"

"No it wasn't. We had a lot of requests for that song, but they were all for the Little Richard version."

Bernie nodded.

"Why?" asked Pam.

"Oh nothing... Just interested."

Bernie was very interested. Of course Pat Boone would be Margo's preferred choice. He may not have been British, but he was white, and he was an avowed Christian whose professed belief in sexual abstinence before marriage was frequently and widely publicised. These were pleasures which should only be experienced within the confines of wedlock, and he frequently exhorted his teenage fan base to aspire to his lofty ideals (he already being in a position to enjoy all the home comforts of matrimony himself).

Bernie wondered what Margo's reaction would be if he enlightened her by explaining that, before it was sanitised for public consumption, Little Richard's composition originally contained lyrics which were a paean to the inestimable pleasures of anal sex - of the non-heterosexual variety. *'Tutti Frutti!.. What a booty!..'* *'Nice and greasy!.. Slips so easy!..'* not to mention the graphic images to be conjured up by the onomatopoeic intro - *'A wop bob a loo bop, a lop bam boom!'*

'Straight and narrow?' Bernie chuckled. To his eternal regret, Bernie knew that was a conversation which was never going to happen.

Margo made no eye contact with Bernie whatsoever.

*****

Then Clive Nosary turned up. Bernie didn't know what to make of Clive. If he had been asked to match Clive to a colour, he would have said grey.

He knew he worked in the Gramophone Department selecting records to play on the Light Programme, and therefore had zero knowledge about, or interest in, live music production. But Bernie had no idea what he actually got up to.

Conversation with Clive was a non-starter. He didn't seem to be interested in anything. True to form, he turned up, sat himself down and proceeded to do... well... nothing really... except stare into space.

*****

As it drew closer to the start time of the meeting, others started filing in at increasing frequency. Jeff Griffin was the next through the door.

'Thank God we've got at least one more producer trying to bring the department up to date', thought Bernie.

Looking round the table, it was clear that those who took pop music seriously were still very much in the minority. Jeff nodded, and took a seat next to Bernie.

Jimmy Grant, who was sitting across from Bernie, was a very important part of the minority. In fact, if it weren't for Jimmy, there might not even be a minority, and the Popular Music Department of the BBC Light Programme might still be staffed exclusively by a bunch of conservatively dressed fossils and misfits who sounded like a bunch of refugees from elocution lessons. By way of contrast, in Bernie's eyes, Jimmy was a pioneer.

He was highly educated: maths and science were his forte, and he was a classically trained pianist. But his passion was jazz - particularly modern - particularly bebop. He gigged in bands with well-respected recording artists like trumpeter and band leader Nat Gonella.

Bernie admired Jimmy. Some might assume that, as he was musically talented, he would be some sort of musical snob. Quite the reverse was true. Although he was classically trained, the ethos of jazz placed value on individual, joyful expression over slavish adherence to the rules and regulations of musical notation, so he was quick to recognise the passion and enthusiasm in some of the latest musical trends, even if they weren't always executed in a neat and tidy fashion. Jimmy gave a great deal of consideration to the teenage audience, which was something of a rarity amongst people of his age.

When he took Bernie under his wing on *Saturday Club*, he told him that before he joined the BBC, he thought the second most important person in the BBC - after the Director General - was the producer of *Jazz Club*.

Of course, once on board, he quickly realised that he wasn't going to get much promotion producing *Jazz Club*. And the same went for *Saturday Club*. Jimmy was in the process of moving onwards and upwards.

When Jimmy started spending more time on glitzy productions involving orchestras and big bands, he was more than happy to let Bernie spread his wings. He was pleased with the quality of Bernie's work. The listening figures were rising steadily, fuelled by the surprising success of the new generation of British beat groups who had emerged in the wake of the Beatles.

Bernie was clearly in touch with the latest trends. So, although Jimmy remained in overall control of *Saturday Club*, he had let Bernie loose by charging him with the additional responsibility of producing the entire show every second week.

*****

Then Pat Brennan shambled through the door. Typically, just a minute or two before the production meeting was due to begin.

Until recently, Pat had been in charge of *Lunchtime Pops*. The title was a bit of a misnomer. This show attempted to do something for the young folks between the hours of 1pm and 2pm every day. But it wasn't a record show.

It consisted of live performances by an assorted collection of session musicians, most of whom wouldn't have looked out of place in an Al Jolson movie, all doing their level best to murder the latest hit records. To a man, (they were all men), they despised what they were required to play. This was the downside of *'needletime'* restrictions on playing records, and *Lunchtime Pops* had to make do with second rate live bands performing second rate cover versions.

While in charge of the show, Pat Brennan had taken all these challenges in his stride. Difficulties which might have seemed formidable to those of a more discerning nature just flowed off Pat - like water off a duck's back.

He was in the fortunate position that, when it came to matters of value judgements relating to the production of popular music on the radio, he simply didn't give a shit.

Having the hide of a rhinoceros had other benefits too. Pat was a notorious freeloader. He was liable to turn up at all record business events, invited or not, whether the artist in question had any relevance to the programme he was producing or not. And he never had any problem in hoovering up as much food and drink as his prodigious intestines could accommodate.

He also had a habit of phoning up record pluggers at random, suggesting that they might like to meet him for lunch - at their expense, of course - in order to discuss their latest releases.

In pursuing these endeavours, Pat was surprisingly successful. Most promotion people readily agreed to his requests, although that might have had more to do with the fact that the record company would be picking up the tab - and a valid receipt for an expensive lunch with a BBC producer would, in any case, look good on the plugger's work activity sheet at the end of the month.

Once, Pat had been taken to a swanky restaurant in St James. On being presented with an hors d'ouevre consisting of a single jumbo prawn cooked in its shell, he lifted it daintily with his fingers, explaining to his surprised host, *'You know, you can eat these things whole,'* before popping the crustacean - complete with shell, little legs, antennae, bulging eyeballs and all - into his mouth. Adding, with his mouth full, *'Not many people know that.'*

Pat was based in a BBC office building opposite BH called Egton House. When he found out about it, he seemed quite proud of the fact that his colleagues in the record business had dubbed him *'Egton Ronay'* - after the prominent gourmet, Egon Ronay, who was very fashionable at the time.

Some within these circles might also refer to Pat as *'The face that lunched a thousand shits.'* But if he was ever aware of that moniker, he never said so.

Despite all the bad press, it was hard not to like Pat. Being affable was his redeeming quality. His interest in music stretched as far as the age of the crooner - anything from Bing Crosby to Frank Sinatra - and no further.

Not that he ever voiced any objections to the shoddy material over which he was obliged to preside on *Lunchtime Pops*. He was the perfect employee. Things chuntered along. He didn't make waves. His bosses didn't either. Everyone was happy. Until one day.

That day, Bill Holliday was tuned in to *Lunchtime Pops.* This particular programme was one of a group of Light Programme shows for which Bill Holliday had *'Executive Producer'* responsibilities. Executive Producers didn't produce any programmes themselves. They had no creative role. As a result, they would spend their time trying to improve the various productions under their aegis. Or so they would claim.

The less charitable might opine that, as the Executive Producer class had nothing better to do, they would attempt to justify their existence by constantly tinkering, interfering, unconstructively criticising, getting on people's nerves and generally wasting everyone's time.

Lunchtime Pops wasn't one of Holliday's favourites. However, he probably had little office work that day, so, to relieve the boredom, he had decided to switch his office speaker over to the Light Programme, while leafing dreamily through a brochure detailing the latest features of a flashy sailboat. Boating was Bill's preferred activity. Just then, in the midst of his daydream, through the ether, he subconsciously registered a familiar Irish lilt in a most unfamiliar context. The neurons and synapses in Holliday's brain must have stirred and connected, because, what had initially inhabited the backwaters of his subconscious suddenly lurched to the front of his mind.

"Welcome folks, once more, to *Lunchtime Pops* on the BBC Light Programme. It's Pat Brennan here, your host for the next hour. And what an hour we have in store for you..."

Holliday sat dumbfounded, staring at the loudspeaker in disbelief. When he finally moved, it was to grab a nearby copy of the *Radio Times*, and see who was officially listed as the compère for that particular show. It was not Pat Brennan.

He opened the door to his office, and bellowed to Ethel, his secretary,

"Are you listening to this?"

Ethel blanched, immediately placing her half eaten sandwiches in her desk drawer.

"What's that, Mr Holliday?"

"The radio damn it! *Lunchtime Pops!*"

Ethel scrambled to switch on her own office loudspeaker. When it burst into life, it was on the BBC Home Service.

She preferred the news on the Home Service. It took her a second or two to realise that she was listening to the wrong programme, but, just before Bill Holliday was about to explode, she grabbed the switch and turned it over to the Light Programme. Then she heard Pat Brennan's voice. Then she looked back at Bill Holliday. Totally confused.

"Well, don't just stare at me woman!.. Find out what the hell is going on!"

And with that, he slammed his office door shut.

After a few hurried phone calls, Ethel meekly entered Bill Holliday's office and informed him that, the way she understood it, the regular presenter, Edward Boyd, was scheduled to compère *Lunchtime Pops* that day, but, due to a misunderstanding, he was still away on a trip abroad. He had taken a two week break, whereas the people writing the schedule had thought he was only away for a week.

"And who wrote the schedule?" enquired Holliday testily.

"Ummm..." Ethel consulted her notes, and after quickly deciding there was no way she could spin it otherwise, she finally admitted,

"It was Pat Brennan."

"Well, well..." said Holliday, almost chuckling.

"The man who, for months now, has been trying to persuade me - or anyone else within earshot - to recognise his nascent talents as a radio presenter, just happened to be around to provide on-the-spot emergency cover for someone he (making *'quote marks'* gestures with his fingers) *'thought was away for another week'* "

He paused, exasperated,

"And he would have us believe that he made this inexcusable administrative cock-up in good faith, while any thoughts he might have harboured of engineering an unofficial audition for himself, live on the radio, never sprang into his tiny little mind?" Then, shaking his head, "I could almost admire his audacity."

In that moment, wafting from the radio, he heard the strains of *Diane*. A current hit. A melodious, middle-of-the-road song by the Irish group, the Bachelors. But, of course, this was a cover version by the *Lunchtime Pops* house band. The crooner on this particular cover version had an appropriate, soft, Irish brogue which was, again... familiar?..

"God preserve me!"

Holliday listened intently for a moment, and then composed himself.

"Brennan's meant to be producing this bloody show. How can he be doing that and crooning at the same time?"

He looked around the office to see if anyone could provide any explanation.

"Simon Cutler is producing," offered Ethel. "He was just about to go home after his early start this morning when he got a call from Pat to say there was an emergency at the Playhouse, and that he should get down there straight away to take over the production, as Pat had been forced to take on the compère's role."

"Forced!" scoffed Holliday. "Ethel, get on the phone to the studio and inform Mr Cutler, that I want to see him and Mr Brennan in my office immediately after the show comes off the air. And make sure they both

105

understand that it's not for me to offer them my congratulations."

The upshot of Pat Brennan's special day was that when the pair of them were wheeled into Bill Holliday's office some time later, the interview was short and to the point.

Pat was summarily removed as producer of *Lunchtime Pops* and Simon Cutler was appointed immediately in his place. Pat knew better than to ask why, but as they were both being dismissed as quickly as they had come in, he asked timidly,

"What will happen to me?"

Holliday responded by telling him to get lost, letting him stew for a few days, and then allocating him to *Music While You Work* until he worked out what to do with him in the long term.

Almost twenty years after the war, the BBC was still imbued with attitudes ingrained in days of immediate post-war austerity: that every civilised society had a duty to provide full employment and jobs for life.

Sometimes Bernie wondered to what level of depravity one would have to sink in order to actually get sacked from the BBC?

*****

Pat Brennan smiled at Bernie amiably as he took his place at the conference table. Bernie smiled back and watched as Pat prepared himself, extracting a foolscap notepad from his briefcase.

Bernie knew there was no chance of Pat taking any notes, and he also knew that he wouldn't be bringing up any issues for discussion during this production meeting.

No, from observing his previous behaviour, Bernie knew that the notepad was there to provide him with a suitable writing surface on which he could doodle or play noughts and crosses to help him pass the time until he could get back to doing something less tedious.

Bernie was scanning the disparate faces around the conference table when there was a flurry of activity. As the door opened, the assembled cast half-heartedly sat themselves to attention and Aubrey Small plus entourage swept in to the room.

Aubrey Small's full title was Deputy Controller, BBC Light Programme, although those producers who had young children had dubbed him the Fat Controller - after a jolly character from the popular children's book, Thomas the Tank Engine. Aubrey Small was a portly man in a grey pin-stripe suit. Public school. Aloof. Jolly he was not. He was accompanied by his secretary Edwina Dinsdale and, predictably, by his favourite toady, Rhys Williams, H.O.M.P.

The Fat Controller took his place at the head of the large conference table, while the HOMP installed himself at the right hand of The Father.

The first item on the agenda was the management of the tea and coffee making facilities, and the increasingly sloppy behaviour of those involved in making the refreshments.

All present were told to have a word with their secretaries and encourage them to mend their ways. Bernie knew who the culprits were, and they were not the secretaries. Not that anyone was going to own up, or defend the honour of their faithful colleagues who weren't there to defend themselves. In any case, Bernie made his own tea, and he made sure he kept the place neat and tidy.

Still, standards had to be maintained, and the appearance of the office areas was of paramount importance, particularly when it reflected on the image of the Deputy Controller, Light Programme. Everyone mumbled their assent, and things moved on.

The next item was about the consumption of office stationery, which had been increasing in a seemingly uncontrolled manner - at least according to the Deputy Controller. A point thoroughly endorsed by Rhys Williams whose concurrence he signalled by nodding, gravely, and making some sort of annotation in his big black book with his Parker fountain pen.

And so it went on.... Item after item of what Bernie would have described as housekeeping (if he needed to be polite) - or crap (if he didn't). Almost an hour later, attention spans, which were not particularly resilient in the first place, were sagging noticeably. By Bernie's watch, the meeting was about to overrun, when things took a surprising turn.

"Finally," Aubrey Small declared, "I'd like to us to take a little time to talk about audience listening figures."

Bernie's heart skipped a beat. He was overjoyed that, at last, real issues relating to actual productions were to be put on the table for discussion. This was more like it. In his enthusiasm to embrace the opportunity, he raised his hand and caught the eye of the Fat Controller - who seemed a little taken aback. But Aubrey Small was nothing, if not polite.

"What is it Bernie?" he enquired, indulgently.

"I'm glad you've given us the opportunity to talk about audience reaction Aubrey."

Rhys Williams winced at the familiarity in Bernie's tone of voice.

Bernie didn't intend any disrespect, it was just that he was genuinely excited for once, and a sense of decorum was the last thing on his mind.

"Things have been going very well on *Saturday Club* since the last time we talked about this sort of thing *(Bernie couldn't remember when they'd ever talked about such things).* And if you look at the figures month by month since the beginning of the year, you'll see a marked rise, not only in the number of people listening to *Saturday Club*, but also in the audience appreciation index which shows how much the audience rates the quality of what we're doing."

"We know how these surveys work Bernie," said Rhys Williams, condescendingly.

Bernie ploughed on, "…and the comments canvassed in the latest survey show that since Beatlemania took off, there has been a dramatic increase in interest across all age groups, not only in the Beatles specifically, but also in the British pop music scene in general."

With all eyes looking expectantly in his direction, Bernie made his final, salient point.

"*Saturday Club*, and possible spin-offs from what *Saturday Club* has started, are ideally placed to make the most of this trend."

There was a hushed silence. No-one seemed to know how to respond. Rhys Williams' beady eyes locked on to Bernie's while he assumed the attitude of a weasel, readying itself to strike,

"And precisely what point are you making Bernie?" he demanded in his clipped Welsh tones.

To Bernie, the answer was obvious. "Well…. given the proven success, perhaps it's time to launch more programmes like *Saturday Club?*"

Williams laughed out loud. "Bernie..." he gushed, "Fads will come and go.... We can't just drop everything and rush down each fashionable new rabbit hole as it appears, only for it to vanish again just as quickly."

"The BBC is here to provide a public service to licence payers as a whole, and one quality which licence payers value above all else is stability. We're not here to jump on bandwagons, like some sort of commercial operation..."

Just then, Aubrey Small discreetly laid a restraining hand on Williams' sleeve.

"I haven't had the chance to look at the details you are highlighting Bernie, but it sounds as if you are doing a good job. So, keep up the good work! Rhys and I shall review the issues you have raised and take them into account in future planning."

Then, with Aubrey Small's next statement, it began to dawn on Bernie why the subject of audience figures had been raised at all. And he finally understood that, in raising the subject, his boss's intentions were definitely not designed to open things up for general discussion - as Bernie had mistakenly assumed.

"The reason I wanted to talk about audience data," the Fat Controller announced gravely, "is because the latest survey shows that the BBC Light Programme got record listening figures for the two minutes' respectful silence in remembrance of the War Dead during the last broadcast from the Cenotaph."

On hearing this, Bernie could not resist.

"Perhaps we should do more of those then?"

Another, more deadly silence followed, with the hint of a suppressed snigger or two from around the table.

Bernie's sarcasm seemed to go right over the head of Aubrey Small. But not Rhys Williams'. His measured reaction was to inform Bernie, in his most officious whine that,

"I'd like to see you in my office after the meeting."

Bernie had no doubt what that meant.

*****

The closer he got to Rhys Williams' office, the more anxious Bernie became.

Thoughts of their previous, disastrous confrontation over the Rolling Stones had been running through his head ever since the meeting had ended.

Williams' office door was open, and Prunella waved him through. He stood for a while. On receiving neither an invitation, nor even an order to 'take a seat', he pulled up a chair and sat himself in front of the desk. He wondered what he was in for this time. Was there a BBC rule or regulation which forbade the use of sarcasm in the workplace?

Williams looked up briefly, then continued annotating the important document he had been studying. When he was satisfied, either with his work, or with the enjoyment derived from keeping Bernie waiting, he carefully put pen and paper aside.

"Thank you for coming along Bernie."

'Did I have a choice?' thought Bernie.

"I'd just like to put you straight on how things are done in this department."

'Here we go.'

"You raised an item for discussion during the production meeting."

"Yes I did," agreed Bernie, adding, in his head,

'And a fat lot of good that did me... '

"We can't have issues being raised ad hoc like that. We need these meetings to run efficiently, and if everyone raises whatever issues happen to come into their head at any particular time, willy-nilly, then there would be total chaos. We'd be permanently overrunning, apart from anything else, and we might not have an appropriate amount of time to devote to important matters."

He paused.

"You do see that Bernie, don't you?"

Bernie thought that Williams was being uncharacteristically amiable. Maybe the Fat Controller had, at Bernie's prompting, actually taken a look at the audience figures? Maybe he'd realised that Bernie had a point? Maybe he'd suggested that Williams take it easy on him? Give him some encouragement?

Or maybe pigs had actually taken to the skies?

In his attempts to mollify Williams, he had been nodding respectfully, as if in agreement with his pontifications. Amazingly, Williams seemed to be responding to these efforts. So Bernie decided to see just how long he could keep up the pretence.

Williams droned on... Until...

"So, in future Bernie, if you have anything you want to bring up at a production meeting, have a word with me first, and I'll see if it's an appropriate item for the agenda."

"Absolutely!" said Bernie.

"I mean, if you'd spoken to me about the issue you raised, I could have told you it was not the appropriate forum. So, we could all have saved ourselves some wasted effort."

Bernie felt his hackles rising again. For a few minutes he had been quite pleased with himself, nodding, making vague noises of assent, and, as far as he was aware, avoiding negative body language.

Unfortunately, Williams' comment that a production meeting was *'not the appropriate forum'* to raise questions about production started to gnaw away at Bernie's resolve.

Fortunately, Bernie didn't get the opportunity to react.

"Oh, and one more thing Bernie. That remark about broadcasting further editions of the two minutes' silence was rather tasteless, don't you think?"

Williams had finally taken some time out from his monologue to chide him for his sarcasm - ostensibly the reason for this little tête à tête in the first place - and he was waiting for a response. Bernie was ill-prepared, which was just as well, as he had no time to think up a suitably sarcastic reply.

"Yes… Sorry about that…"

"Well, I'm glad to hear it, so please, let's have no more of that sort of thing."

Williams started to tidy things up on his desk. Clearly, the pep talk was at an end, and Bernie was pleased to acknowledge that it hadn't turned out to be a confrontation. More of a one-sided meeting. All in all, a successful outcome.

Having wrapped up the proceedings, Williams then invited Bernie out of his office.

An invitation which Bernie was only too glad to accept.

The Turn of the Year

Bernie was at his desk when Shirley brought in the post. The usual: a pile of press releases promoting the latest artists, records, performances, tours … Invitations to this and that record reception … Invitations to this or that club to see this or that new band... Not to mention the latest consignment of new singles and albums.

One unusual item which caught Bernie's eye was a postcard. The central feature was a bronze Viking statue with wings on his helmet, blowing a large curly horn. Other scenes were of tidy waterfronts with boats in the foreground and tall spires in the distance. He looked at the strange text in a language he didn't understand until he came to the word Stockholm.

'Who do I know in Stockholm?' he wondered. None of his family had ever expressed an interest in going there. He certainly didn't know anyone who lived there. Then he turned the card over - and laughed out loud.

It was addressed to:

Bernize Andrews
c/o Saturday Club
The BBC
London W1

Remarkably, it had found its way to Bernie's office with no problem whatsoever. He read the message:

Pleez play She Loves Me for everydoby at
No 10 Downer Street.
You remain, sir, my obedient service
J. Winston Lemming

'What a prat.' Bernie smiled, fished out a drawing pin and stuck it, proudly, on the cork board in his office.

The boys were beginning to cause a stir on the continent, and not just in Germany, where they had made a name for themselves in their early days, playing in the fleshpots of Hamburg long before they had a record deal. Now, they were off to Sweden to appear on a national TV show.

The postcard cheered Bernie up immensely and kept his visitors amused for some considerable period of time.

*****

1963 had come and gone. During the festive period Bernie reflected on the ups and downs. The year had arrived in humdrum fashion, but here in the UK, 1963 went out in a frenzy, having seen a total transformation of the music scene.

Only the January before, Elvis Presley and Cliff Richard had been the grand old men of rock'n'roll. Elvis ruled on both sides of the Atlantic, while Cliff shared the spoils as the junior partner in Britain. The cultural explosion originating in the southern states of the USA in the mid '50s had shocked and enthralled the Western World by equal measure.

Unfortunately, this youth-led movement had been gradually subdued and sanitised. The clean-up had been achieved through the persistent efforts of the establishment, which used its influence to water down anything it considered degenerate or subversive.

In this mission, it was aided and abetted by the impresarios, agents and managers of the music business, who increased their efforts to transform their wild men of rock'n'roll into *'all round family entertainers'*.

The received wisdom in showbiz circles at that time was, *'Look son, this rock'n'roll thing is a fad. It's the grown-ups who have the money to spend, and if you don't widen your appeal you're not going to last long.'*

It was a mantra which sounded entirely plausible to the new generation of rock'n'roll stars, most of whom came from humble beginnings. They suddenly found themselves with unexpected amounts of cash in their pockets, and, in the interest of keeping the money rolling in, they listened carefully to their mentors. Although it has to be said that some of the worst damage suffered by the first generation of rock'n'rollers was self-inflicted - much to the disgust of the more youthful element of their fan base.

Up until the end of 1962, the UK charts tended to follow the US charts, particularly at the teen end of the spectrum. Jerry Lee Lewis, the rock'n'roll devil incarnate, described it, deprecatingly, as *'the era of the Bobbys'*: Bobby Vinton, Bobby Vee, Bobby Rydell and all the other clean cut, wholesome, simpering, whimpering crew that the US record industry was so keen to pump out - in deference to the armies of respectable parents who strove to keep their offspring, and particularly their daughters, on what they saw as the right path.

When 1963 arrived, the Beatles blew the doors of repression off their hinges. In the UK, the aforementioned sterilised kitsch was rendered obsolete - at a stroke.

Those who initially dismissed the Beatles as just another fad with funny haircuts soon had to eat their words. Each record release was bigger than the last. Each concert tour was bigger than the last. And the media couldn't get enough. By the end of the year, anything interesting that happened to the Beatles - or sometimes things that hadn't actually happened to them at all - made front page news.

Bernie couldn't believe his luck. A bunch of guys who he initially recognised as a *'promising new group'*, had repeatedly fulfilled that promise. What is more, having befriended them, here he was occupying a front row seat. Once again, he had to ask himself, *'How the fuck did I get here?'*

For Bernie, the highlight of the year had been the 5th Anniversary of Jimmy Grant's wonderful creation, *Saturday Club*. He had persuaded Jimmy, without too much effort, to spend, and then overspend, the usual weekly budget on a star studded line-up. He was adamant that it would break the record for audience listening figures. It did.

The special lineup, headlined by The Beatles and the Everly Brothers, featured many other chart-topping acts of the time: Joe Brown and the Bruvvers, US singer Tommy Roe, Kenny Ball's Jazzmen, Kathy Kirby and Frank Ifield. It was a signal success. When the audience research figures came in a few weeks later, they showed that 20.2% of the adult population had tuned in. That was getting close to fifteen million adults.

In those days, the BBC, in its infinite wisdom, didn't bother canvassing the opinion of anyone under the age of 15. But Bernie knew from the contents of the weekly *Saturday Club* mail bag that under-15s were a significant segment of the listening audience, so the actual audience could be anything up to twenty million - or more. On those Saturdays when it was Jimmy rather than he who was in charge of the broadcast, every time Bernie walked through a street market, into a shop or into a café, it seemed that the raucous tones of *Saturday Club* were ubiquitous. Who knows what the actual audience numbers were. But they were huge.

Bernie's star was rising - marred only by the management fallout caused by his unauthorised *'trial broadcast'* of the Rolling Stones. Since then, he had been trying to follow Jeff Griffin's advice and keep his head below the parapet.

So far so good. Now that 1964 had arrived, he wondered what the next big thing would be?

He didn't have to wait long.

*****

On Thursday, January the 16th 1964, Bernie was sitting comfortably in the armchair by his bed. He was sorting through the sizeable backlog of new releases.

Some records just jump out at you wherever you are and you know straight away that they are going to be successful. Others need to be absorbed in more thoughtful surroundings before they earn their appeal. So Bernie preferred listening to new records, alone, at home, rather than in the hustle and bustle of the office.

In those days, the process of making a hit record was shrouded in mystique and was the source of much fascination to the record buying public.

The music press often ran features about how *'so and so'* was discovered or how *'such and such'* a record was made. When the opportunity arose, the moguls of the record business were not slow to publicise how infallible their talent selection and record production processes were.

Those processes revolved around the A&R (Artistes and Repertoire) man. A constant stream of personal managers and agents would knock on the A&R man's door touting their latest wannabes. After selecting an artist he thought could be turned into a recording star, the A&R man would fulfil his *'repertoire'* responsibilities by trawling his network of song writers and music publishers for a suitable song.

Then he would assemble the necessary producer, musical director, arranger and session musicians in the recording studio where a team of recording engineers would spend vast amounts of time and trickery working their magic, and - voilà! - a new record was ready for release.

It was a complex and expensive process. So when he was listening to this endless supply of new material, Bernie often wondered why so many of these records sounded so competently performed, so expensively produced and so unutterably boring. He could work his way through dozens of them before finding anything that sounded fresh or had any kind of creative spark. To compound the problem, many new offerings were based on the long established principle that, if an artist had a hit, the A&R man would strive to make the next release sound as similar as possible to the previous one. Unfortunately, this approach depressed not only record sales, but often the fans too.

Bernie leaned over to pick up the next record from the box on the floor. He put it on the record player and sat back while taking a few sips of tea. He always started these sessions with the intention of listening to every record all the way through, but that could be a difficult principle to honour, not to mention often being a colossal waste of time.

In the case of the record which was currently spinning on the turntable, Bernie managed to force himself to listen to the track until the end of the first chorus. He knew that sometimes, a nondescript song could be redeemed by a strong chorus - but not in this case.

He lifted the needle, took the record off the turntable and placed it on the largest of the three piles of discs sitting on the table to the other side of his armchair. That was the reject pile. It was, by far, the largest pile. The second, much smaller pile was the *'maybe'* pile. He would try those ones again later, but if they weren't persuasive on a second play, they too would go on the reject pile.

The good ones would go on the smallest pile - the *'yes'* pile - along with the other successful candidates.

Bernie had listened to nearly all of the new releases that particular week, and so far, there were only three records on the *'yes'* pile. *Tell Me When* by the Applejacks (a new band), *Stay Awhile* by Dusty Springfield (one of Bernie's favourite girl singers) and *Not Fade Away* by The Rolling Stones (with an authentic Bo Diddley beat).

He wasn't convinced that *Tell Me When* was destined to be a classic, but it was a very catchy tune. The backing track had a good feel and it was worthy of a play on *Saturday Club*. Unlike most of the dull offerings that week, Bernie thought the Applejacks deserved some encouragement. The record companies had rushed to sign all the talent available in Liverpool and Manchester, and were now moving on to pastures new. The Applejacks hailed from Birmingham. Bernie had also heard on the grapevine that a number of labels were showing interest in a group from Newcastle called The Animals as well as an outfit from Glasgow called Lulu and the Luvvers - the latter fronted by a 15 year old girl of precocious talent.

The search for something new showed no signs of slowing up. Bernie was glad. In his view, it wasn't just the music business that needed to be shaken out of its smugness and complacency. It was society as a whole.

It was well past midnight. Bernie was a bit of a night hawk, but he was getting tired and had decided to go to bed. He was in the bathroom, cleaning his teeth, when the phone rang.

'Who the fuck rings at this time of night?' Bernie wondered.

Assuming the call must be important, he hastily rinsed his mouth with the intention of answering.

Then he heard Terry walk along the hallway and pick up.

It was a surprise to Bernie that Terry was at home at all. It had been quiet when he got back from work. If Terry had been out when Bernie arrived, then he must have come in later, very quietly. Maybe Bernie had been so absorbed in listening to records he hadn't noticed? But Terry would normally have popped his head round the door to say a cheery hello when he got back. Maybe he had company?

The mystery remained unresolved when Bernie heard the most almighty kerfuffle. Echoing down the hallway came a series of whoops and yelps, and a disbelieving *'No!..'* followed by a pause, followed by another *'No!..'*. Repeated again … and again …

Bernie was intrigued. Terry sounded elated rather than angry, so Bernie rinsed his mouth, properly this time, left the bathroom and walked along the corridor, rubbing his face with a towel. As he approached, Terry grinned, holding his hand up and tilting his head back in a *'don't say anything, I'll explain when I get the chance'* sort of gesture. There were several short exchanges which, only hearing one side of the conversation, didn't mean much to Bernie. Then he heard Terry say,

"Yeah... He's right here. I'll put him on."

He held out the receiver,

"It's George. He'll explain."

Bernie knew that the Beatles were in Paris performing a series of concerts at the Olympia Theatre and that they were staying at the George V, the most prestigious hotel in the whole of France. Paris was an hour ahead, so they must have come off stage much earlier in the evening.

"Hi George, what's going on?"

"We're number one in America." said George.

Bernie did a double take.

"What?.."

"When we got back to the hotel from the Olympia, Brian ran in to the room waving a telegram from Capitol Records, shouting '*I Want To Hold Your Hand is top of the US charts.*' "

"That's bloody amazing." said Bernie. "You sound like you've been on the bubbly?"

"Too right!" said George.

"Did you disturb the other diners at the George Cinq?" Bernie chuckled at the thought.

"Oh no! George took us to this amazing restaurant in a wine cellar. It's a massive vault with wine barrels all around, and it has a sort of a theme ..."

"And what's that?" Bernie asked.

George laughed, "Well the bread rolls are shaped like dicks, with massive bellends... and the soup comes in chamber pots... and the chocolate ice cream is served on elegant crockery and looks just like huge turds..."

"I get the idea." It was Bernie's turn to laugh. "And the respectable George Martin took you to this den of iniquity? He clearly has a dark side."

When the amusement had subsided, George turned to more serious matters.

"Look Bernie, you've got to do something on *Saturday Club* about this. It deserves some sort of mention, doesn't it?"

"I'll speak to Jimmy first thing in the morning. I don't know what we'll do, but we'll definitely do something."

They made small talk for a while and then Bernie handed back to Terry who said his goodbyes and hung up.

Bernie was flabbergasted. The British charts were routinely dominated by American recording artists in a way that was not usually reciprocated. OK, within the last year, *Stranger on the Shore* by Acker Bilk and *Telstar* by the Tornados had both reached the number one spot in the US - but they were both instrumentals and considered sort of novelty records. You had to go back to Vera Lynn's *Auf Wiedersehen Sweetheart* in the 1950s to find a British vocal performance at number one in the US charts. To Bernie, the Beatles' new found American success felt a bit different to those isolated events.

Then, a little sadness crept up on him. What if they really did break through in the US? The commercial opportunities over there were in another league entirely. How long before they based themselves in the States and found little time for their adoring audiences in the UK? Had they already made their last *Saturday Club* appearance? Bernie shrugged off these unpleasant thoughts.

"Isn't that bloody amazing?" said Terry. Then he paused, pensively. "I hope this US hit isn't just a one-off."

"They will take America by storm." said Bernie.

*****

First thing in the morning, Bernie was in Jimmy Grant's office.

Jimmy was already at his desk. He wore a suit like most of his colleagues, but whereas they, for the most part, just looked nondescript, Jimmy, by comparison, looked dapper. He wore a suit because he liked to wear one and felt comfortable in one, not because he felt he had to conform or impress. Bernie couldn't quite put his finger on it. Jimmy's suits were always well cut. Maybe he had the knack of choosing fabric which was a bit more easy on the eye than most of the business suits around him - without being too flashy. He wore neatly pressed white shirts, and his ties always added just the right amount of flair. Jimmy was a smart guy.

"Jimmy! You heard the news?"

Jimmy could see Bernie was excited.

"What news is that?"

"The Beatles are number one in the US."

"That's very good," was Jimmy's typically understated reply.

"And they've got another four records in the US Hot 100 this week."

Jimmy looked puzzled.

"Why would their record company do that?" he asked, "It's madness to release all those records at the same time. They'd make much more money if they staggered the releases."

"Ah, well…. It's not just one record company, Jimmy. Capitol Records have first refusal on American releases of everything that EMI produces in the UK. But they turned down the first three Beatles singles."

"Why?" Jimmy interjected.

"Because the Capitol boss is a dick."

"Like Dick Rowe then?" said Jimmy, smirking at his own pun.

"It's worse than that." Bernie sniggered. "If you think the UK record companies initial assessment of the Beatles was pathetic, all that fades into insignificance in comparison with the almighty fuckup presided over by Dave Dexter, the Capitol label boss."

"From what I was told, when he was offered *Love Me Do*, he thought John's harmonica was the worst thing he had ever heard, so, in his words, he *'nixed'* the Beatles. EMI were forced to release the first three Beatles singles in America on a variety of other minor US labels. But those companies didn't do much with any of them."

"So what changed things?" asked Jimmy.

"Eventually, Beatlemania got so big over here in the UK that even the Yanks couldn't ignore it. Walter Cronkite, their top TV news guy ran a documentary style piece on them, and another guy on CBS did a sarcastic television feature."

"It highlighted the stupidity of British teenage girls who were going bananas over a bunch of mop-top airheads, and, congratulated American parents on raising a generation of youngsters who would never consider anything so foolish."

"Of course, the kids in America took one look at the Beatles on the telly and the local radio stations were immediately swamped by phone callers demanding to know why they couldn't get that sort of stuff in the US of A."

"And that sorted it?"

"Well, not quite. Things have been bubbling in America for a few weeks now. George told me that late last year, Ed Sullivan was flying through Heathrow when he saw hundreds of girls mobbing the Beatles at the airport to welcome them back from Sweden. He asked who they were, which helped when Brian Epstein approached him about a spot on Sullivan's TV show. So eventually, Brian negotiates an agreement that the *Ed Sullivan Show* will get the Beatles for an exclusive appearance along with the simultaneous release of *I Want To Hold Your Hand*."

"And?.." Jimmy was clearly enjoying the gossip, and was eagerly awaiting the next instalment.

"A DJ on one of the radio stations decides to contact a girlfriend who's an air hostess on BOAC. He gets her to buy a copy of *I Want to Hold Your Hand* during her next round trip to the UK, and fly it back to the States. So, with one phone call, he manages to do what Capitol Records have been trying so hard not to. He plays the next Beatles single on the radio, only to discover that there is massive demand."

"But that was just one local radio station Bernie?"

"Yeah, Washington DC. But then that guy gives copies to jocks in Chicago and St Louis, and then it snowballs."

"Capitol must have jumped on it then?"

"Oh no..." Bernie laughed long and loud. "Ed Sullivan was furious because he was promised an exclusive appearance and simultaneous release, so he threatened to pull the Beatles from the biggest TV show in the USA. Then Capitol, under pressure from EMI had lawyers delivering *'cease and desist'* letters to all the radio stations playing the record - to which they all replied, *'Fuck off!.. This record is a hit.'* And then everyone involved suddenly realises there's a lot of money to be made - no thanks to Capitol and their total incompetence. So finally, they start getting behind what is clearly going to be Beatlemania Mk II over on the other side of the pond."

"Oh..." Bernie added, "And to answer your question about why there are so many Beatles records in the American charts at the same time, all the other record companies who previously failed with their original US releases have now re-released them. You couldn't make it up."

"That's what I call democracy in action..." said Jimmy. So what do you think we should do this end?"

"I just spoke to Brian Epstein and told him we can get Brian Matthew to make a big thing of it on air this coming Saturday, just before he plays the record, and he can tell everyone what the Beatles are going to get up to in America... Ed Sullivan and all that... Brian can do that sort of stuff blindfolded, so we don't need to plan anything special for that."

Jimmy nodded.

"But then I asked him when the boys will be flying in to New York. He said they're booked on the Ed Sullivan show on the 9th of February, so they'll fly in a couple of days before that. I suggested that maybe we could do a phone interview with them on the day they arrive. Brian thought that was a great idea."

"But it'll be the middle of the night in New York when *Saturday Club* goes out?"

"We could pre-record the interview overnight and then put it out later on Saturday Club?"

"Mmmm…. Transatlantic phone calls are pricey. I don't know if we have the budget."

"Ah… I've got an idea about that," said Bernie. "I spoke to Jenny Solomon in the news department, and they're keen to use bits and pieces of anything we can get. This is a global headline Jimmy. BBC World Service will have it on the news all around the world. And the best bit is that BBC News will pay for the line. All we have to do is provide Brian Matthew to interview them. We won't have to pay a penny for the overseas phone link."

"Sounds great." said Jimmy. "Let's set it up!"

*****

The next few weeks were the most memorable in the history of British popular music.

On Friday the 7th of February, the Beatles landed at John F Kennedy airport in New York. It was besieged by thousands of fans. They did a brief press conference at the airport. Even the hard-bitten US press corps found their impromptu one-liners a refreshing change from the usual crap pumped out by most pop stars and their PR minders:

Q. What do you call that hairstyle you're wearing?
A. Arthur.

Q. Will you sing for us?
A. No, we need money first.

Q. Why does your music excite people so much?
A. If we knew, we'd form another group and be managers.

Q. How do you find America?
A. Turn left at Greenland.

And so on...

This brief interlude was followed by a motorcade through the streets of Manhattan with immense crowds lining the route - a turnout which would have made any religious leader or head of state green with envy.

When they reached the Plaza Hotel, fifty policemen were there to hold the crowds back, but, as scheduled, the first thing they did after checking in to the Presidential Suite was to record an interview with Brian Matthew for *Saturday Club*. In those days, a transatlantic telephone call was an extreme luxury, usually reserved for likes of leading politicians and Hollywood stars.

The next morning, Bernie and Jimmy scored a remarkable scoop when the interview was broadcast to a record *Saturday Club* audience - who couldn't believe what they were hearing.

That evening, a record audience of 73 million people in the USA tuned in to watch the boys take America by storm on the Ed Sullivan Show. The event was instantly embedded in popular US psyche, to be added to a very short list of *'where were you when?'* moments, relating to historic events - such as the assassination of John F Kennedy and the moment Neil Armstrong took his first step on the moon.

Not long after, another postcard arrived, this time addressed to:

Bernardo Android
c/o Saturday Club
The BBC
London W1

Pleez, pleez, pleez – play
Hold Mine In Your Hand by the Beadles
for all who nose me at the RNPDD
(Royal National Prostitute for the Debb and Duff)
With kisses
J. Lemon Esq

Bernie grinned, and stuck the postcard on the cork board beside the one from Sweden. Many more postcards followed in the wake of the Beatles' fantastic adventures around the world.

Bernie had never felt so alive. A few days after the Beatles phone-in, a young man called Jim Waters walked into his office.

Jim was in a band called the Daltons who had scored a few minor hits. Bernie knew they'd supported the Beatles on an early tour, but he had never met him. Jim was there to pitch the Dalton's latest single. It was unusual for a band member to double as a promotion man, but Bernie was, as always, interested in a new record.

However, he felt that it was a mistake for recording artists to get involved in promoting their own stuff.

When making a pitch on your own behalf, how do you get round the elephant in the room that is, *you would say that, wouldn't you?*'

"Are you just promoting your own records?" asked Bernie.

"No. I'm spreading my wings a bit. Doing a bit of freelance plugging in my spare time. So when our new record was up for release, I thought *'Why not?'* "

Bernie went through the motions as he listened to the record. He quickly came to the conclusion that the Daltons' new record wasn't right for *Saturday Club*, but he didn't let on as Jim went through his spiel. Behind the record biz pizzazz, Bernie detected a bit of self-doubt. He had taken a liking to the guy and he wanted to let him down lightly. So he cut him short,

"What are you doing this evening?"

First a pause. Then a slight shake of the head. Then, a tentative,

"Nothing ..."

"Fancy joining me for something to eat?"

Another pause.

"You want me to ..."

Bernie saw where this was going.

"No... I'm not suggesting you take me out on an all-expenses paid blowout to promote your record. That's not my style."

Another pause.

"My treat." said Bernie.

Bernie watched Jim's face as his uncertain expression relaxed into the hint of a smile.

"Why not?"

"Do you know Shepherds Market?"

"Yes."

"There's a restaurant called Tiddy Dols."

"I know it."

"Seven o'clock?"

"Great."

*****

Tiddy Dol's Eating House was Bernie's favourite. It had a cosy, *Olde Worlde* feel to it. Dark oak furniture. White linen table cloths. Little vases of heather on lace doilies in the middle of each table. Copper skillets on the walls. A bit kitsch, but it had a comfortable and welcoming atmosphere. The menu was always interesting, the fare well prepared and the staff were friendly and attentive. The icing on the cake was that Tiddy Dols was just the other side of Shepherds Market, literally a stone's throw from Bernie's front door. Bernie sat in one of the quieter corners. It was only five past seven when Jim walked in. Bernie caught his eye and he bustled over full of smiles and apologies.

"Sorry I'm late. It took longer than I expected on the tube and I didn't realise how far it is from the station."

"It's good to see you," said Bernie, smiling back.

Conversation was easy. If news of significant events in the business was in short supply, there was always plenty of gossip, much of it salacious. And if people ran out of stories of substance to gossip about, then you could just make it up. Little passed for unbelievable in the music business.

They shared a bottle of wine, ate a tasty meal and then Bernie ordered brandies. Jim asked if Bernie minded if he smoked. Bernie said he didn't. Jim pulled out a packet of cigarettes to share.

In a pleasant state of nicotine and alcohol induced relaxation, Bernie asked Jim how things were going.

"You mean with the Daltons? Or with my record promotions?"

"Either... Both..."

Any record biz bravado that Jim had displayed in Bernie's office had gone. The mood was casual and Jim's answer was unvarnished.

"It's difficult ..." he said. "Every week there are new groups, and they look and sound very different to anything that was around before the Beatles. It's not just the music - the whole business is changing."

Bernie nodded. "And what about the record plugging?"

"Well ... I'm not a natural. But the band seems to be falling apart. Kenny has managed to get a few of his songs placed, and he seems more excited about writing than anything the band is doing ... Which is not a lot."

"I think it's just a matter of time before he concentrates on writing full time. To be honest, Pete and I don't have what it takes to function as a duo, but we can't think of anyone who might take Kenny's place."

Bernie was aware how precarious things could be in the record business. No regular salary, no pension plan, no severance pay, and was there anyone you might turn to for career advice?.. Dream on! Although the recompense was hardly munificent, BBC employees were pampered by comparison.

"It sounds as if you're doing the right thing then Jim." Bernie did his best to accentuate the positive. "You're right about the way things are moving. And if you think the band's about to break up, then it's probably best for you to make a move too, as soon as you can. You know a lot about the business and you have lots of useful contacts. Are you interested in anything apart from promotion?"

"I wondered about management," said Jim. "I know all the dodges that people get up to, and I know my way around. That sort of knowledge must be useful to bands who are just starting out."

"Sounds good to me. Maybe you should try that sooner rather than later. Get your nose in front."

Jim thought carefully about Bernie's words. He lifted his brandy glass. It smelt delicate and fruity. And expensive. He took a sip, and after the initial roughness on the back of his throat had faded, he savoured the flavours that settled and mingled.

"I take it you're not putting money on our new single then?"

The question was delivered nonchalantly, but it was an awkward question for Bernie to answer. He felt obliged to be frank.

"You said it yourself Jim, things are moving. You're about to lose Kenny, and you don't have a replacement … And you've convinced me that you need a change. What's more important is, have you convinced yourself?"

Jim smiled. He sat back in his chair, took a drag on his cigarette and thought a bit.

"That's very diplomatic Bernie." He smiled. "You've played back to me pretty much what I just told you." He chuckled. "But you're on the level. And I needed to talk it over with someone I know who isn't full of bullshit. There are plenty of those around. I've been wavering for some time, but I've just come to a clear decision."

With that, Jim lifted his brandy glass and proposed a toast.

"To the future?"

"The future." Bernie replied.

They clinked glasses and drained them.

They chatted for a while. Then Jim looked at his watch.

"Got a train to catch?" said Bernie.

"Last one's at half past."

A few minutes later they left Tiddy Dols, the fresh air hitting them pleasantly in the face.

Bernie didn't know it yet, but he had just made a friend for life.

The British Invasion

1964 was the year of the British Invasion. Or at least that was how the Americans saw it.

As soon as the Beatles had broken through the transatlantic wall, a whole string of British artists followed them into the breach: The Dave Clark Five, The Searchers, The Swinging Blue Jeans, Peter and Gordon, Gerry and the Pacemakers, Chad and Jeremy - all in quick succession.

Then of course, not to be left out, along came The Rolling Stones, belatedly coming to the conclusion that if they wanted to make some real money, they'd have to stop being sniffy about doing anything that didn't conform to what they considered to be pure, black-American R&B. They got themselves into the US charts with a self-penned, poppy tear jerker called *Tell Me*. The kids couldn't get enough.

In the wake of this unparalleled success, stuffy old Britannia had suddenly never been so cool. US industry moguls, never shy of hustling a dime two, threw their doors wide, welcoming with open arms anything and everything from our little island across the water - much to the chagrin of many established US artists, including King Elvis himself.

For Bernie it was hard to keep up with this rollercoaster. He wasn't complaining.

British record companies were in a feeding frenzy, signing up anything that moved in the full expectation that the production line would work as follows: sign a band, make a single, get it on the radio, get it in the UK charts, get it on US radio, get it in the US charts, make loadsa money.

Saturday Club, and therefore Bernie, was very much on the critical path of that production line. Not that he had any commercial interest in this increasingly lucrative business.

While it was exciting to be involved in such a direct way, it made life a lot more stressful. The financial rewards for British record companies had never been greater and as there was so much at stake in breaking new artists and records in the UK, promotional methods became proportionately aggressive.

*****

A few days after his evening out with Jim, a new record plugger presented herself in Bernie's office. Yasmin Lambert's reputation preceded her. Bernie had already heard a few stories about how innovative her promotional methods were.

Yasmin was short in height, but striking. Her long, dark hair framed elegant features and a radiant smile. She was fashionably dressed, beautifully proportioned and her diminutive stature somehow made her appear all the more exotic.

After a brief, eyelid fluttering introduction, she pulled a record out of her bag, sliding it across the table.

"Our latest offering, Bernie. It's totally hot."

Another disarming smile.

Bernie viewed the proceedings with equanimity. He pulled the record over and retrieved the seven inch single from the sleeve. As he did so, a neatly folded pair of twenty pound notes fell out. Bernie looked at the notes, and then at Yasmin, who was unsuccessfully trying to read a reaction on Bernie's poker face.

"Ooh... I wonder how they got there?" she teased.

Bernie shoved the notes back towards her across his desk.

Feigning affront, with brows raised high above wide eyes, she insisted,

"They're not mine."

"Well they're not mine either." countered Bernie, firmly, while sliding the notes as far away as possible.

The first crack of disappointment on Yasmin's face was quickly recovered by another smile. This time a bit more calculated. She casually slipped open the top button of her blouse and leaned over the desk to pick up the notes.

"I'm sure we can find something to interest you..."

"That's very subtle Yasmin," said Bernie, with a chuckle.

But clearly, not the kind of chuckle Yasmin was hoping for.

"Just sit down for a minute, will you?"

Now Yasmin was pissed off, making no attempt to hide the fact, and looking a bit uncomfortable about what might come next.

"Is this the only record you've got in your bag?" asked Bernie.

"Er ... No. Actually... But they're not as good as that," she followed up hastily, pointing at the one on the desk.

"Well, let's see them anyway."

Reluctantly, she unloaded the contents of her bag. Bernie shuffled through the handful of records. He'd already heard most of them via other channels, but there were two which were new to him.

"I've heard these," he said, putting the rest aside.

Then he took the ones he hadn't heard, including the one she most favoured, over to the record player and played them one after the other. He selected one of the three that were new to him - not the one she was pushing - and put it back on the turntable to have another listen. It had a catchy bluebeat feel. The latest thing from the Caribbean. Not everyone's cup of tea, but Bernie was interested. He turned to Yasmin.

"I'll get this one on *Saturday Club* this week." he promised.

Yasmin was pleasantly surprised. "What about the others?"

"Not for *Saturday Club*."

She looked downcast. But then Bernie pointed out two of those he had rejected, giving her some advice about which shows he thought they might be good for, and which producers she might concentrate on. That cheered her up a bit.

"You're a freelance, aren't you Yasmin?"

She nodded.

"And most of your money is paid on results?.. Getting radio plays?.. Chart positions?.. Record sales?.."

She nodded again.

"And the company who is pushing this…" he held up the one that had been offered with incentives, "is promising you a fortune if it's a hit?"

"Well… I don't know about a fortune?" she replied, slightly flushed.

"Yasmin, I'm not a plugger, but if I were, I'd be a bit more selective before investing my valuable time and talents in promoting records of - let's say - dubious quality."

She sat, stony faced.

"My office door is open any time if you want to talk about new records. I get a kick out of hearing the most promising tracks before they become the latest hits. And my success rate's not bad. If you make me your first port of call, then I get in first, which is great for me, and in return, I will tell you very quickly what the prospects are as far as plays or recording sessions go on *Saturday Club*."

Then he went on to mention a few other producers who he considered more adventurous than the average. Those who might take a risk on featuring new artists. Rather than those producers who he considered *'followers'* - i.e. those who preferred to stick to playing established artists, and who would be more inclined to let others give a new act airplay. Then they would wait to see if there was any kind of public reaction before jumping on a new bandwagon.

"I'm just one producer, Yasmin. You should compare what I say with everyone else and make up your own mind. Maybe you'll come to the conclusion that I'm talking crap. But the sooner you can get feedback from as many different people as possible, the sooner you'll be able to figure out which records are likely to make you the most money. And even if some fat-cat is promising wads of cash to break a record, if it's rubbish, the last thing you want to do is to get sucked into spending too much time - never mind anything else - flogging a dead horse."

Yasmin paused thoughtfully. Then she gave Bernie what he thought might be a genuine smile.

"Can I keep these three?" asked Bernie.

"If you're not going to play them, why would you want them?"

"I collect them. I think I've got copies of every single that's been released in the UK since 1958."

"Sure." she replied. "Why not."

Then she stood up and slipped the twenties into her pocket.

"Thanks for the chat Bernie," she said, turning to head out for her next appointment.

"Take care!" called Bernie as she closed the door after her.

*****

Bernie couldn't think of a better job than being a radio producer. He lived in a perfect location and he mixed with a crowd of like-minded people. Fair enough, there were a few potential flies in the ointment at work, but he was getting better at keeping out of trouble.

Those whose opinions really mattered to him thought he was doing a good job, and his confidence grew with his successes. He had grown very comfortable with his work in the studios - to the point that, for the first time in his life, he felt capable of taking on anything that the job might throw at him. Which was just as well, given what was in store for him during his next session.

This time, Bernie was in the BBC Playhouse Studio just off Trafalgar Square. It originally opened as the Royal Avenue Theatre in 1882, staging comic opera, burlesque and farce.

By the turn of the 20th century, George Bernard Shaw had seen his first play performed there. Then, in 1907, the theatre was redesigned and rebuilt, relaunching this time as the Playhouse Theatre, where some decades later, in 1934, a twenty year old Alec Guinness made his stage debut.

By 1951, it had been taken over by the BBC. This was at a time when television was an infant upstart and radio was the only medium which could instantly reach a mass market.

Classic BBC radio comedies like *The Goon Show*, *Hancock's Half Hour* and *Steptoe and Son* were recorded there, which may have been why the Playhouse ranked so highly in Bernie's affections. He had listened to BBC Radio enthusiastically since he was a boy, and particularly loved the humour of *The Goon Show* - emulating it as often as he could, when appropriate, *(and sometimes when not)*.

Like most BBC Radio studios, The Playhouse had seen better days. It was rather careworn. A world away from its Edwardian splendour. But the acoustics were good, and the BBC had retained seating for about three hundred or so in the now shabby auditorium, for those occasions when it was necessary to record a show in front of a live audience.

That day, there was no need for an audience. Bernie had booked the Dave Clark Five. They were one of the first British groups to follow the Beatles across the ocean to America. Their first hit single, *Glad All Over*, had already reached #1 in the U.K. and #6 in the US.

Bernie was highly entertained when an American record review magazine - called, appropriately, Cashbox - reported that *'Glad All Over is a happy-go-lucky pounder...that sports that Mersey Sound with the Liverpool beat.'* The Dave Clark Five were a London band.

They had a new single out which Bernie didn't think was the most beautiful work of art, but it had a relentlessly catchy refrain, and featured a foot stomping sequence which he knew would be irresistible in the clubs and dance halls.

But when it came to the foot stomping bit, the performance on stage at the Playhouse was a bit of an anti-climax. It didn't matter where Nick placed the mics, the thumping refrains sounded nothing like the record.

Unfortunately, the thumping passages were a fundamental ingredient. Nick, Bernie and the band tried everything, from bashing the more conventional percussion instruments in endless permutations, to picking up any loose articles lying around in the studio: mic stands, tape spools, cardboard boxes, desk drawers, shoes, you name it - and thumping them against anything else, fixed or otherwise: the floor, the wall, tables, chairs, the pipes, the radiators, whatever... Nothing worked.

Eventually, a defeated silence settled over the studio. Then Bernie turned to Dave Clark and asked him,

"How did you do this on the record then?"

Dave's face was blank.

"You know... When you were making the record, how did you do the thumping noises?"

"Oh...'. said Dave, "Eh, we got a builder's board and stamped up and down on that."

"What do you mean a builder's board?"

"Well … They were doin' some buildin' work nearby, an' they got one of the wooden boards off the scaffoldin' and put it in the studio, an' we just sort of stamped up and down on it."

"Oh..." replied Bernie jovially. "You should have said that before. I'll just go and get one."

And with that he strode off down the centre aisle of the Playhouse towards the exit with an air of finality.

Everyone was nonplussed. Was Bernie being sarcastic? In a huff? In the wake of Bernie's dramatic exit, Nick broke the hiatus.

"We'll break for ten minutes then guys." he announced.

The assembled cast of band members, roadies and a few hangers-on broke up into small groups and dispersed themselves around the auditorium. Some lounging against the stage or sitting in the audience seats, some grumbling to each other, others smoking quietly, and others smoking and grumbling not so quietly. Nick retreated to the safety of the control room. When he got there, his recording assistant was looking anxious.

"What do we do now?" asked young Phil, a new trainee.

"Fuck knows." came the curt reply.

Then a pause... Then... "I'll wait a while and if Bernie doesn't come back we'll get on with the session."

"Who's going to produce it then?"

"I will."

"But Nick, shouldn't we ring the office and let them know?"

"Nah!.. It'll take them ages to find someone. The session time will have run out by then, and we'll have nothing. Let's just wait for a bit and see if he comes back."

To pass the time, Nick switched the control room loudspeaker over to the radio, just in time to catch a funereal church organ playing the depressing signature tune introducing *A story, A Hymn and A Prayer* - the daily God spot on the Light Programme.

A frown of distaste spread over his face and he quickly switched over to the Home Service. He was just in time to hear a government minister by the name of Robert Boothby vehemently refuting a Daily Mirror headline which, reading between the lines, seemed to be suggesting a homosexual liaison between him and an infamous London gangster called Ronnie Kray.

Nick was intrigued by the interviewer's technique. Since he was broadcasting on the BBC, he was obliged to dance around the subject using arcane euphemism and veiled inference in order to conduct any sort of cross examination. Nick concluded that the whole thing must have sounded totally incomprehensible to most who were listening.

Suddenly, the double doors at the back of the auditorium crashed open. Nick switched the radio off and peered through the control room window to see what was going on.

Striding down the central aisle carrying a large, heavy looking plank of wood with metal reinforcements at each corner was Bernie. He manhandled the plank onto the stage and let it fall with a resounding clatter.

By the time Nick got down there, the band had gathered round and were offering congratulations,

"Wow! That's great! You got a builder's board!"

"Mic it up Nick!" said Bernie as he made his way back to the control room.

Nick did what he was told. The subject of how to mic up a builder's board had never come up on any of his BBC training courses, so he just made it up.

When he got back to the control room, Bernie was struggling to brush the cement dust from his red corduroy trousers with his bare hands.

"They overdubbed the board on the record." said Bernie, as he laboured.

"So we'll record a fresh backing track without the thumps. For syncing purposes, Dave Clark will tap his sticks lightly for the count in and through the gaps, but make sure they are not too loud so they'll be drowned out easily when we overdub the feet stomping on the builder's board."

Time was tight. Fortunately, they succeeded in recording a clean backing track on the next take. Then they tried overdubbing the foot stomps. After a bit of fiddling around, it sounded much more convincing than the previous attempts. Suddenly, Bernie had a thought.

"I still think it could sound a bit bigger."

"What? You want me to turn the thumping noises up in the mix?" said Nick.

"No. I want it to sound like there's more people stomping around on the board."

"How do we do that then?"

"We get more people." said Bernie.

"And I've got my Chelsea boots on. They're the height of fashion you know," he shouted, as he exited the control room door.

Nick watched as Bernie assessed the situation on stage, trying to work out how many extra people in addition to the band could get on the board. Then he commandeered a couple of the roadies and got as many bodies as possible on the board with their arms around each others' shoulders - like they were at a Greek wedding or something.

They made a motley crew - the fragrant and trendily dressed pop stars alternating with the members of their road crew in jeans and t-shirts, some of whom were in need of a good bath, never mind a judicious dab of after-shave. Bernie added the final touch, clad in his cement-dust impregnated red corduroy trousers and shod in his brand new pair of high-heeled leather boots.

"Run the tape and see what this sounds like!" he shouted.

The count-in sounded on the playback speaker and, as one, the assembled cast bashed up and down on the builder's board...

"I'm in pieces
Bits and pieces..."

"I'm in pieces
Bits and pieces..."

After the first chorus, Bernie called a halt.

"How was that Nick?"

"Perfect!" came the reply on the talkback.

"Great! Let's do it!"

This time the track was played back from start to finish, and the Greek wedding party thumped along merrily in time with the music. When the final chorus had faded, the feet continued to stomp with military precision until Nick's voice came over the speaker,

"That's it."

At which point everybody fell about.

The band listened to the end result in the control room, and pronounced themselves happy. It was thumbs up all round. But they also told Bernie and Nick on the way out,

"That was much more fun than the record."

*****

After breaking down the mic stands and tidying up the cables in the wake of the morning session, it was customary practice to retire to the nearest pub for a liquid lunch and a snack. Or maybe just a liquid lunch.

All BBC studios had an adopted pub close by, and the Playhouse was no exception. The name of the pub was the Ship and Shovell. Actually, they were two pubs sitting directly opposite each other in a nearby lane called Craven Passage.

The Ship was reputed to have been the hostelry of choice for coal labourers in days gone by. Because of this association, the name origin of the Shovell was, according to some sources, wrongly assumed to be some sort of allusion to the profession of Marine Stokers, the guys who shovelled coal into the furnaces on steamships.

If the aristocratic portrait on the signboard outside the pub is to be believed, nothing could be further from the truth. Shovell, with two 'Ls' is not an archaic way of spelling the tool of the trade. It is in fact the surname of Admiral of the Fleet, Sir Cloudesley Shovell.

He had a glittering career, but is more often remembered for the worst disaster in the history of the Royal Navy, when he guided his fleet onto the rocks near the Isles of Scilly in 1707, with the loss of all of his ships and 2,000 of his finest seamen - including himself.

Despite this inauspicious tale, the Ship and Shovell were very popular twin watering holes. So when Bernie suggested,

"Shit an' Shovel?"

His team mates assented without hesitation.

"We'll have to go via Villiers Street." said Bernie.

Nick and Phil looked confused.

"I promised the foreman I'd get it straight back."

"You got the board from the building site round in Villiers Street then?" asked Nick.

"Yeah. I remembered there was a building site round there, so I went in and asked the foreman if I could borrow a board for an hour or so. He looked very sceptical about it, and asked me what I was planning to do with it. Anyway, as I was explaining, one of the young lads on the site, well... His ears must have pricked up, and when I said we were recording the Dave Clark Five for *Saturday Club* in the BBC Playhouse round the corner, he got really enthusiastic. That must have been the clincher for the foreman, cos just then he said,

'Aw... Go on then! But have it back by lunchtime!' "

Bernie's tale was received with some mirth as they set off in high spirits for the Ship and Shovell - via Villiers Street.

When they got to the building site, the young lad was first to spot them. A shout of, *'Hey Bert! They're back!'* was enough to bring the foreman out of his hut.

Just before he handed the board back, Bernie stood the board on its end, cleared the dust from a space at one end and retrieved a black marker pen from inside his jacket pocket. Then he carefully inscribed the board:

'Used by the Dave Clark Five, Friday 24 Feb 1964. Signed, Bernie Andrews, Producer, Saturday Club.'

He handed it over, saying, "As agreed."

The young lad and the foreman were beaming by this time, and the ceremony had drawn the attention of quite a few of their co-workers. Bernie said goodbye, the foreman shook his hand, and as Bernie and Co left for the pub they overheard an animated discussion about where the site crew should display their now valuable possession.

"Not often that a bunch of builders get their hands on a rare artefact like that, is it?" said Bernie, chuckling, as they headed off.

*****

On Easter Sunday, 1964, Bernie was sitting at home in his armchair, drinking tea. He had his radio set tuned in to 199 metres on the Medium Wave Band. Bernie felt a frisson of excitement when, at the stroke of 12:00 noon, he heard an unfamiliar voice,

"This is Radio Caroline on 199, your all-day music station. We are on the air every day from six in the morning until six at night. The time is one minute past twelve, and that means it's time for Christopher Moore."

Jimmy McGriff's *Round Midnight* was played in for the first time as Radio Caroline's signature tune. The music was swiftly dipped under Chris Moore's voice while he announced the first record to be played on the new station - *Not Fade Away* by the Rolling Stones.

Bernie was transfixed. It was a teenager's dream. All the latest records being aired in quick succession on the same radio programme. Often it wasn't just the latest singles, but also selected tracks from the latest albums that were in the mix. The presentation was relaxed, almost casual, and as the day progressed, the energy generated by the music showed no sign of flagging, or going stale.

Radio Caroline was run by Ronan O'Rahilly. Bernie knew him as the manager of the Scene Club in London's Soho district. Ronan also managed a number of artists, including one Georgie Fame. Having experienced difficulty in negotiating a record deal for Georgie, he decided to produce and release a record on his own independent label - an entrepreneurial activity which was practically unheard of at the time.

Producing the record was no problem. Getting it played on the radio was another matter.

153

Ronan found it was impossible to compete against the promotional cartels of the big record labels like EMI, Decca, Pye and Philips. Faced by this obstacle, he came up with a brilliant idea. One which would give him as much radio play for his records as he wanted. He set up his own radio station. Radio Caroline.

The first Radio Caroline DJ, Chris Moore, was also the station's Programme Director. His programming policy was simple and direct:

Key:
1 - Pop music - Top 50 - new releases, and old hits up to 5 years
2 - Classic pop - Standards - Sinatra, Peggy Lee, Big Bands, etc
3 - Sound Tracks - Film & Stage shows, Themes, Pop music from films etc
4 - R & B, Jazz, Hip sounds - Jimmy Smith, Booker T, Georgie Fame etc
The sound is to be kept UP TEMPO as much as possible.
The order of the key numbers show priority on programmes.

Bernie was pleased to note that there was no mention of religion, education or housewives. No radio orchestras employing elderly Musicians' Union members were featured, and the 0.0000001% of the population who loved listening to music played on a cinema organ were completely ignored. Most of all, Bernie was pleased to note that no programme on Radio Caroline that day resembled anything like *Music While You Work*.

Radio Caroline quickly gained a considerable audience - to the growing consternation of the UK Government, the BBC Board of Directors, the record companies and the music publishers.

The government didn't like the pirate stations because they had no control over them. The BBC didn't like the pirates, seeing them as upstart competitors.

The record companies and music publishers didn't like the pirates because they paid no royalties whatsoever to them, their artists or their writers for the privilege of playing their records and songs on the radio.

Bernie knew that Radio Caroline had been branded a *'pirate station'* before it even started broadcasting - although, he couldn't understand the reason why.

The radio transmission was coming from a boat anchored in international waters in the Thames Estuary. No laws were being broken. If UK citizens could enjoy listening to Radio Luxembourg transmitting from outside British territorial waters every evening, then how could anyone object to them listening to Radio Caroline during the day?

Bernie also compared the difference in scale between the BBC's operations and Radio Caroline's. The BBC had veritable armies of staff and management spread all across the UK, while Radio Caroline was staffed by a few DJs on a boat, and a handful of support staff on shore. He didn't know what the actual numbers were, but there was no doubt in his mind that Radio Caroline cost a tiny fraction of what it cost to run the BBC Light Programme.

OK, to begin with, the Radio Caroline audience was restricted to those in the South East of England within range of their transmitter. But Radio Caroline was much more economically efficient than the Light Programme in terms of operating costs per listener. That was obvious. And Bernie was convinced that Radio Caroline would soon be joined by other off-shore radio stations all around the UK.

He listened all day, until the station went off the air at 6:00 pm. He wondered how the BBC would react? And he wondered if the shock might force a few changes? Hopefully for the better.

One thing he was sure of. He was sure things wouldn't end well for pirate stations like Radio Caroline. The Music Business, the BBC and the Government would see to that.

*****

The Beatles were a transatlantic phenomenon sans pareil. No one could touch them. On April the 4th 1964, they occupied the top five slots on the US Billboard Hot 100.

They also had a further seven records in the top 100, as well as the top two positions on the Billboard Album Chart. No recording artist had ever achieved anything like that, or come near it.

As a result, by the middle of 1964, Beatles influence reached far beyond their own personal success. Anything and everything that the Beatles were interested in was newsworthy. This curiosity applied particularly to the Beatles cover versions of classic tracks by early rock'n'rollers.

These fulsome endorsements - on record, on the radio and live on stage - had breathed new life into the careers of a number of American 'has-beens'. Beatles' mentors like Carl Perkins, Little Richard, Gene Vincent and particularly Chuck Berry, were soon back on tour in the UK, taking full advantage of the professional resurrection afforded by the latter-day blessing of the Fab Four.

During the early part of 1964, Bernie booked all of these 'oldies' for appearances on Saturday Club, along with current acts like Ben E King, the Crystals and the Ronettes - all from the USA.

In fact, he was so busy, he was obliged to call on his friend and fellow producer, Jeff Griffin, to produce a couple of Saturday Club sessions for him.

These sessions were with Chuck Berry - who else? - and a new girl group from the US called The Supremes.

This last act reflected a new UK trend. American girl groups were now totally cool. The Beatles had recently covered songs by the Shirelles and the Marvelettes, the latter of which, like the Supremes, were to be found on an exotic American label called Tamla-Motown - which few Brits had ever heard of.

Of course, new London groups, like Brian Poole and the Tremeloes and Manfred Mann also found their way onto Bernie's booking sheets along with a growing number from the provinces: the Hollies (Manchester), Dave Berry and the Cruisers (Sheffield), Lulu and the Luvvers (Glasgow), the Spencer Davis Group (Birmingham) and even a young Jamaican girl called Millie, who became an overnight bluebeat sensation. So it was all grist to the mill when Bernie found himself in the studio awaiting the arrival of an emerging band from Newcastle called the Animals.

Their first record, *Baby Let Me Take You Home*, hadn't quite made it into the top twenty. But what was of much greater interest to Bernie was the track that was scheduled to be their next single. *The House of the Rising Sun* was their distinctive version of a folk-ballad of uncertain origins, previously recorded by a stream of artists from Woody Guthrie to Bob Dylan. Bernie had witnessed the Animals playing this song while supporting Chuck Berry on his current UK tour. *'Mind blowing!'* was his take on their live performance. He was convinced it would be a massive hit. So, he booked them.

*****

Bernie checked his watch. New bands were usually prompt, often turning up early. But the road crew hadn't shown yet.

Suddenly, the door of the control room burst open, heralding the entry of one Eric Burdon, the lead singer of the Animals, flaunting a pair of sunglasses. This surprised Bernie. *'It's pissing down outside.'* he thought to himself.

Eric was followed by a retinue, who Bernie assumed were a mix of band members, roadies and hangers-on. The usual suspects.

"I'm Eric." he announced, expansively, thrusting out his hand.

Bernie shook it. "I'm Bernie Andrews."

"Not *THE* Bernie Andrews?" shouted someone in the midst of the retinue.

Bernie looked round, trying to locate the inquisitor, without success.

"Well... I suppose so," he said, with a shrug of his shoulder.

"And who the fuck is Bernie Andrews?" shouted another voice, in a broad, Geordie accent coming from somewhere at the back.

Cue large laughter.

"Shut the fuck up!" said a tall guy with a thick, Beatley mop of reddish brown hair, as he shouldered his way through the throng. "Don't pay any attention to those thickos!" Another Geordie accent, but a more articulate delivery. He seemed amiable. Bernie shook hands once more.

"I'm Chas, the bass player. Where do you want us to set up?"

"Nick, the studio manager, is rigging the mics in the studio. Have a chat with him about the setup."

Chas to Bernie, "OK then." Chas to the retinue, "Come on then!.. Move it!"

"Just before you go," Bernie interrupted, "Can I have a word about the songs you want to record?"

"Sure!" they chorused.

"I saw you doing the *House of the Rising Sun* at the Hammersmith Odeon last week. I think it's a great track, and I would like to spend as much time as we need to get that recorded as well as possible."

"Why don't you just play the record then?" said Eric, smirking, sticking his face right in Bernie's.

"You know why not, Eric," said Bernie. "You must have listened in to hear what other groups sound like on *Saturday Club*?"

"So, you're unbribeable then?" said Eric, with a cheesy grin.

"I'll suck you off if you play the record!" shouted the Geordie voice in the doorway as the retinue departed.

"Oh well, that settles it," said Bernie, rolling his eyes, and turning back to Chas and Eric.

"So, you want us to have a go at the *Rising Sun* first then?" confirmed Chas, restoring some order to the situation.

"Yes, that's what I had in mind. But if we spend a lot of time on that one to get it right, I'll need three more tracks to be done, very quickly, straight after."

"We did the *Rising Sun* on the first take with Mickie Most," crowed Eric.

Chas interjected, "We want to do our first single, *Baby Let Me Take You Home*, and the B-sides of that one and *the Rising Sun*. We can play all of those blindfolded, but we're more fussy about how the A-sides turn out than the B-sides."

"OK, so we'll start with *the Rising Sun* and see how things go from there." said Bernie.

With that, Eric and Chas vanished into the studio.

It was just as well that Bernie had decided to invest a lot of time on *The House of the Rising Sun*. The first take sounded a little uncertain. Bernie knew that Mickie Most, their producer, was not sold on this particular track, and that the band had been obliged to cajole him, persistently, before he gave in and agreed to release it as the A-side of their new single.

Before that decision had been taken, they had recorded the song as a possible album track, so the pressure was off during that particular session. The relaxed manner in which it was originally performed might have been one of the reasons why they got it down so well on the first take. Now, having worked hard to convince Mickie that it was a hot prospect, perhaps they were beginning to doubt their own judgement? Perhaps they needed the *Saturday Club* version to be perfect? Millions of potential record buyers would be listening in on Saturday. Perhaps Saturday would be make or break?

When they came in to hear the first playback, Hilton Valentine's guitar arpeggios on the intro sounded a bit shaky. The nerviness also contributed, in Bernie's opinion, to an over-critical analysis of the drum sound and the reverb on the vocal.

Bernie was patient. He was determined to get this recording the way the band wanted it. He listened carefully to the various comments, and asked them to run it through again so Nick could make the necessary adjustments. When they returned to the studio, he also reassured Nick in the quiet of the control room.

"Don't worry about the carping, Nick. The secret's in the performance. So long as they believe we're doing everything possible to get it right, we'll have the best chance of getting them to relax, and enjoy."

The next take was much better. Bernie could see that they looked pleased with each other. However, he got on the talkback immediately after the fade out, and told them,

"That was great guys. Good enough for me. I can use that. But, don't come in and listen to it yet. While you're in the groove, let's just do one more for luck."

They were on a roll, and they knew it. They didn't need any further encouragement. The number was counted in, they hit the intro perfectly, the vocal entry was supremely confident, and the overall performance was edgy and soulful. After the fadeout, everyone relaxed, looked at each other, and smiled. That was the one.

So it proved on the playback. With spirits high, they returned to the studio and knocked the other three tracks off, first time, back to back. In the end, they finished bang on time.

Everyone was well pleased.

A Frank Exchange

The following Saturday, it was Jimmy's turn to supervise the transmission. Bernie knew *The House of the Rising Sun* was going to be a smash, and it hadn't even been released. So, he was really looking forward to *Saturday Club* scoring another major scoop.

He tuned in his radio set. The signature tune, *Saturday Jump,* sounded the fanfare for pop music lovers all across the nation, and he settled himself in his armchair with a full glass of wine at hand, sipping slowly as the programme progressed.

The Animals' session was trailed by Brian Matthew during the opening announcements.

Eventually, Bernie heard the three filler tracks, *Baby Let Me Take You Home*, *Talkin' Bout You* and *Send You Back to Walker*, mixed in with the other *Saturday Club* contributions that week: Frank Ifield, Rose Brennan, Billie Davis, The Fourmost, Mike Berry & The Innocents and Arthur Greenslade & The Gee Men.

Only after 11:30 did Bernie start to twitch. *The House of the Rising Sun* still hadn't been played. The show went off the air at 12:00 and he wondered if Jimmy had reached the same decision that he would have made if he were running the transmission? Maybe Jimmy was keeping the best till last, with the intention of giving the week's programme a rousing send-off?

By 11:50, Bernie's stress levels were rising. The *Saturday Club* version of *House of the Rising Sun* was over four and a half minutes long. If Jimmy didn't put it on soon, there wouldn't be enough time to play it in its entirety before Brian Matthew closed the show.

So, when it passed 11:55, and Brian back-announced the previous track - *School is Over* by Billie Davis - Bernie was not best pleased.

'Jimmy's going to do an early fade on House of the Rising Sun,' Bernie thought to himself. *'Sacrilege!'*

They had put so much effort into the *Saturday Club* recording, and now it wouldn't even be heard in full. Bernie picked up his wine glass and, as he knocked back the remains, he almost choked when he heard the rest of Brian Matthew's announcement,

"So, here to wrap up the show for this week is the latest single by our favourite Australian smoothie. It's Frank Ifield with *Summer Is Over.*"

Bernie only just managed to control the fluid in his gullet. He swallowed hard, with a splutter, and slammed the wine glass back down onto the side-table. It shattered in his hand. Luckily, it didn't cut him.

He was fuming. What on earth was going on? Jimmy knew how much time and effort had been invested in recording that track. Was he deliberately trying to piss him off? Did he think he was getting a bit too big for his boots? Bernie's mind careered through a whole stream of paranoia.

He walked along the passage to the phone with the intention of catching Jimmy while he and his colleagues were packing up in the studio. Then he decided against it. He needed to calm himself. He went into the kitchen, poured a glass of water from the tap and drank it. Then he walked back to the phone. He didn't have Jimmy's home phone number and he knew Jimmy wouldn't hang around, so he thought he'd better get through to him before he left the studio. He picked up the phone and dialled.

"BBC Broadcasting House," said the lady with the cut glass accent.

163

"Can you put me through to Studio 3A please," said Bernie.

He heard just one ring before the studio manager picked up.

"3A." *(Dave fucking Bisley!!!)*

"Can I speak to Jimmy please?"

"Who's calling?"

"It's Bernie," *(as you well know).* Bernie was losing patience.

"Bernie who?" Bisley insisted.

"You know perfectly well Dave. Just fucking get him will you!"

"No need for the language..." whined Bisley.

Bernie's blood pressure went up a few more notches.

Bernie heard the clatter of the handset as it dropped on to the desk. He heard a bit of verbal discourse in the background and then some fumbling around.

"Hello Bernie, I'm just about to leave. Is it anything important?"

"What just happened, Jimmy?"

"Sorry?.. What do you mean?"

"You know how much work we put into that track."

"Which track?"

Bernie could contain himself no longer.

"*The House of the Rising Sun* for fuck's sake! Why didn't you play it?"

Jimmy was genuinely flustered.

"Well... It's a very long track Bernie, nearly five minutes long..."

"It's going to be a massive hit. It's not been released yet, and you just turned down the chance of a major coup."

"Well, I don't know about that," said Jimmy, collecting himself, and going on the offensive. "Anyway, it's all about a brothel."

"Christ Jimmy, there's nothing explicit in it. In any case, the song has a moral. It's a warning not to get involved in the immoral."

"Well, I'm not in the mood for lectures Bernie. In case you forgot, I'm still the Lead Producer on *Saturday Club*, and I don't think we should be broadcasting stuff like that."

"Oh for fuck's sake Jimmy!.." retorted Bernie, slamming the phone down in a fury.

Bernie stood for a while, looking at the phone. Eventually, the fury abated, and he turned and walked back to his room. He flopped into his armchair put his head back and closed his eyes for a while. When he had gathered his thoughts he cleared up the broken wineglass, fetched a clean one, and poured himself another glass of wine. He slumped into his armchair once more.

'*Bloody Hell!..*' mused Bernie. '*I've done it now. I'll have to apologise to Jimmy when I see him next week.*'

He knew in his heart that his reaction had been unreasonable. He owed Jimmy. Jimmy had taken him on as a junior producer, and had generously shared the production responsibilities. He would have to think of something to make it up to him. But what?

*****

When he arrived on Monday morning, the office was eerily quiet. He wondered if he'd missed a departmental meeting, but, on checking his diary, he was relieved to see that wasn't the case.

He thought he had best take a walk to Jimmy's office, and try and mend fences, but when he got there, Jimmy was nowhere to be seen. Neither was Jimmy's secretary, Gladys. Shirley, his own secretary was also absent, but that's because she was on a week's leave. He had been offered a temp by Rhys Williams, but he told him not to bother. He wasn't a great one for writing memos, and between his own efforts and a bit of help from Gladys, he was sure he could make do.

As he wandered back through the typing pool, he saw Alex Radford floating around.

"Good Morning Alex."

"Good morning to you too, dear boy," replied Alex, loquacious as ever.

"What's going on?" enquired Bernie.

Alex looked confused. His face told Bernie everything he needed to know.

"I don't know. Am I missing something?"

"Probably not," said Bernie, with a shrug of the shoulder.

166

He went back to his office and started working on a running order for next week's show. About 11 o'clock, he decided to go and make himself a cup of coffee. He returned to the typing pool, wandered over to the communal electric kettle, and switched it on. Just then, he noticed Gladys was back in her seat.

"Is Jimmy in then?" he enquired politely.

She seemed unusually hesitant.

"Er... I'm not sure..."

When Bernie looked at her questioningly, she admitted,

"I... think he might be in his office."

Bernie thanked Gladys, forgot about the coffee, and made his way along the corridor. Jimmy's door was shut. He knocked.

"Come in!" came the muffled reply.

Bernie walked in with a placatory smile on his face. Jimmy looked unsettled. Harassed, even.

"What's the matter Jimmy? You look as though you've seen a ghost..."

"It wasn't my doing, Bernie." Jimmy spluttered.

"What wasn't your doing?" said Bernie, brows furrowing.

"Oh!.." said Jimmy... Bernie waited.

"You've not heard then?"

Bernie had the most ominous sense of foreboding.

"Not heard what?"

Another pause. Jimmy's expression was difficult to read.

"I... I think you'd better talk to Rhys Williams" he stammered. "It's better you hear it from him. It was his decision. Not mine. I played no part in it."

'Christ! What the hell is going on.' thought Bernie.

He could see that Jimmy was upset, so he politely apologised for interrupting, and also for the exchange of words over the weekend. Then he strode off towards Rhys Williams office.

As he approached, Prunella fixed him with her bespectacled gaze.

"Now is not a good time, Bernie," she said assertively. "But Mr Williams would like to see you first thing this afternoon, at two o'clock."

Bernie, not a natural optimist at the best of times, fell into the blackest of black depressions. He trudged back to his office. On the way, he ran into Jeff.

"Hi Jeff, heard the news?"

"Yes. I'm really sorry Bernie. I don't know the full story... Would you like to tell me your end?"

Bernie grinned, ruefully.

"Yes, and maybe you can tell me exactly what is going on? As I have precisely no idea."

"Oh God!" said Jeff, putting a consoling hand on Bernie's shoulder. "Let's go back to the office."

*****

Jeff closed the door behind them. They sat down, and Jeff told Bernie what he had heard from the rumour mill: that Bernie was to be moved off *Saturday Club*; that management had no choice; that it was in Jimmy's and Bernie's interests to have a break from each other; and that it was Bernie who would have to move, as *Saturday Club* was Jimmy's baby in the first place.

Bernie sat. Immobile. Jeff's story was pretty much as he had guessed.

"What I don't get," said Jeff, "is how Williams could have known about what happened over the weekend. At first I assumed that Jimmy had done the dirty, but you said you spoke to him today, and you're convinced that he had nothing to do with it."

"Dave Bisley." said Bernie.

"What?.." said Jeff. "How?"

"Dave fucking Bisley was the studio manager on last week's *Saturday Club* transmission, and he took the call when I phoned up Jimmy after the show. Then I had a go at Jimmy. Bisley only heard Jimmy's side of the conversation, but he would have had a pretty good idea of what was being said on the other end. And even if he didn't, he would have enjoyed making it up."

Bernie paused,

"He's pretty thick with Williams. I'm sure the jungle drums were beating long before we got here this morning. Williams has been looking for an excuse to have a go at me for a while. And now, thanks to that cunt Bisley, he's got it."

"Maybe it's just a temporary thing? A break? For a while?" said Jeff, optimistically.

Bernie didn't look convinced.

"Well, you'll just have to bide your time. I'm sure there will be other things you can get your teeth into." said Jeff.

*****

When it came to the actual meeting with Williams, Bernie was glad he had discussed it with Jeff beforehand. Their conversation had taken all the sting out of what might otherwise have been an explosive encounter.

Maybe that's what Williams was trying to engineer? Another confrontation?' thought Bernie.

If so, Williams must have been disappointed. When he finally wielded the axe, his *'management decision'* came as no surprise, and Bernie accepted it impassively. Bernie remained stony-faced throughout Williams' homily, and he managed not to lose his rag.

*****

When he got home that Friday evening, he was full of gloom. The next morning, the phone rang. Terry answered.

"Bernie!.. It's for you... Jim Waters."

Terry handed Bernie the phone.

"I just heard," was Jim's opener.

"Bloody hell! That was quick."

"Yeah, well when major promotional lines of communication get interrupted, the news travels fast. Are you doing anything this afternoon?" said Jim.

"No."

"Well, why don't we go out for a quiet drink together. We can grab a bar snack or something."

"Not sure I'm up to it,"

"Look Bernie, you helped me a while ago. Maybe I can return the favour. In any case, you shouldn't shut yourself away. It's best you get out and about. Try to get some perspective on what's happened. Not dwell on it."

"What do you have in mind?"

*****

Jim had recently found a new flat in Barnes, south of the Thames. He suggested they meet at a nearby pub, The Bull's Head, which had a good view facing the river. The area was well off the beaten track - as far as BBC staff and record biz people were concerned - so it would be easy to talk without being recognised or overheard.

Bernie got off at Barnes Bridge railway station. He was early, so he walked slowly along the pavement, taking in the wildlife on the river and the greenery on the opposite bank. It was a beautiful summer afternoon. Bernie, uncharacteristically, found the whole thing quite tranquil.

When he entered the saloon bar, the quieter of the two, Jim was already there with Bernie's favourite tipple on the table - a double gin and tonic with ice and a slice of lemon. Bernie sat down, thanked Jim and took a nice, long sip.

"That's better." he said, smiling at Jim.

"I'm glad you've cheered up," said Jim.

"Well, I wouldn't say I've cheered up. But I'm trying to come to terms with what's happened."

"So, what are your plans now?"

"I don't have any," said Bernie.

"Well, you encouraged me to make a move a while ago, and it's worked out well for me... So far..."

"I often look at the alternatives," said Bernie, "but there's nothing I love more than working in BBC Radio. I really don't know if I can do anything else. Or want to do anything else."

"Look at the last few years, Bernie. You've produced successful sessions with everyone who is anyone in the record business: Gerry and the Pacemakers, The Rolling Stones, Dusty Springfield, The Searchers, The Dave Clark Five, Cilla Black... That's just for starters. And it's common knowledge that you're on good terms with Brian Epstein and the Beatles."

"That's one of the things that got me axed from *Saturday Club*. Quite a few of my so called colleagues... On the one hand, it's just a job to them. But on the other hand, they don't like it when I can pick up the phone and book the Beatles - and lots of other groups for that matter. I can often persuade artists to come in for sessions when they can't. Because it's common knowledge that it's more than a job to me. Which makes me very unpopular with some."

"Yes, but now you're in a great position to capitalise on your reputation."

"What are you getting at?" said Bernie.

"What about record production?" said Jim.

"Don't think I haven't thought about it," said Bernie. "I've even done a few records... On the quiet... Under a nomme de plume. None of them have been successful."

"Yes, but if you worked under your own name... You'd have everyone falling over themselves to hire you. You'd have the best new prospects with the best new material knocking on your door. Particularly since you know your way around the BBC."

"I've thought about that too. I might get some offers. At least to begin with. But you know better than anyone, if I don't produce the goods - by which I mean immediately make the record company piles of money - then I'd soon have a hard time making a living. I don't get paid a fortune at the BBC, but I like the job security. I'm not really cut out for a hand-to-mouth existence, waiting for the next big thing to come along... "

"I think you underestimate yourself," said Jim. "You're good at spotting potential hits. Sometimes, you see them coming before the record companies do."

"That's very nice of you to say so," said Bernie. "But the other problem is with what you call *'knowing my way around the BBC.'* "

"My contacts are divided into two camps. The first is those who resent me - which is quite a few - and they're not going to do me any favours. In fact, having my name on record labels could well be a millstone around the necks of the artists and labels involved - at least as far as those people are concerned. On the other hand, the few people that I do get on with, and who are likely to be supportive... Well... I'd feel as though I was pimping them out to make myself a living."

"Isn't it worth taking a risk? You might find you enjoy the freedom? What have you got to lose by giving commercial record production a go?"

Bernie stared into his G&T.

" *'Freedom'* is a relative sort of concept, Jim. The board-room execs who run the record companies aren't really interested in the music, or the artists, or the audience, or diversity, or creativity... They're all about making money."

"Those people make a lot of noise about discovering new artists and new trends - but only after the event. After the lucky few have managed to struggle their way through the bullshit. And then, do they want these artists to develop, or to experiment or to evolve? No! All they want them and their producers to do is to churn out one single after another, like on a production line, making the next one exactly like the last one."

After a pause.

"I'm sorry I'm being so negative," said Bernie. "And I appreciate you listening to me. You're one of the few friends I've got who I can open up to like this."

Jim nodded.

"What about the pirates?"

"They're great fun," said Bernie. "But they're doomed. It's just a matter of time."

"Fair enough," said Jim.

"The only other radio station you could work for is Radio Luxembourg. What about that?"

"Yes, I've thought about that too,"

"But?" enquired Jim.

"It's a glorified pay-per-play machine for the record companies. And I'd feel like I was the one being pimped out."

"Oh, you're such a man of principle." said Jim, starting to sound frustrated.

"I'm sorry. And thanks again for listening. At least I've blown off some steam."

"You've ruled out all the realistic possibilities. What's left Bernie?"

Bernie sat for a while, collecting his thoughts.

"There are two sets of people who desperately want to get together. You have emerging talent who know there's a young audience out there waiting for them, and that young audience will do anything to hear what this new talent has to offer.

I'd like to see the BBC devote a bit more airtime to younger audiences, and to take a few more risks in the choice of music."

"And whatever airtime we decide to devote to the younger audience, it should be focussed _entirely_ on the younger audience. For example, on _Saturday Club_, we shouldn't be mixing up what they want with middle-of-the-road pop like Frank Ifield and Rose Brennan, and trad jazz and folk groups... There's plenty of that stuff elsewhere on the Light Programme. _Saturday Club_ is the only two hours a week where the kids can be sure to find what they're looking for. And they have made it abundantly clear that beat groups are the way of the future."

They both sipped their drinks.

"We're a public service. So I think we should be living up to that principle. Look at BBC Manchester. They got the Beatles on the radio while all the major record companies were turning them down. Now I don't know what part those radio appearances actually played in eventually getting them a record deal. There's no way of measuring that. But even if early coverage on the BBC made no difference at all to the Beatles' eventual success - which I very much doubt - it speaks well of BBC Manchester that it brought the next big thing to millions across the country before the record companies ever dreamt they could be the next big thing. That kind of no-commercial-strings-attached talent development is exactly what we should be doing."

"Given what's just happened Bernie, do you think there's any way that a maverick like you could have the slightest influence on the course of the BBC?"

"Maverick?" Bernie laughed. "I've heard myself described a lot worse. To answer your question, I wouldn't put money on it.""

"But I'll just have to stick with it for the time being. Play the game. Be patient. Try and come up with some new programme ideas."

"For how long?" asked Jim.

"I don't know. But I'm not willing to give up yet."

*****

Bernie's alarm went off at 6:00 am. During the previous evening, he had been up late, and had also sunk a few. He was not in the brightest of moods. Then he remembered why the alarm was going off at such a preposterous hour. This morning, he was down to produce *Music While You Work*. Bernie's mood turned from not bright - to dark! He hated early starts. He also hated *Music While You Work*. Doubly so. Because it necessitated an early start.

Music While You Work had been a weekday regular on the BBC Light Programme since 1940. During the war, factory production across the UK was crucial to the war effort, and it was deemed a good idea to boost morale and productivity by relaying *'non-stop light music at an even tempo on factory loudspeakers'*.

'But it's 1964, for Christ's sake!' thought Bernie, as he dragged himself out of bed.

He forced himself into the bathroom trying to focus on the routine that he knew would have him washed, dressed and on the road up to BH, just in time for rehearsals. *Music While You Work* went out live, every weekday, from 10:30 to 11:00 am, so the whole show had to be rehearsed, checked and timed well before 10:30 am.

As Bernie shuffled through the door of the control room he was confronted by a large man dressed in tweeds, with a pile of cables in his hand. His voice was as loud as it was posh.

"Bang on time, Bernard. Your orchestra awaits."

If you didn't know Eton-educated Charles Clarke-Maxwell, your immediate impression might be that he was a bit of a toffee-nose. But, in Bernie's book, Charles was one of the most amiable Studio Managers at the BBC. Not that he would have been happy for Charles to mix the likes of the Animals or the Dave Clark Five. But in this case, when Bernie - like so many of his Light Programme colleagues - didn't really give a fuck about what he was preparing to put out on the radio, he was very content to share Charles' hearty company.

'An easy going studio manager for an uninspiring show.' he thought to himself. *'Could be worse.'*

"How do you want to go about this, good sir?" quoth Charles.

"You've done it all before," said Bernie. "You've got the running order there. Just run it through. If you or the band has any questions, just give me a shout."

Bernie got his stopwatch out and placed it on the desk. Shirley, his secretary, had already typed up a list with an estimated running time logged against each number. All of these timings had been added together to calculate a total running time for the whole programme. Bernie checked the sums carefully. He'd been caught out before. Not by Shirley, but once by a temp, whose arithmetic wasn't too good.

It's very uncomfortable if the producer looks at the clock towards the end of a live broadcast and suddenly realises the programme is running short.

He or she is then obliged to get straight on the phone and explain to a panicked continuity announcer that, with very little notice, they will be obliged to face a nice, big, brown BBC microphone and fill a couple of minutes of dead space on the radio with a load of waffle before the handover to the next programme.

Charles started the run through. Bernie dutifully clicked his stop watch at the beginning of each number and then proceeded to read the neatly folded newspaper on his desk. He found the newspaper immeasurably more interesting. At the end of each number he would click the stopwatch again and check the logged time against the estimate on the running order.

The rehearsal was, predictably, uneventful. A bunch of aging musicians scraping and blowing and thumping along next door; everyone intently reading their parts on their music stands; everyone playing in perfect sync; and everyone performing with absolutely no feeling whatsoever.

There were occasional attempts to relieve the boredom. Once or twice, Charles gave Bernie notice of minor adjustments to the sound balance together with the reasons why they were needed. Bernie inevitably failed to detect any measurable impact after these minor adjustments. Then Bernie asked Charles to check and make sure that *Deep In The Heart of Texas* was not on the running order.

"Are you taking the piss, dear boy?" boomed Charles.

"Of course I am," replied Bernie.

Deep In The Heart of Texas was a jolly 1941 ditty by Bing Crosby, which involved a bit of audience participation.

It proceeds thus:

The moon at night
Is big and bright

(Audience) Clap, clap, clap, clap

Deep in the heart of Texas...

The clapping bit is childishly simple. The most unmusical in the audience can join in with relish.

The joke was that, even in 1964, there was still a BBC Standing Order to the effect that *Deep In The Heart of Texas* must never be played on *Music While You Work*.

This regulation was put in place to obviate the possibility that over enthusiastic factory workers might pick up spanners or hammers or any other tools that happened to be lying around at the time, and bash them vigorously against the valuable plant or machinery on which they were working. I mean we wouldn't want any explosive incidents in the torpedo factories, would we?

The tedium continued. Bernie clicked his stopwatch on and off. He surreptitiously opened and folded the newspaper between numbers, so he had a fresh page to read each time. Not that Charles was fooled. He didn't give a fuck either.

Towards the end of the rehearsal, Bernie saw that Shirley's estimated timings were accurate. He also saw that there was a relatively long number programmed as the last item. His arithmetic told him that the total running time was likely to overrun the half-hour slot on air by about a minute or so, which could be solved by fading out the last number to time at the end of the programme.

Perfect! If, up to then, Bernie had been merely apathetic, then after making his calculations, he was now totally relaxed and apathetic.

Sensing Bernie's mood, Charles, very helpfully, informed Bernie in his perfectly enunciated English,

"Oh by the way... you may have noticed that Mr Beaumont, the band leader, has a microphone in front of his guitar."

"'Yes?..." said Bernie.

"Well, it's not plugged in," said Charles.

"Why?..." Bernie enquired, vaguely interested.

"We find him such a bad guitarist, we consider it better not to broadcast his contribution," explained Charles.

In that moment, the complete futility of it all came home to Bernie. He descended once more into a black depression.

"Excuse me!" he said to Charles. "I must go for a piss."

Charles continued with his task while Bernie got up and made for the toilet.

He went to the furthest urinal, stood up on the footrests and started to relieve himself. As he did so, he leant forward and put his hand up against the wall while bumping his forehead against it, muttering,

"Fucking Hell!.."
"Fucking Hell!.."

...an incantation which he continued even after his bladder had been completely evacuated. The door opened and Fred Unwin, who regularly manned a nearby edit suite, walked in.

"You alright Bernie?" asked Fred.

"Yeah... Hunky Dory... Never better..." he lied.

*****

As Bernie predicted, within a few weeks, *The House of the Rising Sun*, was topping the UK charts, and after a month or so, it made the #1 position in the US Billboard singles chart. Bernie and Jimmy never discussed the matter - ever.

Tedium and frustration became the focus of Bernie's life. He found it difficult to adjust, but gradually, adjust he did. He did his chores - for that was what he considered them to be - without complaint. Standard fare was producing innocuous orchestral covers of middle-of-the-road pops, show tunes or light classics - what the BBC described as *'light music'*, and which Bernie would affectionately refer to as *'shite music'*. Such delights were conjured up daily by the likes of the *BBC Radio Orchestra*, or *Paul Fenhoulet and his Swinging Strings (more like 'Dangling Strings' according to Bernie)*. Then, of course, there was lots and lots of *Music While You Work*.

Thankfully, he was still considered a prime target by record pluggers, so the promotional copies and white labels kept coming in. He assuaged his *Saturday Club* withdrawal symptoms by immersing himself, whenever possible, in listening to the latest record releases.

Jimmy was kind. He always spent time with him in the canteen and on passing in the corridors.

Bernie also continued to pass comment on the latest releases to both Jimmy and Brian Willey, who had taken over Bernie's responsibilities on *Saturday Club*. He never laboured the point, but once or twice, he thought that he might have influenced a play or two. But there was no denying, he was a fish out of water.

So he kept his spirits up in producing a constant stream of *'programme suggestions'* - either by verbal descriptions on paper, or sometimes in the form of tape-recorded *'pilot programmes'* - provided that he could blag the necessary studio time and voice talent required.

He got a kick out of doing these try-outs, but, each time he submitted the results for consideration, he didn't hold his breath.

Into Top Gear

One afternoon, he received a phone call summoning him to a meeting in Aubrey Small's office. Bernie wasn't sure how he should feel about this.

At the appointed hour, he knocked on the door, was admitted, and offered a seat at a large table opposite a trinity in the form of the Fat Controller in the centre, Edwina, his secretary on the left, and, Rhys Williams, of course, at the right hand of the fatter. Aubrey Small and his secretary seemed affable enough. He didn't get the same vibe from Williams.

"Thank you for coming along, Bernie," said Small.

Bernie nodded.

"Now, as you may, or may not be aware, a number of unofficial radio stations have started transmitting off the coast at various points around the British Isles. They are not big operations. They broadcast from boats moored in international waters, just outside UK jurisdiction. They can hardly compete with BBC Radio in terms of scale and coverage, but we're keeping an eye on them. Of course, the Government is looking at the legality of these cowboy operations, and we've been asked to assess their impact on our own programming."

Bernie was suddenly very interested in what the Fat Controller had to say. It was the first time he had sensed a fear of competition emanating from BBC Management. And he liked it. But he wondered what on earth they wanted from him?

"Now, as I understand it, you haven't been working on *Saturday Club* for a while,"

'You could say that', thought Bernie.

"And you have been submitting ideas for new programmes which, well… Let's say they seem to have something in common with the kind of thing these pirate radio stations are getting up to."

Bernie was beginning to get excited, but was determined not to show it. He sat still. Poker faced.

"So, I've been talking to some of our senior producers, and we think you should have a go at something along the same lines. You know… Top forty format… New releases that are likely candidates… And so on."

Bernie sensed that the Fat Controller wasn't completely au fait with what he was talking about. He seemed to have switched into some sort of parroting of a party line which Bernie suspected might have come from a bit further up the chain than Aubrey Small's lofty position.

"After all, we at the BBC always strive to be ahead of the curve. Don't we?"

Bernie had to call on all his self-discipline to stop himself falling off his chair in hysterics. Eventually, he managed to cough out,

"Yes. Of course."

"Good." said Small with an air of finality. "That's settled. I'll leave you to work out the details with Rhys here,"

Williams' face was fixed in a waxen smile. Bernie knew exactly what was going on underneath.

*****

The subsequent meeting with Williams was fascinating.

He told Bernie that they were giving him a regular slot on Thursday evening to - more or less - create a show which would point in exactly the same direction that he had been trying to steer *Saturday Club* in the months before he was sacked. Then Williams expounded on how management had deliberated at length, carefully analysed audience figures and reaction, and sifted through listener feedback in detail before coming to this momentous decision.

'What a load of old cobblers', thought Bernie.

Williams had turned the whole thing around, effectively claiming that all market analysis and creative thinking had fallen on the part of the execs - which had resulted in handing down to Bernie a well-considered management directive, telling him to do exactly what he had proposed in his most recent *'programme suggestion'* - without any *'help'* from above.

Bernie wasn't sure what his dominant urge was. Did he feel like strangling Williams and stuffing his management directive down his throat? Or did he feel like laughing in his face, pulling down his trousers and using the management directive to wipe his arse?

In any event, Bernie steeled himself to make sure that his body language remained neutral, and he employed the *'Yes sir! No sir!'* routine that he had learned so well during his RAF days. Then he went into the zone and just let the rest of Williams' monologue float over his head.

Suddenly, Bernie was jerked out of his trance by the realisation that Williams was actually asking him a question.

"Pardon?' said Bernie.

"What should we call our new show? What name should we give it?"

He really didn't want to be knee-jerked into deciding something that needed a bit of careful thought. But he knew that Williams wouldn't like it if he tried to fob him off. Williams was probably more interested in having a name - any name - to drop into the memo which he would soon circulate, and in which he would claim credit for his wonderful new programme idea. But he would be too wary of suggesting a name himself, in case he exposed himself to public ridicule. As Williams himself knew only too well, *'What do I know about the latest fashions in music?'*

"Well, come on then Bernie!..." he cajoled.

Bernie scrabbled around in his brain for the right thing to say. Anything that would buy him some time. Then it came...

"I know... Why don't we run a competition and see what the music fans think? They're the ones who will listen in.... Why don't we ask them to give us their ideas?"

"What a brilliant idea." said Williams.

(That you've just had), thought Bernie.

"You work out the logistics, and I'll deal with the internal communications on this." he pronounced.

'Williams, you're as subtle as an air-raid, and totally predictable,' thought Bernie. *'I do the work. You take the credit.'*

In view of the fact that he was being handed the second chance of a lifetime, Bernie ignored all the bullshit. He knew this was the best deal he was going to get.

*****

Bernie had thrown himself into his new project like a fury. But there was so much still to do. He had a confirmed slot for his new programme. It was scheduled to go out from 10.00 pm to 11.55 pm every Thursday from the beginning of the next quarter - which was not far off - and he still hadn't finalised the bookings for all the recording sessions.

At least he had a name - *Top Gear*. He had hastily organised a competition open to anyone listening who felt like writing in to suggest a name. Jimmy Grant helped out by getting Brian Matthew to promote the competition on *Saturday Club* during the run up to the launch. Brian was well pleased, because Bernie had asked Brian to present the new programme - so he was about to get his voice on two different pop music programmes each week.

At that time, the idea of one BBC Radio programme putting out a trailer for another BBC Radio programme was considered outlandish by the powers that be. It smacked of commercialism and competition. The BBC was a Public Service for goodness' sake. So, apart from the exceptional dispensations granted to him by *Saturday Club*, Bernie bypassed those publicity limitations by calling on his contacts in the music press to help out. They were only too glad to get involved in spreading the word that there was about to be a new, pop music friendly radio programme on the BBC.

In the end, two teenage girls came up with the same suggestion. They came from different ends of the country.

A sixteen year old girl from the Home Counties called Susan and an eighteen year old girl called Fran from South Shields had both, quite independently, proposed that the new programme should be called *'Top Gear'*. Apart from the obvious allusion to high-speed motor racing, the Beatles had imported a great deal of Liverpool *'lingo'* into the popular lexicon. One of these expressions being, *'it's the gear.'* - i.e. It's *'top class.'* Or *'spot on.'* When Bernie bounced this idea off Ringo in the flat one day, Ringo's reaction was,

"It's the gear!"

So, *Top Gear* it was.

The prize for choosing the winning name was a special invitation to come into the studio and see the first programme being broadcast. Home Counties Susan was beside herself with joy at the prospect, but, unfortunately South Shields Fran was at a boarding school. For her, a jaunt to London was totally out of the question. So Bernie called in favours from all his record company contacts. He collected as many of the latest releases he could get his hands on together with all the promotional merchandise he could find. Then he had these treasures parcelled up and sent on to Fran. She too was overwhelmed with joy when she received this bounty. Her special treat was duly reported during the first broadcast, live, on-air, along with her own, special record request. But before all that took place, the last few weeks before launch were frantic.

One bright spot was that the Beatles were in the UK at the time, and when Bernie phoned up Brian Epstein to ask if they might be available to record the inaugural session for *Top Gear*, Brian's answer was,

"Of course Bernie. It would be our pleasure."

Not only that, Bernie was able to get the boys involved in creating some trailers for the new show which would go out on *Saturday Club*. When he explained to the lads what was happening, he was delighted to see that, despite their phenomenal worldwide success, they seemed to be as enthusiastic about the project as he was. And when he mentioned the 'launch' of the new programme, they were soon waxing lyrical about,

"Bernie's new ship..." "...sailing off into the sunset..." and any other nautical imagery they could think of.

'They are nothing, if not inventive,' thought Bernie.

He brought a portable tape recorder into the flat, and recorded the trailers in the front room. One of his favourites started with John, in falsetto voice and posh accent, enunciating imperiously in the fashion of Her Majesty the Queen,

"I name this ship, *Top Gear*."

(vocal sound effects imitating a champagne bottle smashing over a ship's bow)

"God bless her, and all who sail in her."

That opener was closely followed by Paul, George and Ringo running through the musical attractions that would be on offer that Thursday - not least of which would be special BBC recordings of tracks they had written for their forthcoming album, *A Hard Day's Night,* which was scheduled for release just a few days before the launch of *Top Gear*.

'Astonishing!' thought Bernie. *'The biggest group in the world are doing trailers for my new radio programme - for free!'*

Bernie also managed to get Joey, the mynah bird, in on the act. He spent ages trying to wean the bird off its favourite,

'Hello Ringo!'
'Fuck off, Ringo!'

And on to a new call in the form of,

'Top Gear!'
'Top Gear!'

The bird eventually picked up *'Top Gear!'*, but Bernie was never completely successful in disentangling it's penchant for mixing up the bland *'Top Gear!'* with the more exotic *'Fuck off, Ringo!'* However, with a bit of judicious tape editing, he was able to produce a splendid result.

The anarchy continued into the studio when the Beatles recorded the first ever *Top Gear* session. The centrepiece was the eponymous single, from the new album.

After the fade out, the tape was still running, and so was George - doggedly picking out the distinctive closing arpeggio on his 12-string Rickenbacker.

At this point, John put the talkback key down, shouting something like,

"That's enough... It's over..."

George started clowning around, pretending he couldn't hear what they were saying, and sticking to his post like a good soldier. This larking about was all caught on tape.

Bernie thought the mayhem was funny, and, what is more, it made the point that this special *Top Gear* recording was quite distinct from the record. So, although Brian Matthew wasn't actually there at the time, Bernie got him to overdub a few more catcalls later. And when George finally came to a standstill, Brian finishes of the lunacy by shouting,

"Here! Ringo!.. Have a banana!.."

No-one would ever have dreamt that such crazy gems would make it into the archives to be pored over by Beatles aficionados all around the world more than fifty years later.

But there was a problem with this recording. A big problem.

In the middle of the record, George Martin had overdubbed a piano riff in unison with George's guitar break. The boys had asked George if he could come in to the BBC and record the same overdub. He had initially agreed, but then it turned out that he was urgently needed somewhere else, so he had to pull out.

On the session, Paul tried to emulate George's piano overdub - without success. So the tape was left with only George's guitar line in the middle. This was very different to the record. It wasn't bad, but the boys thought the piano break was sorely missed.

Bernie told everyone not to worry. He promised he would sort something out. He wasn't saying how, but they took him at his word. Later, he took the newly-released album into an edit suite and transferred it onto tape. Then he cut out the few bars of instrumental where George Martin had overdubbed the piano, and cut that piece of tape into the BBC *Top Gear* recording. Unfortunately, the two recordings had been performed at slightly different tempos and in slightly different pitches. The edit was obvious.

So, he experimented. By speeding up the album version, ever so slightly, he found, to his joy, that it fitted into the *Top Gear* version perfectly. Now, this was a trick that George Martin himself would adopt a few years later, when he spliced the front end of one version of *Strawberry Fields* onto the back end of another - each performed at a different speed, in a different pitch. But Bernie wasn't to know that yet. He was just relieved that it all worked. He was very proud of his edit.

When he played it to the boys, they liked the result. But when he explained how he had done it, he was met with a barrage of feigned outrage!

"Ooooooh!.. Aaaah!.. We'll have to take this up with the Musician's Union you know..."

Until John put on his best Winston Churchill,

"Nevah.." In the field of human fakery... grrrr... Has so much... Been owed by so few... grrrr... To our Bernie..."

Cue laughter...

*****

"I'm surprised they had the time to do all that," said Jeff. "Every time I look in the music press, they're off on some tour or other."

"I was lucky to catch them in between,"

"When did you check out the edit with them? Getting them all together in one place must have been tricky?"

"More luck," said Bernie. "We had a party at the flat, just before they flew out again."

"Good party?"

"Loads of showbiz faces… Tommy Cooper and his wife were there, Dusty and Alma Cogan…. the lads… Apart from Paul… He's always otherwise engaged with a girl called Jane Asher. Bit of a stunner by all accounts. But the other three were there, and they OK'd the edit. They were sure it would be fine with Paul."

"During the party, John told us about the autobiography that Brian Epstein's writing. Well, actually it's his PR guy, Derek Taylor who's ghost writing it. John took great delight in explaining to us all that he thought it should be called *'Queer Jew'.*"

"Well, everyone's falling about laughing - except me - and eventually John says, *'Why are you looking so po faced Bernie?'* And I said, *'Well, Brian might not be unique.'* John went a bit quiet, and I could see he was thinking… Maybe he was trying to figure out if it might be one, or the other, or maybe both?"

"Anyway, he said, *'I didn't mean any harm Bernie… It was just a joke…'* So I had to stop him apologising. He seemed genuinely upset. So I laughed it off. Made him feel at ease. But I made the point that it wasn't as if Brian had done him any harm was it? I mean, Brian had been very good to them, hadn't he? And Brian's got enough problems without adding to them, hasn't he? By this time John was looking contrite, and I began to feel a bit sorry for him. He had a hellish childhood you know?"

"Yes, I heard about his Mum dying in a car accident when he was seventeen." said Jeff.

"Tragic." agreed Bernie. "But that's not all... Even at the age of five, the war was on, his Dad had vanished and his Mum, Julia, was living with another bloke. Then his aunt Mimi, his Mum's sister, complained to social services about the way Julia and her boyfriend were looking after John - or not - and the upshot was that Mimi got custody. Then his Dad suddenly reappeared and got back into the act. Apparently, at one stage, the poor little bugger was told by his Dad that he had to choose between him, or Mimi and his Mum, who visited John at Mimi's every day. So, long before Julia was hit by a car, he was a pretty mixed up kid."

"That's tough," said Jeff. "Must have been very difficult for him."

"Yeah... I think John is basically a kind and sensitive guy who has had to develop a pretty hard shell in order to cope with life. And I suspect that when he sees things that make him feel uncomfortable, he makes a joke about it - and the more tasteless and shocking the joke is, the better he likes it."

Bernie paused for a while to think.

"But he often regrets shooting his mouth off. He's a bit like me... Which is probably why I like him so much."

*****

Bernie was back on form. He had his own radio programme which he could put together exactly the way he wanted.

The first week featured the Beatles, Dusty Springfield, Carl Perkins, Mark Wynter and the Nashville Teens. The next week, it was the Rolling Stones, PJ Proby, Elkie Brookes and Joe Brown and the Bruvvers. The third one was Billy J Kramer, The Animals, and Elaine Delmar.

And after that, the Merseybeats, Cilla Black, Sounds Incorporated, the Fourmost, Lulu, the Searchers, the Barron Knights, Brian Poole and the Tremeloes, Georgie Fame and the Blue Flames, Brenda Lee, Gerry and the Pacemakers, Dave Berry... And so on...

But it wasn't just Bernie who was on top form. The pirate radio stations were going great guns too. Every week there were stories in the press about how fast they were extending their reach and growing their youthful fanbase.

The media was full of contradictory rumours:

'The BBC must be restructured...'

'The pirates must be squashed...'

'The BBC must learn to compete with the pirates...'

'The pirates must be legalised...'

It seemed there was a new rumour each day.

"There's no doubt about why they are so popular with the kids," Jeff remarked to Bernie during a coffee break.

"They don't have any needletime restrictions and can play any records they want, from dawn till dusk. They don't pay royalties to the artists and writers, and they don't even pay for the content in their news bulletins. All they do is listen to the BBC News on the hour, and within 15 minutes, they're broadcasting exactly the same bulletins. They may not have the pre-recorded clips that BBC News has, but the main headlines on their stations are always up to date."

Bernie nodded,

"The Government will have to do something about it. But the question is what?"

"Maybe they'll legalise commercial radio?" said Jeff. "Regulate them properly? Make sure they pay their dues? Maybe even licence them to operate on the mainland? If they did that, I'm sure that well-managed stations would have no problem raising money for investment. The potential for generating advertising revenues on a national basis has to be massive."

"Well, that might create interesting opportunities for a lot of people in the BBC," said Bernie. "I can see a job-creation scheme that would appeal to those who work in the gramophone department. All they do is play records all day - just like the pirates. The opportunity to boost their salaries in a competitive environment would be right up their street. Except they'd have to seriously start thinking about what the public wants to hear, instead of just pleasing themselves."

*****

It was around this time that Jeff put his own pilot programme together. A one hour radio concert recorded in front of a live audience. A double bill featuring Manfred Mann and Georgie Fame and the Blue Flames.

For a long time Jeff's show stayed in some high ranking executive's office drawer until, eventually, it was pulled out and broadcast on the BBC Light Programme as a one-off special. It was used as a filler during the evening of the General Election in October that year.

On the one hand, Jeff was pleased that it got an airing, but on the other hand, he was pissed off because during the transmission, they kept interrupting the programme so they could bring listeners the latest updates on the election results as they came in.

Afterwards, he received no response from management about the prospects for his idea of regularly broadcasting live R&B concerts on the BBC Light Programme.

Which was surprising. The pirates would have had great difficulty competing on a national basis with an idea like that.

*****

For Bernie, it was all systems go. Everyone who was anyone appeared on *Top Gear*: The Kinks, the Who, the Yardbirds, Them, Donovan, Chris Farlowe, the Small Faces... There seemed to be no end to the constant stream of new talent.

When Harold Wilson was elected as Prime Minister, he recognised the significant political benefits to be gained by awarding the Beatles the Order of the British Empire - an act which had old soldiers like Rhys Williams choking on their scotch and sodas.

Bernie was delighted by just how topsy turvy British society was being turned. He had never paid much attention to which old buffer got which honours at the end of each year, but he took heart at the way things were changing - to his way of thinking - for the better.

It wasn't just British pop music that went global. British fashion trends for girls, like sexy miniskirts with eye catching makeup and accessories, exploded onto the streets, while the boys responded by emulating regency dandies with copious locks flowing down over the flamboyant cut and outrageous colour of their latest couture. Post war austerity was a thing of the past.

Bernie grinned when he read a newspaper article in which some toff or other observed ruefully that, "If you walk down King's Road these days, it's impossible to tell the difference between the debutantes and the commoners. They all dress the same."

It wasn't just the teenagers who were clamouring for change and freedom. Universal access to birth control had revolutionised family planning. It had also radically altered the public's attitude to premarital sex.

*****

Author's note: *At this point, I wanted to quote a verse by a leading poet of the 1960s called Philip Larkin. I wasn't able to get clearance. If you Google* **Annus Mirabilis** *by* **Philip Larkin** *and read the first verse, you'll find a witty commentary on how the young people of the early 1960s, within a very short period of time, roundly rejected the sexual repression that had been selectively and hypocritically imposed on society by the establishment for as far back as anyone could remember.*

*****

Debate on *'the permissive society'* - a pejorative term coined by those who disapproved - raged on. Not only with regard to conventional boy-girl matters, but also on same sex relationships, which many thought should be legalised.

The judiciary had recently lifted the ban on D H Lawrence's novel, *Lady Chatterley's Lover*, which had previously been deemed too obscene to publish. Around the same time, the Minister for War had been outed for deceitfully denying in Parliament that he was having an affair with Christine Keeler - a striking young lady who wasn't backwards in coming forwards, and who was simultaneously on intimate terms with a Russian spy.

All this was a gift for television, which had rapidly superseded radio as the most effective way to communicate with the masses. Politicians were no longer treated with deference. They frequently found themselves suffering bruising encounters with aggressive reporters in front of television audiences which were counted in the millions.

One of Bernie's favourites was a weekly programme called *That Was The Week That Was*, which took a highly irreverent look at current affairs in a format employing comedy, music, satire, parody and lampoon as never before. The establishment hated it.

But Bernie wasn't working in television. The big question for Bernie was not how BBC Radio would deal with this massive social upheaval. The big question was whether BBC Radio was equipped to deal with any sort of change at all?

*****

A memo arrived from the Controller of the BBC Light Programme. This missive announced that, without any warning or prior discussion, *Top Gear* was to be axed from the beginning of the next quarter. He wasn't the only one to suffer. There were a few other changes to the programme schedule which Bernie didn't think were particularly forward looking. In fact, in his view, things seemed to be going backwards.

Bernie also saw accompanying communications - from one R. Williams, H.O.M.P. - informing him that for the first couple of weeks of the following quarter, he would be responsible for a variety of shows involving - in no particular order - the recording of brass bands, Wurlitzer

200

cinema organs, light orchestral music, and, of course, *Music While You Work.*

Bernie was numb.

The move seemed so arbitrary that he couldn't really muster any feelings of anger. There seemed to be no-one he could focus his anger on. Yet another mindless decision had been imposed from on high - without explanation.

What's Going On?

Bernie took a walk along to Jimmy Grant's office.

"Hello Bernie!"

"Hi Jimmy. You've heard about *Top Gear* then?"

"Yes. I'm sorry about that."

"When they asked me to do it, they mumbled something about taking on the pirates. But now, they seem to have changed their mind. Although, true to form, no-one's giving any reasons why. Have you heard anything?"

"Well, I don't know much more than you Bernie."

He thought for a bit.

"The only thing I might say is that I talk to Richard Douglas in Current Affairs now and then in the club. He's got a pretty good nose for what's going on in politics - both at Westminster and in the BBC. He told me that the Board of Governors and the DG are in a bit of a state because of the pirate radio situation. Well, I mean, up to now, successive Governments have kicked this one into the long grass... All too difficult... But Harold Wilson has finally decided to grasp the nettle. Probably because of the incident last month. I mean, you can't have the Radio Atlanta boss shooting the Radio City boss in broad daylight, just 'cause he feels like it... Like it's the Wild West... Can you?"

"Do you think anything's actually been decided?" asked Bernie.

"Well, there hasn't been any methodical Inquiry or Government White Paper or think tank analysis, or anything like that. Richard's reading of the situation is that Harold Wilson has just told his ministers and the BBC to sort it out."

"They're not going to do that by cutting *Top Gear*, are they?" scoffed Bernie. "*Top Gear*, *Saturday Club* and the weekly Top-20 countdown on *Pick of the Pops* are the only things on BBC Radio that appeal to potential pirate radio listeners."

Jimmy nodded, "But my guess... And it's only a guess... Is that those upstairs are in a bit of a tizz. There's probably a progressive faction who want to shake things up, and a more conservative faction..."

"You mean the dinosaurs?.." interjected Bernie, " ... who want to maintain the status quo. And by the looks of it, the dinosaurs have won this round?"

Jimmy nodded again.

'And I know exactly where I might look for some more information on this,' thought Bernie.

*****

In communal spaces like the canteen or the club, there was never any shortage of conversation at the BBC. One day, you might share a table with someone who was a sports commentator, and the next, you might be talking to a personnel manager or an electronics expert, or an actor. Everyone was always interested in what everyone else was doing in the BBC.

That was how Bernie had come in contact with a studious looking young lady called Katy Fielding. Katy worked in Audience Research.

She wore large, black-framed glasses, and had dark hair, long on the sides, with a fringe cut just above her eyes. Her clothes were fashionable, but on the well behaved side of fashionable. Restrained enough not to draw too much attention to herself in the office. The glasses helped with that too.

Bernie had never been much interested in BBC Audience Research. He knew they ignored the views of anyone under the age of 15, which must have skewed the figures they produced - certainly with respect to the kind of programme he enjoyed producing. And he also suspected that the people who conducted BBC Audience Research interviews on the street would have a natural bias towards those who looked as if they might be *'licence payers'*, which would result in a tendency to ignore the opinions of people under the age of 25 or so.

On one occasion, Bernie and Shirley were sharing a drink in the club when Katy walked over to their table,

"I'm a big fan of Chris Farlowe and the Thunderbirds, and I've heard a rumour that they're going to be on *Top Gear* soon. Is that right?"

Bernie looked at Katy, thinking to himself, *'Yes… Lose the glasses and don a pair of knee high boots, and you wouldn't look out of place at the Marquee or the Flamingo.'*

"Actually, we're recording them a week on Wednesday at the Playhouse," said Bernie.

"Fabulous." cooed Katy. "When will we hear them on the radio?"

"The Thursday after," came the reply.

Then Katy asked all sorts of questions about the groups Bernie had broadcast and those he was planning to book in the future. But the information flow wasn't all one way. He asked her about the music she liked, and while most of her replies didn't surprise him, she talked about a couple of bands who were just beginning to make a name for themselves in the clubs.

Bernie asked her where she worked. She explained that she had interviewed for a job as a studio manager, unsuccessfully. Her next move was to ask the Personnel Department if there were any other posts available within the BBC. They said that they only had secretarial posts open at that time, but if she was interested, and as she had a degree in economics, there was a position available in Audience Research. It wasn't really what she wanted to do, but she took the offer anyway, with the intention of trying again for a studio manager's post when the opportunity next presented itself.

"Can you get next Wednesday afternoon off?" Bernie asked.

"I think so. Why?"

"If you come down to the Playhouse, you can sit in on the session."

"Gosh!" said Katy. "That would be fantastic."

Then Bernie gave her a few tips on what kind of things she might need to bone up on, to increase her chances of getting a Studio Manager's job in the future.

After that exchange, Bernie regularly nodded to Katy in passing. But now it was he who wanted something. She was only a secretary in the Audience Research Department, but she might know something of interest.

He looked up the Audience Research Department in the internal phone book.

"Can I speak to Katy Fielding please?"

"Speaking."

"Hello Katy, it's Bernie Andrews, from *Top Gear*."

"Of course... Hi Bernie! What can I do for you?"

"Well, this might sound a bit strange, but I'd like to ask you some questions about your job. Could we talk about it over lunch in the club sometime. "

"My job." Katy laughed out loud. "What on earth would you want to know about my job?"

"Can I explain that when we meet?"

"Sure. When?"

"Would today be OK?"

"Yes."

"Excellent. Just after 1.00 in the club alright?"

"Yes."

"I'll see you there."

Bernie got there early and chose the quietest table in the corner. When
Katy appeared, he asked if he could get her a sandwich from the salad bar,
but she said no, she never ate much at lunch. So, he bought her an
orange juice as requested, and ordered a G&T for himself.

"What's this all about then Bernie?"

"Well, to be honest, I don't know if you'll be able to help me or not. I
don't even know what your job consists of, and I don't know if you'll have
access to the kind of information I'm looking for."

Katy looked puzzled.

"Oh... And even if you have got any information that I'd be interested in, I
don't know if it might be confidential... Or whatever... And I wouldn't
want to get you into any trouble. So, if you can't help, just say so."

"Try me!" said Katy, intrigued.

"As you probably know - or maybe you don't - *Top Gear* is for the chop."

"Oh no!"

"Now, I can't figure out what's going on. But I'm wondering if it's got
something to do with the pirate radio situation... How BBC Radio might
position itself in response to competition? And I wondered if Audience
Research might have been consulted?.. Maybe asked to conduct a survey
or two on what kind of inroads the pirates have been making into our
share of the audience?"

Katy thought for a while.

"Now before I say anything, like you said, I'm just a secretary. I don't conduct any audience research, and I don't write up any statistics or commentary. But I see a lot of paperwork passing across my desk, and I often have to type up reports and such…"

"What I'll tell you is my own idea about what has been happening. It's not the official line. In fact, it may have nothing to do with the official line. Frequently, I see conclusions being drawn from AR data which I think are written up more to tell the people who receive these documents what they want to hear, rather than formulating any clear and logical conclusions. You know what I mean?"

"I know exactly what you mean," said Bernie.

"The pirates don't have national coverage like the BBC. But in some areas where the pirates are active, during the daytime, they are capturing an audience about 15% of the size of the BBC Light Programme."

Bernie raised his eyebrows.

"The thing is… In those places, the Light Programme numbers have hardly changed. Which means that the listeners who are tuning into the pirates are a completely new audience - I am sure - of young people like me, who hardly ever tune into the radio during the day, because there's never anything on that they want to listen to."

"That means," Bernie interrupted, "that there is a significant youth audience out there that is unserved by the BBC during daytime hours."

"Quite." said Katy.

"Which is what I have always felt, but have never seen any evidence to back it up."

"Apart from analysing the contents of our postbag. Which is continually growing."

Katy nodded.

"OK," continued Bernie. "So, let me do some thinking aloud, and see if you think my ideas fit with what you've seen. It seems to me that those upstairs who are trying to figure out what to do about the pirate radio stations will fall into a number of camps."

"The first camp consists of those who want to get rid of the pirates and set up a new BBC Radio service for those who currently listen to the pirates. Opposing that idea will be those who are scared out of their wits by the potential upheaval involved in restructuring BBC Radio."

"The second camp consists of those who would be happy to see the pirates legalised, so that BBC Radio can avoid upheaval and just keep trudging on in the same old way. Opposing that idea will be those who are scared out of their wits by the possibility of commercial competition, and the threat to the survival of BBC Radio."

"The third camp consists of the *'head in the sand'* lot. They won't see any reason why BBC Radio should be forced to change just to satisfy a bunch of foolish youngsters, and they won't see any reason why the Government shouldn't just ban the pirates. That approach will get rid of all the problems with a single stroke. And I can't get a mixed metaphor out of mind," added Bernie. "A bunch of dinosaurs sticking their head in the sand. I suspect that those upstairs who support some sort of variant of the third case are currently in the ascendant, and are in the process of rearranging the deckchairs on the Titanic."

"I think that's a fair guess," said Katy.

*****

As it happened, Bernie wasn't the only one who was upset by the axing of *Top Gear*.

'Why have the BBC parcelled up their Top Gear listeners and handed them over to the pirates?' screamed the commentary in the UK music press.

Bernie was quite touched when a band of *Top Gear* fans mounted a public demonstration outside Broadcasting House petitioning for the programme to be reinstated.

He knew it was all a waste of time.

*****

"So what are your plans now?" asked Jim.

Bernie finally managed to get the cork out of the bottle of Mateus Rosé he had brought in from the kitchen. Just then, the doorbell rang.

He put the bottle down on the coffee table and put his forefinger to his lips, signalling Jim to keep quiet. Then he turned out the light and walked across to the sitting room window overlooking Shepherds Market. He quietly, but firmly drew up the sash window, and popped his head out. Then he popped it back in again, once more putting his forefinger to his lips while a mystified Jim looked on, riveted. Bernie carefully picked up the bucket of water that was standing on the floor below the window sill, gingerly marshalled it into place on the window ledge, carefully took aim, and then smartly turned the bucket upside down.

There was a brief moment as the water fell through the air, until cries of,

"You bastard!.. What the fuck was that for?.. Show your face, you bastard!.." echoed up from the doorway directly beneath the window.

Bernie quietly closed the window, and turned round with a contented smile.

"Glass of wine?" he offered.

"What was that all about?" asked Jim.

"The tart downstairs... Miss Veronica... Some of her customers can't read. Or maybe she's busy and can't come to the door, so her desperate punters start ringing the other doorbells... I don't know why? Maybe on the off chance that other tarts are available?.. Anyway, the upshot is that our doorbell goes off all hours of the day and night. I don't mind daytime. I don't retaliate during the hours of daylight. I'd probably get spotted anyway. But at night, let's say I like to give those horny buggers a bit of incentive to ring the correct doorbell the next time they come around."

Jim hooted with laughter. "You'll get arrested... Or assaulted, more likely, one of these days."

Jim resumed from where he had left off, "So what are your plans now?"

Bernie downed a mouthful of wine.

"One thing is for sure. Things aren't going to stay the way they are. Everyone knows that something is going to happen about the pirates. And the way I see it is that either the Government will legalise the pirates, or they will put them out of business on condition that the BBC finally does something sensible to cater for the kids who currently listen to the pirates."

"So you're going to stick it out for the time being then? See which way the wind blows?"

"Exactly." said Bernie.

*****

Bernie was in limbo - again. It was easier this time. He was sure that change was coming.

As before, he kept in close touch with what was happening in the music business. He also kept an eye on who was getting booked for *Saturday Club* sessions, and would surreptitiously - and illegally - record each programme for his own archive.

In the meantime, what he needed was a creative project to keep his brain ticking over. And he had a good idea what that project might be. An office makeover.

Bernie had somehow managed to get himself his own office. At first, he wondered why he was the beneficiary of such generous treatment. But as autumn progressed and the rain became heavier, he began to understand. One of the windows in his office, the one farthest from his desk, was prone to leak. And when the rain was heavy, this leak turned into a torrent.

He got on to Building Services. While his complaint was duly noted, nothing ever seemed to get done about it. Eventually, he had to resort to bringing in an old towel to soak up the water. During heavy rain, he was obliged to wring out the towel and put it back on the window ledge, regularly. He even brought it up at a departmental meeting, receiving an assurance that his complaint to Building Services *'would be escalated'* - whatever that meant?

Weeks later, there was still no action. So, he took a trip to the nearest sports shop and identified the items he wanted. They were expensive, but he thought they would be a good investment.

When the next departmental meeting was due, Bernie, uncharacteristically, had not taken his seat by the time the meeting started. It was a strange feeling. Despite his reputation for hating early starts, he'd never been late for a meeting. When he was sure that proceedings had kicked off, he donned his props and, with some difficulty, made for the conference room. As he entered the room, all fell silent. All eyes turned to the door to see who was making such a conspicuously tardy arrival.

Bernie precariously stalked his way through the doorway, like a refugee from Monty Python's Ministry of Silly Walks. As he did so, the first thing that everyone's eyes registered was a large pair of fluorescent pink frogman's flippers. When he had cleared the door, he came to a stop, and announced,

"I am sorry I am late. The flood waters in my office caused me some delay. But I am here now."

One or two couldn't suppress their laughter. They soon quietened down when they saw that the socially acceptable reaction was shock and disdain.

The Fat Controller remained silent. As usual, it fell to Rhys Williams to deal with the situation.

"We take your point Bernie. I shall address the matter of your leaky window with you off line. Now please go away, and return properly dressed."

"Thank you." replied Bernie.

He turned around and strutted his way back out of the door like a retreating flamingo.

*****

Time went by, and still nothing had been done about Bernie's leak. So Bernie decided to take things into his own hands.

The windows were vertically hinged 1930s style metal frames which opened outwards, and the faraway window frame had warped. As a result, it didn't make an effective seal when closed. He was sure he could make do with only one fully operational window. So, he hatched a plan.

After a rain-free spell, when he was sure the window would be properly dried out, he retrieved from his cupboard a large tube of builder's caulk which he had acquired specially for the purpose, together with a metal applicator which squeezed the sealant out of the nozzle like an oversized tube of toothpaste.

Bernie wouldn't have described himself as a handyman, but he made a decent fist of it, and, having effected a permanent seal all the way round the offending window, he finished it off quite nicely with his finger. He wouldn't be able to open that window any more, but at least, the seal would stop the leak. He hoped...

After the next heavy rain, not a drop of leaky water was to be seen on the windowsill. Bernie pronounced his building work a success. Functional, it was. But it didn't look very beautiful. So, he decided to repaint the window frame.

At first, he was thinking of conforming to Building Services regulations and repainting the window frame in the same drab colour as the original, but he had no idea where he was going to get a match.

He could ask Building Services, but they were bound to ask what he was doing, and would not be impressed by his custom modifications. In any case, what did he owe Building Services? What had they ever done for him?

It was then that Bernie had his brainwave. He would repaint the window frame in whichever colour caught his fancy. Not only that, he might as well go the whole hog and redecorate the entire office. What joy!

For days, he pored over swatches and colour charts, even acquiring some samples to try on the walls and the window frame to see what they might actually turn out like.

He plumped for a bright yellow called *'Wild Primrose'* for the walls, while he complemented that base colour with a golden shade called *'Honey Beam'* to highlight the window frame and the skirting boards. Finally, he went for *'Moroccan Flame'*, to add a dash of orange outrageousness to the terracotta tiles on the windowsill.

One weekend, he sneaked in all his tools and supplies along with a ladder and a pair of overalls. By the Sunday evening, his work was done. Although the Good Lord had managed to complete his work by the sixth day, Bernie didn't manage to complete his until the seventh. But like the Good Lord, Bernie saw all that he had made, and saw it was good.

For a few weeks after, visitors to Bernie's office did a double take on entry. The unanimous verdict was, *'brilliant!'* Bernie never heard another peep from either management or Building Services about his interior design project.

One day, Bill Bebb arrived in Bernie's newly decorated office.

Bill had graduated from the skiffle and trad jazz scene and, from Jimmy Grant's point of view, was the perfect producer to take over from Brian Willey when he moved on from *Saturday Club*.

"Hi Bernie," said Bill, affably.

'I wonder what Bill wants?' thought Bernie.

"I'm sure you've read about this Jimi Hendrix guy," said Bill.

"Yes, I saw him down the Bag 'O Nails last week."

"I thought you'd be interested. Look… I've booked him for *Saturday Club*, so if you feel like it, and you have the time to spare, I thought you might like to sit in at the back of the control room. See what's going on?"

"I would like that very much," said Bernie.

"OK. See you in S2 on Wednesday," said Bill, and then left.

*****

At the appointed hour, Bernie turned up at the control room of Sub Basement Studio 2 in the bowels of Broadcasting House - the same studio in which he had first encountered The Beatles.

Bill and Pete Harwood, his studio manager, were already buzzing around, organising things. Then Chas Chandler, Jimi's manager, walked in.

"Hi Bernie, how're you doing?" he asked, shaking Bernie's hand heartily. Their paths had crossed many times in the days when he had been the bass player with The Animals.

"Oh, I've just come down to have a listen," said Bernie. "This is Jimi's first broadcast, isn't it?

"Aye," said Chas in his broad Geordie accent.

"Well, don't let me hold you up, Chas. I'm just here to watch and listen. Bill's producing."

Eventually, the band started up, and Bill, who had been standing in the studio right beside Jimi's amp, walked back into the control room looking a bit shaken.

"Christ! It's fucking loud out there." was all he said.

The volume being generated in the studio was incredibly high. As a result, Pete was darting around putting attenuators in all the mic cables, so that the amplifiers in the mixing desk didn't overload. Then Bill leaned over and faded out all the mics on the control panel. There was still an incredible rumble coming through the wall. Bill leaned over and pressed both of his hands against the large control room window.

"Fucking hell!" he gasped. "You can feel the window vibrating."

Bill pressed the talkback key down,

"Er… Jimi… Is it possible you could turn the volume down a notch or two?"

Just then, Chas Chandler pulled Bill's hand off the talkback key,

"You can't do that man!" he exclaimed. "That's his sound!"

Bill looked at Chris, a little puzzled. Then shrugged his shoulders,

"OK then."

Then he turned to Pete and said, "Have at it!"

Pete looked a bit harassed, but after sorting out the attenuators, he eventually sat down, got the levels under control, and balanced the sounds coming from the studio. Bernie was studiously keeping his mouth shut. In any case, it was starting to sound pretty good. The band was tight and Jimi was an amazing performer.

Towards the end of the session, a prim, middle-aged lady who had the air of a civil servant walked into the control room. Bill and Pete were in the process of recording a track called *Love or Confusion*. The confusion part seemed very much in tune with the look on the middle-aged lady's face. Bill didn't notice her standing behind him until the end of the track, when Pete had faded out. He clicked his stopwatch, and leaned over to log the time. That was when he noticed.

"Oh... Can I help you?" he asked.

"Yes," said the lady. My name is Cynthia Featherstone, and I'm a producer on the Third Programme."

The Third Programme was the BBC Radio station for classical music and the arts.

"Yes?" said Bill questioningly, wondering where this was going.

"'I'm producing a string quartet in the Concert Hall..."

The Broadcasting House Concert Hall was the main classical music studio in Broadcasting House, two floors above S2.

"...and we are picking up the sound of an electric guitar... very clearly... on our microphones," explained Cynthia.

"Well, look... I've only got one more number to record here, and then we won't be bothering you any longer. So, you can go ahead with your recording in a minute or two."

"No, you don't understand. We're not recording. We're going out live!"

'Oops!' thought Bernie. *'I wonder how Bill's going to deal with this one?'*

Without missing a beat, Bill replied,

"Alright Cynthia, I take your point. As I said, we only have one more number left to do, so I will go into the studio and ask the band to turn down the volume as much as possible, and then we will record the final item as quickly as possible. How about that?

"Thank you," said Cynthia.

Bill stood up, surreptitiously winking at Chas as he escorted the lady out of the control room, and then making a beeline for the studio as soon as he was sure that she was on her way back to the Concert Hall.

After shooting the breeze for a couple of minutes with Jimi and his guys in order to ensure that Cynthia Featherstone was well on her way, he got back to the control room to record the last number. Luckily, The Jimi Hendrix Experience put down a spirited version of *Foxy Lady* on the first take, thereby averting the possibility of any further diplomatic exchanges between Bill and his colleagues two floors above.

In the process, Bernie noted that he had just witnessed Jimi Hendrix' first live broadcast: a muffled and totally random electric guitar accompaniment to a classical string quartet, live, on the BBC Third Programme.

As they were packing up, Bernie said his goodbyes to Chas, Jimi and the band. On the way out, Bill commented,

"Bit different to the days of skiffle and jazz, eh?"

"Certainly is." replied an amused Bernie.

*****

Bernie turned up at work to hear the dramatic news that on the 30th of September, 1967, the three existing BBC Radio stations, the BBC Light Programme, (for mainstream listeners), the BBC Home Service (for more serious and regional listeners) and the BBC Third programme (for culture vultures) would be no more...

They were to be replaced immediately by Radio 1 (aimed at the younger audience, and a substitute for the pirate stations), Radio 2 (for the older, middle-of-the-road segment of the BBC Light Programme - soon to be referred to, by some, as *'the geriatric service'*), Radio 3 (mainly classical music and arts - for what the cognoscenti like to call the *'highbrow'* audience) and Radio 4 (which would focus on news and current affairs).

In addition to the restructuring of BBC Radio, the Government outlawed the pirate stations.

Aubrey Small, the Fat Controller, was now the Deputy Controller of Radios 1&2 - a position which was, no doubt, sold to him as a promotion.

Was he pleased about this? No-one would ever know. But probably not, since the launch of the brand new Radios 1&2 had been entrusted to an outsider by the name of Robin Scott.

Robin was an import from BBC Television, which BBC Radio old-timers considered the upstart branch of the service. However, more objective observers thought Robin Scott had a lot going for him. He had devised very popular TV programmes, like *Miss World, Come Dancing* and *It's a Knockout*, and he had also written a #1 hit called *Softly Softly* for a very popular recording star called Ruby Murray. So, the radio people couldn't pull the wool over his eyes when it came to the worlds of commercial recording and song publishing.

Worst of all, for the dinosaurs and Luddites of the Popular Music Department of the BBC Radio Light Programme, he was used to working in a competitive environment. How vulgar!

From Bernie and his like-minded colleagues there was a loud cheer.

*****

Inevitably, when the excitement subsided, the immediate thought on everyone's mind was, *'What job will I get?'*

Rumours flew, imaginations ran riot and no end of theories were postulated about the possible structure of the new organisation - most of them fantastical.

Bernie was of the more stoic, *'let's wait and see'* school of thought. If pushed, he would confide in those he trusted that, "It's a once in a lifetime opportunity. And I have every reason to believe that the BBC will seize that opportunity with both hands - and fuck it up!"

Salvation

A week or so later, Shirley Jones popped her head round the door.

Bernie turned off the record player. Shirley had been his production secretary during his *Top Gear* days. After the programme was axed, she had decided to take the offer of a job in the USA, and had vanished for a year or so. She had never discussed the matter with Bernie, but he wondered if some of the motivation for her departure was related to the shabby way in which *Top Gear* had been treated.

In the meantime, Shirley had returned from her *'year out'* - quite a radical move at a time when transatlantic job-hopping was considered impossibly exotic - and she had since nabbed herself the post of Personal Assistant to Robin Scott, the new Controller of BBC Radios 1&2. A considerable move up in the world for our Shirley. Bernie often caught up with her during coffee breaks and over lunch.

That day, all Bernie could see was Shirley's head as she peered around his office door. However, she looked happy. She had a conspiratorial smile on her face, and a twinkle in her eye.

"What's with you then?"

"You're going to be alright," was Shirley's enigmatic reply.

"What do you mean?" said Bernie, now anxious. "You mean the reorganisation?"

"Yes," she nodded, giggling quietly.

"What do you know?"

"I daren't say Bernie. But just take it from me, you're going to be alright."

"Oh, come on!.." Bernie was now pleading, although in a hushed tone.
"You know me, Shirley. All secrets will be safe with me." He put on his
best, little boy lost look, "Why don't you come in, sit down, and tell me
what you can?"

Shirley hesitated, thought for a bit, and then decided.

"Oh... All right then."

She came into the office, closed the door carefully behind her and took a
seat at the desk opposite Bernie. He waited, impatiently.

"Robin's been working on the schedules for Radio 1..."

'Tell me something I don't know,' thought Bernie.

"...and most of the daytime shows have been given to producers from the
old Grams Department."

*'That figures,' he thought. 'So Radio 1 will turn out to be more like a Light
Programme 'Lite', rather than a substitute for the pirates. It'll be the same
old faces trying to pretend they're all new faces.'*

"So where does that leave me?" asked Bernie, feeling a bit dejected.

"Well, one evening, we were working late, and Robin was scratching his
head. I could see he was having a problem, so I asked what was up. It
turns out, he had a spare spot left on a Sunday afternoon, and he wasn't
sure what to do with it. I asked him if it was all needletime, and he said
no. There would only be enough needletime for about half the
programme each week."

"So I said that if he wanted a programme that was musically adventurous like the pirate radio stations, but which would be able to sustain that sort of feel even with a lot of in-house sessions, he might think about reviving *Top Gear*. Then he asked all sorts of questions about *Top Gear*, including, *'Why was it taken off?'* to which I answered, *'You'd better ask Aubrey Small and Rhys Williams!'* Well, he just gave a little smile. Then he asked, who the producer was, and I told him it was you. So then, he said, *'Thank you Shirley. That's a very good idea.'* and he wrote *'Top Gear, producer, Bernie Andrews'* on the schedule."

Shirley looked at Bernie. Bernie looked at Shirley in disbelief.

"And I've since seen it all typed up. Ready to go!" she assured him.

"Bloody hell, Shirley," Bernie exploded. "That's unbelievable!"

"Shhhhhhh!!.." said Shirley. "Keep it down. We don't want anyone asking us what's going on."

Bernie calmed himself,

"Can I offer you a celebratory cup of coffee, and half of the vanilla slice I just got from the baker's round the corner?"

"Perfect!" said Shirley.

*****

Shirley had gone back to Robin Scott's office, and Bernie was gazing out of the window in a kind of a trance. What was it? What was this feeling? Oriental mysticism was becoming very fashionable. Nirvana, he wondered?.. Maybe that was it?..

During the past year or so, one of the ways in which Bernie had succeeded in dealing with stress at work was to put himself in *'the zone'*, as he called it. He would try and switch off all negative thoughts. Just put them out of his mind. And in the pursuit of this ideal state, he would roll the occasional spliff at his desk. He never had more than one a day. He always shut his office door, and opened his remaining functional window - wide.

In those days, most people were not familiar with the scent of smouldering cannabis - at least not in the BBC. So, if anyone came into his office and smelt something *'funny'*, he would explain that the aroma was from *'jazz cigarettes'* - i.e. cigarettes made from tobacco of Turkish origin which had aromatic herbs added. A variety which was very popular in the clubs - particularly jazz clubs. So he said.

This was an explanation which invariably satisfied those who were not in the know. Those few within the BBC who were in the know, studiously avoided asking questions.

But today, Bernie was indulging himself. It was not for therapeutic reasons that he was toking. This one was purely for pleasure. He took a last, deep drag from the joint and breathed out a lungful of the delicious vapour, very, very slowly. Then he crushed the butt, carefully secreting it in a tobacco tin which he kept in his office drawer, and which he removed from the office every night.

One prominent feature of career development within the BBC which Bernie thoroughly despised was the *'old boy network'*. That sort of cronyism was anathema. And yet, here he was, a grateful beneficiary of just such a dodgy selection process. He asked himself,

'Do I still despise the 'old boy network?'

The answer was a resounding,

'Yes!'

Then he asked himself,

'Do I have the slightest feeling of regret or guilt in taking advantage of the 'old boy network'?'

The answer was a very definite,

'Do I fuck!'

*****

By the time the official announcements came out, Bernie was already planning his next moves.

The psychedelic era was in full swing. The music business was much more transatlantic. There was mutual respect and increasing co-operation between US and British musicians, and the US and UK charts often displayed a high degree of commonality - at least much more so than before the Beatles. But it wasn't just the music that was transatlantic. Young people on both sides of the pond seemed to be questioning the very fabric of the society they had been brought up in.

The first generation to grow up in the apocalyptic shadow of the atom bomb was coming of age, and a significant number of them were fed up. They were fed up with paternalistic and repressive attitudes to class and sex. They were fed up with authority in all its forms: parental, educational, military, political, the church... They were fed up with racial and gender discrimination...

Above all, they were fed up living in constant fear of the Cold War between the East and the West escalating out of control - and particularly of one specific manifestation of that Cold War - American involvement in Vietnam.

They rejected established western culture. They considered it oppressive, complacent and corrupt, and fantasised about a counter-culture: a world of freedom, and even anarchy.

With hindsight, this was maybe not the most constructive or realistic manifesto, but one which often raised pertinent questions about fundamental social and political issues. Their elders and betters found these questions increasingly difficult to answer. Their clarion call, coined by Timothy Leary, one of the leading hippy philosophers of the time, was *'Turn On, Tune In, Drop Out,'* - a slogan which encouraged the younger generation to *'Wake up to what's going on.'* *'Understand what's happening.'* and *'Don't conform to things you don't believe in.'*

While often impractical, hippies could be passionate about their beliefs, and their music frequently gave voice to those aspirations. Bernie wasn't so sure about some of the beliefs and values, but he was very interested in the music, which, in keeping with the motivating philosophy behind it, could be quite wild and abandoned.

He also suspected that many on the London *'underground scene'*, as they liked to call themselves, were equally selective about which parts of the hippy doctrine they espoused.

While they seemed a tad less interested in the political struggles of their more earnest brothers and sisters in the USA, they were only too ready to answer the calls to *'Turn on'* (take drugs), *'Tune In'* (listen to music) and *'Drop Out'* (avoid working for a living). Not quite the interpretation that Timothy Leary had in mind.

Bernie also knew that while there was a hard core of hippies at the centre of the London underground movement, he sensed that there was a much bigger and broader audience out there. These potential listeners were even less interested in the intellectual and philosophical debates than the lukewarm London hippies, but, like Bernie, were fascinated by the consequent explosion of creativity in the music scene which all this free thinking inspired.

Whatever the driving force, Bernie's instinct told him that the stuffy image of the BBC was not one to which hippies and free thinkers would readily migrate after the Government had outlawed their favourite pirate radio stations and taken them off the air. In fact, they were more likely to see the BBC as Government agents. Which was a fair perception in Bernie's mind.

He was astute enough to realise that what he needed was a DJ who was respected among this fast growing *'alternative'* culture. Someone who would attract this influential audience to a new BBC programme which, if it wasn't running on exactly the same format as the pirates, would offer enough cultural freedom and musical adventure for them to turn on and tune in - for at least an hour or two each week.

*****

After his original *Top Gear* slot was axed, Bernie had plenty of time on his hands, and he found himself listening to the pirate radio stations, casually, on an increasingly frequent basis. However, now that he had new objectives in his sights, his reasons for tuning in had become anything but casual. He needed a new DJ for his new show.

He listened to as many DJs as he could, and drew up a short list, discussing possible candidates with Jeff Griffin, Jim Waters, Jimmy Grant and anyone else who might have a useful opinion on the matter.

In the end, Bernie's decision owed more to serendipity than an exchange of expert opinion.

*****

Jeff Griffin's secretary was a lady called Gill. After work one evening, Jeff, Gill and Bernie walked round to the Coach and Horses. Gill's boyfriend, Steve Brown, had arranged to meet Gill there. Before they departed for a night on the town, Steve and Gill decided to stay for a while, share a drink and have a chat with Bernie and Jeff.

Steve was the Artist Liaison Manager for Dick James Music. One of his protégés was a young singer and pianist called Reg Dwight. Reg was on the books as an in-house songwriter, but he had strong ambitions to make records in his own right. In pursuit of that ambition, he'd confided in Steve that he'd like to change his name to something a bit less humdrum. Reg was well known to Bernie and Jeff as a session musician and backing singer.

"What sort of name is he thinking about?" asked Jeff.

"He said he was thinking of Elton John," replied Steve. "During his days with Bluesology, Elton Dean was the sax player, and his best buddy, Long John Baldry, fronted the band. So, he came to the conclusion that Elton John might sound a bit better than Reg Dwight."

"Sounds good to me," said Jeff.

Then Bernie steered the conversation around to the problem that was foremost in his mind - his search for a new DJ for *Top Gear*.

"Have you heard John Peel?" asked Steve.

"Who's he?" came the reply in unison.

"He does a late spot on Radio London starting at midnight."

"Can't be much of an audience at that time," said Bernie.

"Actually, considering it's on so late, John Peel gets extraordinary listening figures. Mostly from the underground community. He has a very loyal following, and it's growing fast."

Bernie's interest was immediate. He made a note to listen in.

"Is the underground hippy audience specifically targeted by Radio London on that late night spot?" he asked.

Steve laughed. "Nothing could be further from the truth. The only reason Peel got that spot is because none of the other Radio London DJs wanted it. The received wisdom is that nobody listens in after midnight, so the advertisers steer clear."

"But Radio London management must be aware that the listening figures are much better than expected?" said Bernie.

"You'd like to think so," said Steve, "but because the advertisers aren't interested, neither are the management. No revenue prospects - to their way of thinking. In fact, that's probably why it's become such an underground success. When John Peel eventually realised that none of his bosses were listening to his show, he decided to ignore their guidelines and started broadcasting anything he felt like. Stuff that wouldn't go out on mainstream radio in a millions years. Brought in a whole new audience."

Bernie was fascinated.

"They must have realised sooner or later?" said Jeff.

"Oh yes… Eventually… When they started reading glowing reviews in the music press and Brian Epstein wrote to the station boss to congratulate him on putting together such an adventurous programme."

"So, what are Radio London's plans now?" said Bernie.

"Well, not much," said Steve. "They've got a death sentence hanging over them. They'll soon be outlawed, so they don't have any incentive to change anything. Just see out their time."

Bernie nodded. He absorbed the moral of this tale. Radio bosses took interest in their programme output in direct proportion to the number of listeners they thought would be tuning in. If they thought the listening figures would be high, they would be crawling all over the producers, telling them what to do. On the other hand, during periods when they thought the audience numbers would be low, they might even ignore what was being broadcast altogether. As far as Bernie was concerned, the absence of management interference was a radio producer's dream - and a total absence created the ultimate opportunity for creativity on the airwaves.

Later that evening, when Bernie got home, he tuned in to Radio London, waiting for midnight to strike. His first impression was that John Peel had a most lugubrious voice. However, he was highly articulate and Bernie could tell from the content of his fan letters that he had a real connection with his audience. He listened, intently, for the next two hours.

Bernie quickly came to the conclusion that Peel was knowledgeable and had eclectic taste, often reading poetry in between records and quoting from a canon of esoteric books which the hippies revered, like *Lord of the Rings*.

His midnight slot was called *The Perfumed Garden* - after a fifteenth century Arabic text, whose full title was *The Perfumed Garden of Sensual Delights* - another hippy favourite.

Above all, Peel seemed to have a genuine love for the music he played. For Bernie, this was essential, and a characteristic not always displayed by Peel's fellow DJs. It seemed to Bernie that the enthusiasm many of them professed for the records they played often sounded artificial, and if they loved anything, it was frequently themselves.

The other thing that set John Peel apart was his low-key sense of humour, which the casual listener could easily miss. His audience was anything but casual, and if *'Turn On, Tune In, Drop Out'* was their mantra, then John Peel was clearly tuned in.

When Bernie proposed John Peel for the *Top Gear* slot, predictably, the reaction from management was, "Who?" However, as Robin Scott seemed to be on side, underlings like Aubrey Small and Rhys Williams just shrugged their shoulders and moved on to the next item on the agenda.

*****

However, before Bernie made John Peel a formal offer, he wanted to be sure that John understood what he was taking on. So he invited him to a special meeting.

He didn't call it an interview. That would have been too *'establishment'*. But both parties knew it was an interview. He suspected that John would have trouble assimilating to BBC culture, and he wanted to be confident that expectations were effectively managed.

When he first entered Bernie's office, John was rather diffident.

Like the rest of his pirate radio colleagues, he made no secret about how much he despised the BBC. However, it was clear that he found the experience of applying for a job at the BBC intimidating. No doubt, he was also trying to figure out how, if he got the job, he would explain his career development policy to his fellow BBC-despising hippy friends.

John Peel was an unprepossessing character. He wouldn't be seen dead in a suit and tie. He had long hair, almost down to his shoulders, although his hairline was already showing signs of receding early, leaving him with a pronounced widow's peak. On the lower part of his chin, he sported a neatly trimmed beard.

His preferred attire was jeans and a sweater and he liked something suitably ethnic on his feet. Moccasins, for example. In the summer, he might even wear sandals. From his neck, he would frequently hang amulets or other decorative objects - alluding, more than likely, to outlandish cults, philosophies and religions. At least that's how the more conventional thinkers in the BBC would have judged them.

"Have a seat," Bernie offered.

Pleasantries were exchanged. They compared notes on new releases by Al Stewart and The Move, as well as the kind of music that was currently developing in the clubs. John seemed pleasantly surprised when it became clear that Bernie was genuinely enthusiastic about what was happening on the *'underground scene.'*

As John relaxed, he eventually got round to a question which Bernie fully expected, and for which Bernie was fully prepared.

"Who'll choose the music on *Top Gear*?"

The BBC could dress up *Wonderful Radio 1* and present it to the public any way they liked, but what they couldn't do was deny the fundamental differences between the now defunct pirate stations and the new Radio 1 setup.

DJs on the pirate stations were given broad guidelines from which to choose the music they played and they could pretty much manage their own shows in the way they wanted. In fact, they were expected to. The results often appeared anarchic - or, at least, spontaneous. Which was exactly why their audiences loved them so much.

"What have you heard about who chooses the music John?" asked Bernie.

"I've spoken to a lot of jocks who'll be on the regular weekday shows, and they tell me that they'll have no control over what they play. I mean... They can suggest records, and sometimes their ideas are accepted, but in the main, their shows reflect what Radio 1 management think they should be playing. Sometimes their producers aren't even in control. They just do what they're told by the top brass. And that lot, whoever they are, insist that Radio 1 should be filling time by running mindless competitions on-air, and reciting cooking recipes and stuff like that."

Bernie looked John straight in the eye. "That's a fair analysis John. But it's not the whole story."

John leaned back in his chair, his body language indicating, *'Let's hear it then!'*

"That's what happens on daytime slots during weekdays," said Bernie. "Those are the slots which they expect will attract the maximum listening figures. I'm not going to dress it up John. If anyone thinks that Radio 1 is going to replicate the pirate stations on the BBC, they are going to be sadly disappointed."

"Yes, the majority of those on the Radio 1 DJ roster are ex-pirate DJs, but Radio 1 will be trying to retain the maximum number of listeners who previously tuned in to the Light Programme as well as anything they can get from the pirate radio audience. Yes, there's going to be a lot more pop music on Radio 1 than there ever was on the Light Programme, and if they are lucky, Radio 1 will get some of the pirate radio audience tuning in along with the younger end of the Light Programme listeners. But, in order to maximise Radio 1 listening figures, they will have to cater for a middle-of-the-road audience, albeit a relatively young middle-of-the-road audience."

"Where does that leave *Top Gear*?" asked John.

"We're a weekend show John. There won't be such intense interest in our programming. We won't be under that sort of scrutiny. In fact, with a bit of luck, the top brass, as you call them, will be uninterested, hopefully, to the point that they won't bother to tune in at all. Which will give us the sort of opportunity that you took so successfully on your midnight slot on Radio London."

"But you mailed me some of their programme proposals, or whatever they call them, and whoever wrote up the stuff on *Top Gear* is talking about some sort of *'magazine programme - looking beyond the horizons of pop'* or whatever... Involving trotting down to the London Palladium and interviewing people like Lulu and Dusty Springfield... I mean, if that's what I'm being hired to do, I might as well jump on a plane to the US and try and pick up where I left off over there."

"I agree John. But that guff doesn't reflect my ambitions either."

Bernie gathered his thoughts.

"Look, if you decided to delay taking a plane to the US, say, for three months or so?.. Would that make so much difference? If you give it three months, I will do my best to get us the leeway we need to put together a good show. Then, if it doesn't work out, you can be on your way.

Bernie continued,

"One of the things I have learned about the BBC, John, is that it's not a good idea to confront management. The best way to get the result you want is to never complain, do the absolute minimum you have to in complying, and over time, just move things, bit by bit, until you're where you want to be. So, OK, we might have a session by Lulu early on in the schedule, and do a token interview or two with a few more middle-of-the-road artists. But I promise you, you will have a hell of a lot of latitude to do your own thing, and build the audience you're after."

John still didn't look convinced. Bernie ploughed on.

"Here's how I'd like us to do the show. As far as records are concerned, I will split the choices with you 50:50. You can choose anything you want - so long as there's nothing which would be judged illegal to broadcast. As for sessions, I will take your input, and by that, I mean I will listen very carefully to any suggestions or requests you have, but the final decision on booking sessions will be down to me. How does that sound?"

Bernie knew that he was offering something that was strictly off-limits as far as BBC management was concerned. Some years before, he'd been hauled over the coals for giving the presenter, Brian Matthew, the opportunity to pick only a record or two on *Saturday Club*. As far as management was concerned, that sort of practice was ceding editorial control and was therefore totally unacceptable.

But he knew that in this brave new world of broadcasting, handing over at least some editorial control was essential, and he would, if necessary, suffer the consequences.

"Obviously, I'm happy about the fifty per cent of the records that will be my choice Bernie. But what about the other half? Is what you're likely to choose going to be compatible with what I choose? Or will the programme try to be all things to all men, which, it seems to me, is what Radio 1 will try to be?"

"The kind of material I've got in mind are tracks from artists like Cream, Jimi Hendrix, Pink Floyd... that sort of stuff. And I'm not just talking about singles. Album tracks are in the mix too. You know as well as I do, the way things are going, a lot of bands are putting much more emphasis on albums rather than singles. There will definitely not be any middle-of-the-road or bubblegum pop on *Top Gear*."

"What about these studio sessions? Because of Musicians' Union rules, we're obliged to use them. How will they fit in?"

"Most BBC producers hate it when they can't just fill up their show playing records. If they run short of needletime on their programme, they are often forced to hire second rate session singers and musicians to record second rate cover versions in order to fill the gap. Clearly, we're not going to hire the BBC Northern Dance Orchestra to perform a cover version of *Purple Haze* - or anything like that. But I think we can turn the needletime restrictions into an advantage rather than a handicap."

John looked sceptical.

"*Top Gear* is all about looking forward. We shouldn't just be looking for the next record by an established artist. We should be bringing new artists to our audience. Those who have never been broadcast."

"And that audience will be hungry for something different. These new acts may not even have record deals. In fact, some of them may already have been turned down by the record labels. In America, the radio stations only play records. So, over there, you can't get on the radio if you haven't been signed by a record label. But why should the record labels get to decide what the public gets to hear? They've got a track record of ignoring the obvious until it's staring them in the face. So, instead of filling up spare airtime with crap cover versions, we should be looking for the next big thing."

"But you said you wanted control of all the session recordings Bernie. Where are you going to find all this talent?"

"I didn't say that John. I didn't say I wanted to control everything. I just want the right of veto. If I don't think a particular act is up to being broadcast, I will say so. I'll keep an eye out for new talent in the clubs, and you should do the same."

John sat pensively for a while. Then sighed out loud, seemingly resigned.

"It seems to me I don't have much of a choice. The pirates are gone, I'm out of a job, and all that's on offer is *Top Gear*. I suppose I'll have to take it then.

'*Don't be so fucking enthusiastic John!*' thought Bernie.

He put a brave face on it and stood up, offering John his hand.

They shook on it.

*****

John and Bernie were sitting in his office deciding which records they would feature on the first show. John would choose his track, and then Bernie would choose his - until they had used up all the available needletime.

When the list of records was finalised, John asked what sessions Bernie had lined up.

"Traffic, Pink Floyd and Tomorrow," said Bernie.

"Can I make a suggestion for a future session?"

"Fire away!"

"I think we should book Tyrannosaurus Rex."

"Who are they?"

"You remember a group called John's Children?"

Bernie nodded, "Lift up your skirts and fly?"

"Yeah... The BBC banned that record because of those lyrics. Unbelievable!.. Anyway, the guy who wrote and sang it is Marc Bolan, and he's just formed a new band. He's called it Tyrannosaurus Rex."

"For any particular reason?" asked Bernie.

"I've no idea," said John, shrugging his shoulders, completely oblivious to Bernie's teasing.

"I've known Marc for ages, and Tyrannosaurus Rex often turn up at my gigs. In fact, I get on so well with Marc and Steve, that I've become something of an unpaid booking agent. Every time I get a new gig, I usually manage to persuade the promoters to book them as well."

"Where can I hear them?"

"You can come to my next gig on Friday.~

"Where's that?"

"Plumstead."

"What's in Plumstead?" said Bernie.

"A great little club called The Astral Plane," enthused John.

'Astral Plane?' thought Bernie. 'Probably some dump in a cellar with a strobe light on Plumstead High Street.'

That wasn't far from the truth. Plumstead was an hour or two by car, and Bernie didn't own one of those.

John could see Bernie calculating the hassle involved.

"I could give you a lift?" suggested John.

Then, he had a brainwave.

"Actually, I can do better than that. I forgot. I've got a couple of acetates in my bag."

"That's more like it." Bernie grinned.

John retrieved two discs in dog-eared dustjackets. He pulled one out and placed it on the record player. As the needle hit the groove with a bang, a heavy crackling sound scraped out of the loudspeakers. Acetates only sustained a limited number of plays, and this one had clearly been played a few times too many.

"That's the sound of the astral plane, is it?" asked Berne, mischievously.

John got the teasing this time. He was not amused.

Suddenly, through the mush of the astral plane, Bernie heard a high, quavery voice accompanied by an acoustic guitar along with what sounded like a guy thumping away on a pair of bongo drums.

Bernie listened intently. The song was all about a girl called Deborah. The lyrics made that point persistently. But it had an insistent rhythm, and the vocal, while it conveyed a feeling of fragility had some sort of hippy charm, which was quite hypnotic. He could understand why it might go down well in a club with subdued lighting and a - literally - pleasantly high atmosphere.

"If all you have is acetates, I assume they don't have a record deal?"

"They're not commercial enough." sneered John. "So say the moguls of the record business. I've spoken up for Marc and Steve frequently in the *International Times*, but none of the labels are budging."

"Not commercial enough." muttered Bernie. "That's what they said about the Beatles, isn't it?"

John looked at Bernie, quizzically at first, and then hopefully.

If it were his decision alone, Bernie probably wouldn't have given them a second hearing. But he could see how keen John was, and this was precisely why Bernie had hired John - to provide an alternative, informed opinion. He decided.

"I'll book them."

*****

Radio 1 was launched by Tony Blackburn on his *Breakfast Show* at 07:00 on Saturday, the 30th of September 1967. The next day, during the afternoon, *Top Gear* was launched - for the second time - by Bernie's new DJ, John Peel.

It went well. Even John seemed to be enjoying himself, despite the limitations of working at the BBC. The first record was *Lovebug, Leave My Heart Alone* by Martha and the Vandellas. This Tamla-Motown track was probably as far as Bernie was able to push John towards the middle-of-the-road. But it was vital. Bernie knew that the management, and particularly the detractors among management, would be listening in - at least to the handover from the previous show. He was betting on them losing interest fairly quickly after that, and preferably before the first record came to an end.

As the programme progressed, the material grew increasingly *'far out'* with contributions from US bands like Country Joe and the Fish and The Doors as well as the specially recorded *Top Gear* sessions from Pink Floyd, Tomorrow, and Traffic.

The show was positively received by the British music press. Disc and Music Echo said:

'The programme had a definite theme - new sounds from Britain and America - and it seemed to be approached seriously and intelligently.'

'Seriously' and *'intelligently'* were not words that would have been bandied about in the music press just a few years before. *'Fab'* and *'groovy'* would have been more their thing.

'How the world has changed.' thought Bernie.

*****

Reviews continued to be positive. *Top Gear* wasn't a substitute for the pirates, but it was earning a unique place, not only in the music business but also with the wider listening public - or, at least a tuned-in section of it.

If Bernie's record selections were the more obvious *'underground scene'* favourites - like Canned Heat, Tim Rose and Vanilla Fudge - John was continually pushing the envelope to the extremes with the likes of Quicksilver Messenger Service, Ultimate Spinach or Captain Beefheart. And *Top Gear* did something that no pirate station ever did. It broadcast artists who were on the fringes, those who might only have a cult following, or hardly any following at all - specially recorded at the BBC.

If you became a regular *Top Gear* listener, one thing you could be quite sure of was that you were always in for a few surprises. Even in those early days, *'doing a Top Gear session'* became a rite of passage, a badge of honour even, for those looking to make their mark.

Of course, many of these new bands would record a session or two, and never be heard of again. Others might go on to limited success within a specialised circle of followers. But then there were more than a few who became very successful. And some went on to become the most successful recording artists of their time.

It soon became apparent that *Top Gear* was a very effective shop window for those seeking a record deal.

Not only that. Those who already had recording contracts might suffer because their more adventurous artistic endeavours were being constrained by their own, risk averse, record companies. So, they were often eager to prove themselves by broadcasting the more *'outta sight'* items in their repertoire - those numbers which their labels were reluctant to gamble on a commercial release, unless they were pushed. And an increasingly effective way of pushing them was to get a favourable reaction on *Top Gear*.

By way of contrast, the pirates had been strictly about the charts. They were cautious about promoting unknown artists, and would never have played private recordings by bands who didn't have a recording contract. Any pirate DJ who did that would have been taking a grave risk with his credibility and his reputation.

Risk was what *Top Gear* was all about.

Rising Tensions

If the music press showed increasing enthusiasm about *Top Gear*'s programme policy, it was an enthusiasm that was not shared by Radio 1 management.

Bernie came under constant pressure to share and rotate Peel's DJ duties on *Top Gear* with other DJs. He persisted contrarily, defending John Peel as often and as loudly as he dare. He had to be careful. His efforts might be viewed kindly by Robin Scott, but he knew there were others in places higher than his who were not so kind.

On the one hand, Bernie was enjoying putting together an adventurous new programme with John Peel. On the other hand, he could sense increasing intolerance, an enmity even, from above. He found the situation most stressful and as a result was always looking for ways to relax.

Getting high all day was out of the question. Apart from the obvious threats to his career, it was expensive. He'd bought a book on yoga and tried meditation. But sitting cross-legged on a mat in excruciating pain for hours on end, and trying to empty his mind of all thought - well, that was not Bernie. He was far too much of a bag of nerves for any of that stuff.

That was when he hit on the idea of fish. Not to eat. Or to catch. But to watch. Bernie had always been fascinated by fish, particularly tropical fish. He could study them for hours in an aquarium, and he found the experience soothing. So, he decided to install a fish tank in his office.

After measuring the available space on top of his filing cabinets, Bernie trooped off to a pet shop. There, he looked at what was on offer, and picked up some leaflets on how to install a tank and look after the inhabitants.

Having learned which fish and how many of them would co-exist peacefully in the tank of his choosing, Bernie finally got it all sorted out.

With great ceremony, he switched on the electricity, which would regulate the water temperature and oxygen supply, thus ensuring that the micro-environment he had designed for his fish would be maintained in a healthy state. Then he fed them their first meal.

The rest of the afternoon passed in a most pleasurable manner. Bernie stared at his new friends in wonder until it was time to go home. On making his way out, he carefully switched off the tank light and shut the door.

He had been told that the fish would get stressed if you left the light on all the time. Maybe the yellow walls in the office would be too much for them? He would have to keep an eye on that, and if they showed any signs of getting upset, he might have to rethink the office colour scheme?

A couple of minutes later, he was back in the office. He took a sheet of paper out of his office drawer and wrote a notice, which he attached with adhesive tape to the electrical plug connected to the fish tank:

DO NOT
UNDER ANY CIRCUMSTANCES
TURN OFF THE ELECTRICITY
FISH WILL DIE.

*****

In the face of constant carping from middle management, Bernie and John gritted their teeth and carried on regardless. Then, the BBC Audience Research Department circulated their first report on Radio 1 listening figures. Bernie had calculated that no drastic action would be taken regarding Radio 1 schedules until the first set of programme reviews. It seemed he was right. But now the results were in, all bets were off.

The figures for daytime listening during the week, and particularly the *Breakfast Show*, had exceeded everyone's expectations. Bernie was pleased because success on that front meant that attention would be drawn away from other areas - and particularly from *Top Gear*.

But when he saw the numbers which *Top Gear* had actually achieved, he was much more than pleased. Granted, Tony Blackburn's *Breakfast Show* was showing listening figures in the tens of millions - and *Top Gear's* were a lot lower than that. However, if you looked at the number of people who listened to *Top Gear* compared to those who had tuned in to the same Sunday afternoon slot before the launch of Radio 1, there had been a significant jump in the listening audience.

Comments gleaned from individual listeners were also very positive. That meant a lot to Bernie. It meant that he and John were getting through to the audience they wanted - although he knew that sort of thing would cut no ice with management. Listeners' comments might be used to justify management decisions, but they could just as easily be ignored if they didn't suit management's purposes. On the other hand, it was more difficult for them to argue with increased listening figures.

Rumblings continued. Bernie heard stories on the grapevine that some behind the scenes were lobbying to get rid of John Peel. Bernie considered John essential. The younger generation were growing up. They took a much more serious interest in their music, and they expected the media to do the same.

If management were actually aware of these social changes, they made every effort to signal that they didn't want to know.

A memo landed on Bernie's desk. It announced that a trainee producer called John Walters had been hired, and that he would be trailing a number of different producers in various departments. *'Trailing'* was a standard training process. Trainee producers would be assigned to a programme and follow the producer around - watching what was involved in the job, and asking pertinent questions. After a suitable period of trailing and, subject to feedback from those producers whom the trainee had trailed, the new member of staff would be let loose to produce on his or her own. Sometimes this was done under supervision, but more often than not, newbies were thrown in at the deep end to get on with it.

Bernie noted that *'Top Gear / Bernie Andrews'* was high on the list of John Walters' trailing assignments. There was also a comment warning all addressees that John would be doing the rounds, introducing himself in order to make arrangements for specific assignments.

Bernie already knew John. He was a trumpet player, jazz-oriented, and he had recently been a member of the Alan Price Set - a spinoff group from The Animals, of which Alan Price had been the original organ player. Bernie had recorded them a few times, and knew they were a very professional outfit.

About a week later, John Walters knocked on the door.

"Hello Bernie. How are you?"

"Very well John. Welcome to the BBC!"

They chatted. Having previously enjoyed John's company in the pub after recording sessions on numerous occasions, Bernie knew he was a social animal. He was a brilliant raconteur, and could make the most mundane events seem funny, just by telling things in his own inimitable way. Eventually, Bernie thought they should get down to business.

"This is my schedule for the coming week. Feel free to join any production activities you see there. You don't need to give me any notice. Just turn up at whichever studio or edit suite I'm in, according to how it fits with your plans. Also, if you want to sit in with Peel and I when we're choosing records for the show, I've highlighted those sessions and venues."

"That's great Bernie. Thanks," said John. "That's a lot more casual than some others I've been dealing with. Much more my style."

"The thing is, John, you already know a great deal about session work. And that's the trickiest part of production as far as I'm concerned. The rest of it is admin really. So, I don't think you'll have any problem fitting in."

And that was how it went. John Walters took no time at all to find his feet and fit in.

*****

Towards the end of the quarter, Bernie attended a management meeting. Unlike previous meetings, he had a specific objective.

He wanted John Peel's contract renewed. He had discussed the matter with Peel's agent, Clive Selwood, who had also heard that John was in danger of being sacked. So they agreed a strategy to defend him under extreme circumstances.

Predictably, most of the meeting time was taken up discussing the weekday shows - those which drew the massive listening figures. They were deemed the most important, and, as a result, they were analysed, cut, sliced and diced ad nauseam before orders were handed down to the producers involved.

After an hour or so, the meeting seemed to be wrapping up, but just as Bernie was about to raise the subject, he was beaten to it by Aubrey Small.

"Does anyone round the table have an opinion on John Peel's presentation skills?"

"I do," piped up Rhys Williams. "He mumbles, and I still can't understand him when I turn the radio up quite loudly."

Bernie saw a few heads nodding. Robin Scott remained impassive. He was looking at Bernie, no doubt expecting a return of fire.

"I don't know what the pirates saw in him, but I think he is totally unsuitable as a BBC presenter. "

"Can you be a bit more specific?" challenged Bernie.

Williams hesitated.

"Well... His voice... Is very provincial."

"He comes from Liverpool. Like the Beatles," said Bernie. "We haven't banned them - yet."

This rejoinder was received with some levity.

"Don't be facetious Bernie. There's a big difference between the skills necessary to become a successful radio presenter and those required to be a pop musician."

Bernie said nothing.

"And I find him decidedly morose," said Small.

"He sounds like a bit of a druggy to me." said Williams, emboldened, and smirking when one or two sniggers were heard around the table.

'I'm up against a tag team here,' thought Bernie. *'This has been rehearsed, and I'm not getting drawn into an argument. If I retaliate, I'll lose my temper, and it won't end well.'*

Then the Fat Controller announced, gravely,

"I propose that John Peel's contract should not be renewed."

"I agree," said Williams, following swiftly.

They both looked at Robin Scott, waiting for a response. It was then that Bernie decided on the nuclear option.

"Er... I'm afraid that will be impossible."

All eyes on Bernie.

"How so?" demanded Aubrey Small, his brows furrowing.

"I've already agreed a three month extension of his contract," said Bernie.

"What do you mean, *you've* agreed an extension?.."

It was the first time Bernie had seen the Fat Controller spluttering. He was usually so... controlled.

"You can't!.. That's not possible!.." insisted Williams, his voice at an uncharacteristically high pitch. "You have no authority to do that. All contracts must be approved by management, and negotiated through the Contracts Department."

"This is a farce." scoffed Small.

"Actually... It's not a farce." returned Bernie. "I spoke to his manager, Clive Selwood, a few days ago, and we verbally agreed an extension."

Small, Williams and quite a few others looked on, aghast. Robin Scott was observing the proceedings with what Bernie thought was an air of detachment.

"It's quite a good deal... Really... On exactly the same terms as his first three months... I'm sure the Contracts Department wouldn't have done any better."

Small's expression had shifted from aghast to grim.

"Well, you'll just have to pick up the phone and tell Selwood that the deal's off."

"Is that advisable?" Bernie asked quietly.

He saw a few brains ticking round. The penny was beginning to drop. A verbal contract is as legally enforceable as a written one - provided you can back it up with evidence. Even if management instructed Bernie not to back up a claim for compensation by Clive Selwood, the press would have a field day if they heard anything on the matter.

Silence.

Eventually, Robin Scott reassumed control of the meeting.

"Well, it's an irregular way of going about it, but it seems there's nothing further to discuss. Meeting closed!"

*****

Bernie was filing out with the others when Williams pulled him to one side,

"Stay behind. We need to talk."

Bernie wasn't sure what might come next, but he was sure it wouldn't be pleasant. When everyone had left the room, Williams suddenly grabbed Bernie's lapels, and rammed him up against the wall.

"Learn that in your hand-to-hand combat training?" said Bernie, to a WWII veteran who had served his time in England, consigning truckloads of tinned food to Folkestone.

"Now you listen to me you piece of filth. If you ever pull a stunt like that one... ever again... I'll..."

"You'll do what?" said Bernie. "In your lofty position as H.O.M.P. take me outside and duff me up?"

He could see that Williams was squaring up to do exactly that, except for maybe skipping the *'take me outside'* bit.

Just then, the door opened. Williams swiftly unhanded Bernie and took a pace back, assuming a normal stance.

It was Alex Radford. He looked at them, puzzled, then realised that he was interrupting some sort of exchange.

"I left my note pad," he explained.

Alex retrieved his belongings then smartly left the room.

Williams had regained his composure by this time. He gave Bernie a look of disgust, gathered his things and left. He had clearly reconsidered resorting to violence, calculating, correctly, that Bernie would be able to use any such transgression to his advantage.

Bernie was quite disappointed.

Floyd, Hendrix, Zeppelin, T Rex, Bowie et al

Things quietened down. Bernie and John got themselves into a rhythm - which they knew would last for at least the next three months. Positive coverage in the music press continued to grow, and so did the listening figures.

One day, during a break, John asked Bernie how he'd managed to persuade Pink Floyd to come in and record a session for the show.

"The story I heard was that they vowed they would never record another session at the BBC?"

"You're right. That was after the last session they did for *Saturday Club*, which was a disaster," said Bernie.

"Bill Bebb told me about it. He said that the band were there and ready to go - all except for Syd Barrett, who was nowhere to be seen. They had long finished setting up and a lot of session time had already been wasted when Syd decided to show up. You know what Syd's like. He's got a few personal issues. And he might have been, let's say, in a state of stimulation when he got there."

"At EMI, they have top class recording equipment, and as much time as they want to work on it. So, he walks into the control room in the Playhouse, looks at the primitive facilities on offer and freaks out. *'How am I supposed to work on this heap of shit!'* was probably the nicest thing he had to say.   So Bill, who's a lovely guy, but more used to jazz bands and session musos coming in and getting on with it... well... he's a bit blunt. He says, *'OK Syd, are you doing the session or not?'* And Syd comes back with something like, *'Do you want a Pink Floyd session for Saturday Club or not?'* "

"So Bill's getting impatient now. He's old school… And he says, *'Look Syd, The Great British Broadcasting Corporation lasted all through World War Two without going off the air, so I am sure Saturday Club can manage perfectly well without a Pink Floyd session.'* To which Syd throws a wobbly and flounces out of the control room, leaving the rest of the guys wondering what the fuck is going on."

"Then Bill goes out to the studio, and tells the rest of the band that, even if Syd could be calmed down and brought back to the studio, so much time has already been lost that there's no way they are going to get anything sensible out of the session. And, in any case, there'll soon be another band turning up for the next session, so there's no way they can overrun. Then everyone packs up and goes home."

"So what changed for *Top Gear*?" asked John. "Our crappy recording facilities are still exactly the same."

"Well, I've managed to increase the session time for a start. I recently pushed Programme Ops into allocating double sessions for *Top Gear*."

"How do you mean?" asked John.

"A normal BBC session is three and a half hours, including a half-hour break in the middle for session musicians to have coffee during a run-of-the-mill orchestra or dance band session. But the studios aren't in use all day long - in fact, quite a lot of the time, they lie unused. So I twisted Programme Ops arm and got them to arrange afternoon starts in studios where there's nothing booked in for the following evening. That immediately doubles the session time to seven hours. If you're not a jobbing session musician, and you aren't too fussy about coffee breaks and how long your meal breaks are, then you can spend a lot more time on getting the recording the way you want it."

"Then I had a meeting with the Floyd and their manager at their offices and I grovelled a bit. I apologised for the state of the sound mixing equipment, but I pointed out that *Top Gear* sessions would be double sessions from now on, which would ease the time pressure a lot, and would allow them to do as many retakes as they wanted in order to get things right. I told them I was arranging for the best sound engineers to look after their sessions. Guys who were familiar with their work, and who would be in tune with what they were doing. Then I played them a few sessions that we already had in the can. I think they were quite impressed with some of those. So, in the end, they agreed. Even Syd agreed."

"That's great Bernie," said John. "Maybe management will take note? That's the way things should be done."

"Don't get too excited. Apart from anything else, although the studio managers get paid for their time, I don't get any overtime for double sessions. With two or three sessions a week, I'm often doing a seventy to eighty hour week. I love it. Otherwise I wouldn't do it. But it's causing a lot of bad feeling with some of the production staff. *'How come Andrews gets all that session time?..'* and all that. When I pointed out that there's nothing stopping them from putting in the same hours as me, they start asking about overtime. And when they realise they won't get paid any more for putting in the extra hours... That's when they go into trade union mode, complaining that I shouldn't be doing all that extra work for nothing. Makes them look bad... And all that stuff..."

John laughed out loud. "You're a real martyr, aren't you Bernie?"

"Martyr is a new one John. *'Evangelist'* is one of the more positive adjectives I've unintentionally overheard, but *'maverick'*, *'rebel'* and *'pain in the arse'* are the more usual ones."

"Well, I'm glad you're producing the show," replied John. "Shall we go round the pub?"

*****

His self-imposed, work-yourself-to-death lifestyle forced yet another problem onto Bernie's shoulders. There weren't enough days in the week for him to personally supervise all the double sessions he needed to fill the airwaves. As a result, he needed a deputy. Someone who knew how live music sessions worked. Someone with the patience and experience necessary to deal with the unconventional. Someone he could trust.

As luck would have it, a very talented young sound mixer by the name of Bev Phillips had recently earned himself a place as a fully-fledged producer in the Popular Music Department. Bev had helped Bernie on countless *Saturday Club* sessions, and Bernie considered him to be *'one of the good guys'*. So when Bernie asked if he would be interested in sharing production responsibilities, Bev was only too happy to agree. That was the easy bit. The next hurdle was to persuade the management to allow Bev to take up those responsibilities. To his amazement, when Bernie made the request, no objections were raised, whatsoever.

Bev was immediately immersed in recording some of the most adventurous *'alternative music'* sessions of the time. More than a few of these turned out to be timeless classics. Jimi Hendrix was a case in point. When the Jimi Hendrix Experience recorded their first BBC session for *Saturday Club* in February 1967, Jimi was a relative unknown, and the concept of Radio 1 was inconceivable. By the time Jimi turned up at the BBC Playhouse just eight months later, he was a transatlantic phenomenon, having shocked and thrilled the crowd in equal measure at the Monterey Pop Festival in California during the summer.

Jimi's appearance at that festival signalled the first time an American audience had been exposed to heavy rock music featuring high volume delivery, controlled feedback and the, literally, incendiary stage presence of Jimi Hendrix. Rock music was changed forever. Americans perceived this transformation as a British phenomenon, even though Jimi hailed from Seattle. In their minds, the Jimi Hendrix Experience - sporting a British drummer, a British bass player, and innovative, high-powered British guitar amplification - was a British band.

So when Stevie Wonder - already a global phenomenon in his own right - decided to check out this amazing new performer, he found a convenient break in his UK touring schedule and showed up, unannounced, at Jimi's *Top Gear* recording session. Bev and his mixing engineer, Pete Ritzema, didn't bat an eyelid.

Before the session started, Stevie decided to break the ice, not by introducing himself and exchanging pleasantries, but by conversing with Jimi in quite a different way. Musically. Stevie sat himself down behind Mitch Mitchell's drum kit, picked up a pair of sticks and with no introduction whatsoever, initiated a jam with Jimi and his bass player, Noel Redding.

The guys in the control room were switched on enough to set the tape machines running, and, although it was clearly a jam, the improvised interweaving of themes from *I Was Made to Love Her* and *Ain't Too Proud To Beg* were captured for a grateful posterity. Although it wasn't broadcast at the time, decades later, this gem found its way on to commercial release - no thanks to the official archiving policy of the BBC. If anyone was in any doubt about the impact that a fresh, new, Cool Britannia was having on global popular culture, this was a glorious affirmation.

In resurrecting *Top Gear*, Bernie's primary aim was never to fill the airwaves with chart topping singles or tracks from best-selling albums. His ambition was to expose the public to as many new ideas as possible. Having said that, some of these new ideas turned out to be very big new ideas.

Tyrannosaurus Rex was, perhaps, the first case in point. Mind you, they took a very long time to get to the point. After their first outing on *Top Gear*, they managed to land the recording contract they had been so desperately seeking. But, it was only after a series of commercially unsuccessful record releases, a couple of years of persistent effort, a decision by Marc Bolan to dump the acoustic guitar and go electric, and a shortening of their name to T Rex, that they charted - not just in the UK, but across the world.

This was a career profile which was previously unheard of in in the record business. Back then, the received wisdom was, *'You're as good as your last single.'* Even if you were an established recording artist, if your next single flopped, you were likely to find yourself without a recording contract shortly afterwards. John and Bernie's persistence in supporting Tyrannosaurus Rex through an initial period of poor record sales was the first example of such loyal patronage. But it wouldn't be the last. Other artists who benefited from Bernie and John's unwavering help during their early struggles included Supertramp, Thin Lizzy and David Bowie.

Not long after the first Tyrannosaurus Rex session, Bernie produced what he considered to be one of his very best, with a new Birmingham band called The Idle Race. They had just issued their first single, and had applied for a BBC audition - which Bernie deftly bypassed by inviting them in for a *'trial broadcast'*.

By this time, Bernie had established the *'trial broadcast'* as standard practice when booking new bands to appear on *Top Gear*.

The audition panel still got to hear the tapes, but they became a little more cautious about the opinions they passed. Maybe some of them were beginning to feel a little out of their depth?

The Idle Race session involved hiring in extra instruments: two timpani, a glockenspiel and a wah-pedal. Both Bernie and the band were knocked out by the results. Their lead guitarist was a guy called Jeff Lynne, who some years later, went on to distinguish himself in ELO (The Electric Light Orchestra) and The Travelling Wilburys - as well as becoming a very successful record producer in his own right.

On entering the rarefied world of record production, Jeff Lynne would later confess that, on his first session as a producer, he chose to wear a pair of corduroy trousers. This was because Bernie Andrews had worn a pair on Idle Race's first *Top Gear* session. And from that day onwards, Jeff considered corduroy trousers to be *'the right trousers for a producer'.*

Led Zeppelin was a different story. Bernie's and Jimmy Page's paths had crossed often and over many years. They first met during Jimmy's earliest days as a session musician, and then later when he joined the Yardbirds, playing alongside Jeff Beck. When that band split, the remnants morphed into Led Zeppelin.

One of the first major decisions this new band took was that they weren't going to bother recording singles. The constraint of a three-minute format was not for them. Touring rock bands were playing large venues - sports stadia and the like - and were performing sets featuring numbers which were way too long for release as singles.

These performances often involved prolonged passages of improvisation. As a result, by definition, these songs were never going to get airtime on Radio 1's middle-of-the-road record shows.

So, when Bernie phoned up Jimmy in the hope of booking them for *Top Gear*, he had to be at his most eloquent in order to sell him the idea. Even after they arrived for the session at Maida Vale and were setting up in Studio 4, not all of the band seemed to be totally persuaded.

"Have you seen our live show Bernie?" asked Robert Plant.

"I saw you when you were the New Yardbirds, but I haven't seen you since the name change to Led Zeppelin."

Robert threw a concerned glance at Jimmy.

"We've got this number called *Whole Lotta Love*. There's a lot of improvisation in the middle with feedback and tape echo... It sometimes goes on for five minutes - or longer."

Robert looked at Bernie.

"Are you OK with that?"

"No problem." said Bernie.

Robert raised his eyebrows.

Bernie called Pete Ritzema over.

"Robert, this is Pete, my studio manager today. Pete, Robert's got some ideas for improvisation in the middle of a big number with special effects, including tape echo.

Could you talk to Robert and Jimmy, and figure out how we can do this please?"

Bernie left them in the studio to talk about the technicalities and went into the control room to sort himself out. A few minutes later, Pete returned from the studio.

"All sorted?" asked Bernie.

"Yup." said Pete.

Whole Lotta Love was laid down on the first take. It lasted just over six minutes, and when the band came in to hear the playback, their feedback was,

"Terrific!"

The rest of the session went without a hitch.

Many years later, when Led Zeppelin released a CD of their sessions from the BBC archives, Jimmy Page was fulsome in praising Bernie for anticipating what was happening in the music business at that moment, and for giving them the time and space on a *Top Gear* session to do things the way they wanted.

*****

Almost every week, *Top Gear* featured artists and bands who, if they weren't already, were soon to become big names: Arthur Brown, Jimi Hendrix, The Small Faces, The Kinks, The Bee Gees, The Who, Fleetwood Mac, Ten Years After, Pink Floyd, Joe Cocker, Deep Purple, Free, Jethro Tull, Black Sabbath, John Mayall, Georgie Fame, The Nice... and too many more to mention.

However, John and Bernie did have a difference of opinion over one particular artist. That artist was David Bowie. When Bernie suggested booking David for a session, John's initial response was,

"Sounds like a cheap imitation of Anthony Newley to me."

"Well, I think we should book him anyway," said Bernie. "I really think he's got something. It might not yet be fully apparent, but I think we should give him a chance."

John took the huff. Perhaps he didn't think an Anthony Newley impersonator would go down so well in the *'underground scene'*? Bernie tried some sweet talking.

"Come on John! There have been times when you've persuaded me to book sessions I wouldn't otherwise have considered. Your mate Marc Bolan being a case in point. So, please go along with me on this?"

Bernie had a right of veto. John didn't. But Bernie didn't want to pull rank. He wanted co-operation. Eventually, with a bit more wheedling, he managed to get John on side.

"But don't expect me to be effusive." John warned.

Bernie chuckled. *'Effusive'* was not an adjective commonly associated with John Peel.

On Top of the World

Top Gear was well into its second year, when, one morning, Jeff Griffin rushed into Bernie's office. Bernie had just arrived, and hadn't yet sat down at his desk.

"Have you seen this week's Melody Maker?"

Bernie shook his head. Jeff slapped the latest edition on Bernie's desk. *'JOHN PEEL - A VICTORY FOR THE MUSIC!'* the headline trumpeted. Prominent sub-headlines followed up with, *'Top Gear Voted #1 Radio Programme,'* and *'John Peel Voted #1 DJ'*

Bernie sat down and studied the story, a smile growing on his face. When he had read enough, he looked up. "Bloody hell! That is not going to go well with those upstairs, is it?"

"Yes, well don't let it go to your head Bernie!" joked Jeff, on his way out of the door.

*****

Radio 1 Management fully expected the DJs on the big daytime shows to pick up all the prizes. Predictably, there were no messages of congratulations to either Bernie or John Peel from those upstairs.

On the other hand, the mainstream media picked up the story with relish. Suddenly, John Peel became a household name. Reactions varied from that of confused surprise, to those who saw the judgement as an indictment of the BBC's failure to provide a credible alternative to the pirate radio stations. One thing was clear. *Top Gear*, fronted by John Peel, was now the most respected music broadcast in the UK.

Bernie was beside himself. This accolade was vindication of all his efforts, ups and downs over the years. His fervent hope was that this recognition would help him in achieving his dream to continue working on *Top Gear* for as long as possible, while suffering as little management interference as possible.

*****

Bernie knocked on the door of Jim Waters' flat in Barnes. They had arranged to meet at his place and then go out for the evening. Jim wasn't quite ready, so Bernie took a seat in the living room while Jim finished dressing. The week had gone well, and Bernie was feeling chipper.

"Have you heard about Robin Scott then?" Jim shouted through the open door of the bathroom.

"What about him?" Bernie shouted back.

"He's on his way back to television."

Bernie went quiet.

'Surely not? Surely I would have heard about it? Someone in Radio 1 would have heard about it?'

He tried to shrug it off, but the thought just stayed there, niggling away at the back of his head. Eventually, Jim appeared, looking smart in his black flares, maroon velvet jacket and a pink, open necked shirt with wide lapels folded over the collar. Bernie couldn't resist further interrogation.

"What exactly have you heard about Robin Scott then?"

"They think he's done well launching Radios 1&2, so he's been invited back to television to take up a new role as Controller, Light Entertainment. High powered job, by all accounts."

"Who told you this?" asked Bernie, increasingly worried.

"My old band mate, Kenny Jackson. He's been doing really well in music publishing. He's got contacts over at Television Centre, and he often hangs out at *Top of the Pops*. He says he's heard from a number of sources, including the producer, Johnnie Stewart."

Now Bernie was really worried. This didn't sound like an unfounded rumour.

"That won't affect you, will it Bern?"

"I hope not," said Bernie. "Robin's been really supportive of *Top Gear*, and he's protected me from a lot of the crap that I used to suffer before he came on board. I'll just have to hope that, now we've established *Top Gear* as a successful programme, whoever takes over from Robin - assuming he really is moving on - will see from the results that they should just leave us to get on with it."

Jim sensed the concern in Bernie's voice. "Well if it is true," said Jim, "if I were you, I'd be careful for a while. Don't go upsetting anyone." He looked at Bernie. "Anyone! You hear me?"

Bernie nodded, looking uneasy.

"Come on! Let's cheer you up."

They departed for the pub.

*****

The following week, Bernie heard the news from the horse's mouth. All were summoned to a special meeting. Robin Scott confirmed that the rumour was true, and that the management handover would take place in precisely one months' time.

Bernie didn't make any effort to show his disappointment. But what he really wanted to know was who would take over? Would it be another import from television? Maybe an outsider? His thoughts were pre-empted when Robin made a further announcement.

"My replacement as Controller of Radios 1&2 will be no stranger to you. He has been my deputy these last two years, and he has done a splendid job. So, please join me in a round of applause for my successor... Aubrey Small.

Bernie scanned the room. He noted that reactions were mixed. The producers of the daytime record programmes beloved of management sycophantically applauded him to the rafters, while those who worked on live music, many of whom Bernie considered *'the good guys'* were rather more restrained. Then he realised that, of all the people in the room, he was the only one who wasn't applauding. So he belatedly joined in, half-heartedly, in a token effort. He was sure that Aubrey Small, who was also scanning the room, had already noted his lack of enthusiasm.

'That's it then,' thought Bernie, resigning himself to a difficult future. *'But at least Top Gear is established. It's an award winning show, with a rapidly growing base of followers. The Fat Controller will surely think twice about interfering too much?'*

During the following weeks, Bernie found it difficult to put his worries completely out of his mind.

He could cope when he was working in the studios. Busying himself with matters of musical performance and recording processes provided suitable distractions. However, in quieter moments, when his mind found more time to wander, he sought increasing refuge in the privacy of his office, feeding his fish, and dismayed to find that he couldn't resist relieving the tension by indulging in spliff therapy at a steadily increasing frequency.

Apocalypse

When Bernie received his assignments for the next quarter, he opened the envelope with trepidation. Now, he might get some kind of sense of what the future held for him.

He was relieved to see that he retained responsibility for *Top Gear*. However, he noticed other things. Very unpleasant things. His heart sank. He had been allocated additional production responsibilities for *Music While You Work*. Bernie thought he had earned the right to progress beyond that sort of thing. After *Top Gear's* conspicuous success, he had taken it for granted that he would never again be asked to do another *Music While You Work*.

He was incensed. He could see Rhys Williams' handprints all over the schedules, so he immediately phoned his office.

"Mr Williams' office," intoned Prunella.

"Yes. Bernie here. Can I speak to Rhys please?"

"Mr Williams is otherwise engaged," she retorted, snottily.

"It's really most important," insisted Bernie.

"I'm sure it is." Prunella stood her ground. "Would you like to book an appointment?"

'For fuck's sake!..' thought Bernie. He steadied himself.

"When can I see him?" he asked politely.

There was a long pause.

Bernie was beginning to wonder if she had disconnected when suddenly, she was back on the line.

"I can do this Thursday at 14:00."

Bernie looked at his diary. He was due to catch up with Jim over lunch in the West End. It was official business. Jim was promoting a new singer, the hospitality was on record company expenses, and, if they had the leisurely lunch they were planning, Bernie wouldn't make it back to the office in time.

"Have you got anything else?" asked Bernie.

"Not this week." came the unambiguous reply.

'For fuck's sake!..' thought Bernie again, fighting the urge to vent his frustration.

"OK." He gritted his teeth. "I'll be there at two o'clock on Thursday.

*****

At the appointed hour, Bernie showed up outside Rhys William's office.

Prunella motioned to Bernie to take a seat. No small talk. That suited Bernie. What didn't suit Bernie was that he was kept waiting... And waiting... Finally, after twenty past, Bernie could keep silent no longer,

"Has Rhys got someone in there with him?"

"No."

"Do you mind if I knock on his door then?"

"Yes I do. He's a very busy man you know."

"Maybe he has forgotten about the appointment?"

"He's well aware of your appointment Bernie. Please be patient!"

Just then, the office door swung open, and Rhys Williams leaned through.

"Right then Bernie. Please come in!"

Bernie settled himself down in the chair in front of William's desk.

"What do you want to see me about Bernie?"

"It's about my new production schedule."

"What about it?"

"You've given me some extra *Music While You Works* in addition to my regular *Top Gear* assignments."

"And?"

Bernie was beginning to bristle.

"Well... You know that I put in a lot of unpaid overtime to make a success of *Top Gear*. Sometimes I'm working seventy or eighty hours a week, and sometimes from Monday to Saturday... I mean, I can't take on any more workload - particularly if there are early starts after late recording sessions. I never finish before 11pm on late ones, and sometimes they overrun. A 7.30 start the day after one of those is a killer."

Bernie thought he was getting a bit too emotional, so he shut up.

"That's precisely the problem, Bernie. You put in far too much unpaid overtime," Williams smirked. "In the words of some of your hippy friends, *'you're too into the music, man.'* He sniggered at his own jibe. "Not only is it unhealthy, but it upsets the other staff. They don't think you should be hogging all that studio time."

"But I'm not taking studio time away from anyone else." insisted Bernie. "The studios would be lying empty otherwise. In fact, by booking double sessions, I'm getting more value out of our resources."

"That's debatable, Bernie," Williams countered, blandly. "All the other producers I talk to say they can produce the same amount of material in half the time - on a single session."

'I'm not going back to that,' Bernie thought to himself. *'The bands I book think BBC recording equipment is laughable, and allowing them double time to work round the limitations is the only way I've managed to persuade any decent bands to come in.'*

"But if they want the extra studio time, they could do the same as me," defended Bernie. "All they have to do is put in the extra hours."

"But that's the other problem," Williams reasoned. "Our union minded friends are most unhappy about unpaid overtime. We might have a serious problem with them if double-sessions become the norm." He smiled again, "And that wouldn't do any of us any good, would it?"

Bernie didn't know how to respond.

"And another thing," said Williams, "Your colleagues don't think you're pulling your weight."

Bernie bristled once more.

"We all have to pitch in and do some of the more mundane jobs now and again. And we all have to take our share of early starts. That's only fair, isn't it? I mean, I often hear complaints that *'Bernie Andrews only works on one programme - his favourite programme.'* and I've often been asked the question, *'Does Bernie Andrews write his own work schedule?'* Now, you may not have intentionally fostered that perception, but surely you can understand why some noses are out of joint?"

'I know one nose that I'd very much like to see out of joint,' thought Bernie.

"So, I think it's only reasonable that you should take on a broader mix of responsibilities, like your colleagues, and you should do that by spreading yourself around a bit more. Even if that means cutting back on your *Top Gear* commitments."

"But *Top Gear* will suffer if I do that." Bernie blurted out. "Its success is totally dependent on the way I've organised the production. It's one of the main reasons why we've been voted #1 radio programme and John Peel has been voted #1 DJ. Surely you can see that?"

For the first time, there were signs that Williams was getting irritated. He wasn't used to his subordinates questioning his orders. He took a long time to compose himself, and when he did, he chose his words very carefully.

"Bernie, are you saying that you won't be able to find the time to take on any broader production responsibilities if you continue to produce *Top Gear* the way you want?"

"Pretty much."

"Thank you very much for your input Bernie. You have given me a lot to think about, and we must find a solution. Somehow. I'll get back to you on this."

"Is that it?" said Bernie.

"Yes," said Williams. "You can go."

*****

Jim came round to Mayfair that night. He'd phoned up earlier to talk about a band he'd seen at the Lyceum, but Bernie had sounded withdrawn. Despondent even. Monosyllabic grunts were not Bernie's style. He knew something was up, so he told Bernie he'd call round later. Straight after work, he made his way round to Shepherds Market.

Bernie let him in, offered a half-hearted greeting, and padded down the passageway in his slippers. Jim followed. Bernie went off to make him a coffee. Terry was out, so there was a deadly hush. The only thing that broke the silence was the lonesome whistle of the kettle coming to the boil in the kitchen.

'What the hell is up?' thought Jim.

He was sure Bernie wanted to talk. But, as always, it was a matter of choosing the right moment. He'd have to take it slowly. Bernie came back with the coffees, and they sat, once more in silence.

"I saw the Jeff Beck Group last night."

"Right." was Bernie's perfunctory reply.

"They were tremendous. Rod Stewart's such a powerful vocalist. I'm sure he could manage without a PA system."

Jim's feeble attempt at humour was lost in the black hole.

They sat in silence again. Jim tried a different tack,

"How was your day then? What did you get up to?"

Bernie buried his head in his hands, struggling with his thoughts. Then he looked at Jim,

"They're up to something."

"Who's up to something?"

"Them. The bloody management. Williams... Small... Whoever..."

Jim could restrain himself no longer. "What's happened Bernie?"

"They've put me on *Music While You Work*... On a regular basis."

"Well, I know you don't like the programme. In fact, I know you hate it. But they're your bosses. It's not unreasonable for them to ask you, is it?"

"Only when they take absolutely no consideration of how much work I'm putting in on *Top Gear*. They have no idea what I've had to do to make the programme a success. Yesterday, Williams suggested I cut down on the session time to make more room for *Music While You Bloody Work*. It's a joke."

By this time, Bernie was getting quite heated.

"I told Williams. I told him that double sessions are essential to the success of *Top Gear*."

Jim didn't like the sound of the story he was being told. "What was the outcome then?" he asked.

"Nothing. I was just told to go away, and they'd have a think about it all."

Jim carefully considered whether he should say what he wanted to say. Eventually, he decided to say it, regardless of what the consequences might be.

"Please be careful Bernie. If you're too dogmatic, you might put your job on the line. From what you tell me, your managers don't seem to give a toss about *Top Gear*, so they're probably not going to be swayed by any logical arguments you come up with based on listening figures, or opinion polls. Maybe, at least for a while, you'll have to make some compromises?"

Predictably, Bernie exploded. "Compromises! What do *THEY* know about compromises? When have *THEY* ever done anything except please themselves, and run things exactly the way *THEY* want, in exactly the same crappy way *THEY* always have?"

Once more there was a silence. A long silence. And then,

"Why don't we take a tube over to Balls Brothers. I'll buy us a nice bottle of wine, and you can forget about all this stuff. At least for tonight."

Bernie looked up. He looked very tired. Then a hint of a smile appeared on his face for the first time that evening.

"I think that's a good idea."

*****

The following morning, Bernie made sure he was in the office at 9:00am on the dot - despite a slight hangover. Williams had left Bernie in limbo the day before. He wasn't sure what might happen next, but, if Williams did decide to get in touch, he didn't want Prunella charging around, demanding to know why Bernie was not at his appointed place of work.

He didn't have to wait long. Just after 10:00 his phone rang. He had been summoned to return to Williams' office at 14:00.

This time he was ushered straight in. He was already nervous and anxious. But his anxiety rose even further when he saw that David Forbes, the Radios 1&2 Personnel Officer, was sitting at the table alongside Rhys Williams. Then Prunella, instead of returning to her desk, shut the door and took a seat to the side, pulling out a notepad in the process.

'This is a fucking ambush.' thought Bernie. He sat. Williams began,

"Thank you for coming along Bernie. I've asked David to be here as I want to be absolutely sure there is no misunderstanding regarding our discussions."

"And what's Prunella doing?" asked Bernie.

"Prunella is taking minutes."

Bernie's blood ran cold. He did not like the way things were moving. Not at all. Perhaps he'd better be prepared to make some sort of compromise? Appear reasonable? Try and make the best of it?

Bernie nodded. Williams resumed.

278

"Now Bernie, when we left it yesterday, we had reached the point in the conversation when I asked you, (he put on his reading glasses to read his notes), and I quote, *'Are you saying that you won't be able to find the time to take on any broader production responsibilities if you continue to produce Top Gear the way you want?'* "

He looked Bernie directly in the eye. "And your reply was, *'Pretty much.'*"

Williams paused. "Is that a fair summary of where we left it?"

Bernie hesitated. "Er... I suppose so."

"Good. We're agreed. And I said I would go away and do some thinking about it."

Bernie nodded.

"Well, I have applied some thought to the matter. Very careful thought. And I have therefore revised your production responsibilities. In doing so, I've taken account of all of the significant issues we raised yesterday. First of all, I take your point, Bernie, that your health will suffer if you continue producing *Top Gear* in your chosen manner as well as taking on the wider production responsibilities we asked you to. I accept that there is a health issue, and the BBC, as your employer, must be fully cognisant of that."

Bernie sat, uncomprehendingly.

"Also, as your manager, I am very concerned that you don't seem to have a coherent career development path. In context with your work experience, you are what might commonly be referred to as a *'one trick pony'*. And that one trick is *Top Gear*."

"Now, there is no denying that you have made a success of that programme, if judged within the context of a very limited and specialist audience. But we at Radios 1&2 need producers who are good all-rounders in serving our mass audiences; producers who can work across the whole gamut of our output; producers who can put their hands to anything at a moment's notice, and deliver the goods."

At this point, he turned to David Forbes. On cue, Forbes nodded sagely. Williams took a typed sheet of paper, turned it round, and placed it in front of Bernie so he could read it.

"So, we've decided not to limit your opportunities for wider programme experience as per your original work schedule. In fact we're going to be a lot more ambitious in terms of providing you with career development opportunities. And the reason that you'll have the time to take on these challenging new roles is because I've spoken to Aubrey, and he and I both agree that you should move on from producing *Top Gear*."

Williams' words ceased to have any meaning.

The planets stopped in their course around the sun.

Time was frozen.

All Bernie could see was the revised work schedule that Williams had placed in front of him during his speech. All he could see was more organ programmes, more light orchestral sessions, more half-baked pop music cover versions performed by half-baked session musicians, and, of course, more *Music While You Work*.

ALL HE COULD SEE WAS NO MORE *TOP GEAR*!!!!!!!!!!!!!!

"Who's going to produce *Top Gear* then?" Bernie asked weakly.

"We're going to let John Walters have a go at that."

By the time he registered the words, *'Do you have anything to say?'* Bernie realised it wasn't the first time he'd been asked. He looked up from the work schedule and looked at Williams.

He felt sick.

Williams asked once more, "Do you have anything to say Bernie?"

Bernie was numb. He said *'no'* quietly and stood up to get out of the office as quickly as he could. As he got up, Williams called to him,

"Bernie! You'll need this."

Bernie hesitated, turned round and took the piece of paper Williams had in his outstretched hand.

"Thank you," he muttered, and left the room.

*****

On the way back to the office, a few colleagues said hello as he passed by. He didn't respond. Not because he was ignoring them, but because he didn't hear them. When he got to his office, he closed the door and put on an old country LP by Hank Snow. One of his favourites. It was melancholy, but it always calmed him down. There was a knock on the door, and Jeff came in. He obviously knew something.

"You look ill Bernie. You should take the day off."

"You heard then?"

"I heard a rumour. What's the news?"

Jeff could see that Bernie was almost in tears. He could hardly bring himself to say it.

"I'm off *Top Gear*."

"Christ!" said Jeff. "What did they do that for?"

"Because they'll never forgive me for disobeying an order by keeping John Peel's broadcasting career alive after they told me to sack him."

"Because they'll never forgive me for getting him and *Top Gear* to #1 in the polls."

"And because they'll never forgive me for being a royal pain in the arse."

Jeff was relieved to see that some vestige of self-effacement was still alive in Bernie's demeanour.

"Look." said Jeff, "I'm going to phone for a taxi, and then I'm going to take you home."

"But Williams will be on my case." hissed Bernie. "Or at least his watchdog Prunella will."

"I think that'll be the least of their concerns right now. If anything comes up, I'll say that you were taken ill. You look ill. You are ill, as far as I am concerned, so they can't object to you taking some time off."

As soon as reception rang Bernie's office to say the taxi had arrived, Jeff took him downstairs, got into the taxi with him and they left for Shepherds Market.

*****

After dropping him off, Jeff went straight back to work, just in case he had to field any enquiries about Bernie. He didn't hear a thing. After work, he phoned his wife, Rita, and explained that he would be late home, and why. Then he went back round to Bernie's.

He'd alerted Jim during the day, so when he got back to the flat, he found Jim and Terry already there, commiserating with Bernie on his bad luck. Bad luck was an understatement as far as Bernie was concerned. It was the end of the world. Inevitably, discussion came around to what Bernie planned to do next.

"We've been through all that before," said Bernie dismissively. "I don't know that I can do anything else. I'm a radio man. Always have been. Always will be."

"I could have a word with Brian?" offered Terry. "I'm sure there would be plenty of openings for you at NEMS?"

Bernie responded with a weak smile. "Thanks Terry, I really appreciate it. But what would I do? By all accounts, George Martin is doing a great job with the lads..."

There was a huge roar of laughter all round. At least the sense of humour was intact.

"No, really. Like before, I'm going to have to sort this out myself.

But whatever I do, I can never put so much of my heart and soul into a project like *Top Gear*. Never ever again."

The Big If

Who knows what Bernie would have done with the rest of his broadcasting career if management had relented? If they had allowed him to return to *Top Gear*, or given him another radio programme that offered the same sort of creative scope? The fact is, they never did.

John Peel and John Walters were shocked by Bernie's demise. Peel went into print more than a few times on the subject of how unfairly he thought Bernie had been treated. But management ignored all appeals. And the show went on. From strength to strength.

Bernie never resented the continued success of *Top Gear*, or its successor, the *John Peel Show*. And he never held anything against John Walters or John Peel for what had happened. He knew how things worked. He knew that neither of them had been involved in the skulduggery. He was in no doubt about whose vindictiveness had resulted in his humiliation and heartbreak.

In fact, whenever he could, he continued to help out on *Top Gear*. He would occasionally sit in as a producer on Peel sessions if they were short-handed, and if he heard any records or saw any bands that he thought Peel and Walters might be interested in, he let them know.

However, Bernie was interested to note that when John Walters took over as the producer, there was absolutely no question of reverting *Top Gear* recordings to single sessions. *Top Gear* sessions were always double sessions, weren't they?

Equally, there was no question of asking John Walters to take on an early start like *Music While You Work* on the morning after a late *Top Gear* recording session. That would have been silly. Wouldn't it?

Ironically, around the time of Bernie's demise, Jeff Griffin's career was on the way up.

Almost five years after Jeff had tried, without success, to persuade the BBC Light Programme to let him produce live radio concerts featuring emerging talent, Jeff finally succeeded in his quest.

Radio 1 gave him the go ahead to record the latest heavy rock sensation, Led Zeppelin, in front of a live audience. A talented young studio manager by the name of Tony Wilson was only too glad to help him out with that one.

It had taken Jeff a long time to persuade the powers that be that pop shows on the radio needn't be like glorified variety shows with a mix of artists performing a little bit of this, and a little bit of that. But it was worth the wait. His Led Zeppelin concert proved that rock bands really were capable of sustaining a continuous one-hour performance on the radio.

The following year, in 1970, Jeff launched a weekly series based on the format which he had tried and tested with Led Zeppelin. He called the series, simply, *In Concert*.

Despite Bernie's own run of bad luck, he was thrilled about Jeff's good fortune, observing,

"Now you've got a chance to do for live rock concerts on the radio what I've been trying to do for rock music sessions."

Bernie never spoke a truer word.

In the first year of the series, Jeff broadcast concerts by T Rex, Free, David Bowie, Deep Purple, Yes, Elton John, Fleetwood Mac, Black Sabbath, Mott the Hoople, Procol Harum, Rod Stewart and the Faces, Pink Floyd, Supertramp, James Taylor and Joni Mitchell - among many others.

Jeff continued to produce *In Concert* on a regular basis right up until he retired in 1994. During that time, he and his crew made such a name for themselves in producing top class live audio that BBC 2 started bringing their cameras along to his concerts so that the TV pictures could be transmitted simultaneously with Radio 1's stereo soundtrack. These *'simulcasts'* went under the name of *Sight and Sound* and eventually became the template for the biggest rock music event of all time - *Live Aid*.

In later years, Bernie would often remark, wryly, "Jeff was much better at *'managing'* the management than I ever was."

*****

The 'psychedelic' era gave way to the days of 'progressive rock', and then that era was superseded by something called 'glam rock'. So said the many people who could perceive these differences - so long as they could see how the artists were dressed and made up. To many who used only their ears, it all just sounded like rock'n'roll, although, if they were worried about their street credibility, they might have been circumspect about exactly who was within earshot before they made that particular confession.

The Rolling Stones had no such qualms. In 1962, they had proclaimed *'We hope they don't think we're a rock'n'roll outfit. We're an R&B band!'* By the late '60s, they were being universally promoted as, *'The Greatest Rock and Roll Band in the World.'* It is to be hoped that Mick put the errant straight.

A Band Called Queen

About three years after Bernie was sacked from *Top Gear*, Ronnie Beck walked into his office. Ronnie was a song plugger with a well-known publishing company. He had a tape in his hand, and he asked Bernie to have a listen.

"Why are you asking me?"

"You've got good taste Bernie. I'd like to know what you think."

He put the tape on his office tape machine and pressed the start button. After the first track had faded out, and the second one was starting up, he asked,

"How many tracks are on this tape Ronnie?"

"It's a complete album."

"It's very good... Excellent, in fact. But what do you expect me to do with it?"

"Just do me a favour Bernie. Listen to it all the way through. Indulge me! There's a slap up lunch in it for you - at the Ivy."

Bernie didn't need any further encouragement. He liked what he was hearing. After the final track faded out, he turned again to Ronnie.

"When's it released?"

"That's the thing. These guys have done a deal with the owners of Trident Studios to record during studio down time - usually overnight - and they've got this amazing album in the can."

"But?.."

"But they can't get anyone interested. All the record labels have turned them down."

"Unbelievable!" Bernie chortled. "Here we are... Ten years after the Beatles were *told 'you have no future in show business... guitar groups are on the way out.'* and the record business establishment are still the same old bunch of cloth-eared donkeys... What's the band called?"

"Queen."

Ronnie handed Bernie a 10 x 8 black and white photo - studio shot - moody lighting - stylised posing. Bernie took one look at it, and pointed,

"He the singer?"

"Yeah."

"Queen!" he giggled. "Makes sense."

"Now, now Bernie! Don't judge a book by its cover."

"Right." said Bernie, still smirking. "I'll tell you what I'll do. I'll take the tape to Walters and Peel, and see if they are interested."

"Brilliant!" said Ronnie. "I was hoping you would say that."

"But no guarantees." said Bernie.

"None expected." Then they shook hands, and the pair of them jumped in a taxi and headed to The Ivy.

As promised, Bernie took the tape and dropped it off in John Walters' office. The next day, John dropped by Bernie's office.

"Hi Bernie!"

"Hello John. What can I do for you?"

"That tape you left on my desk… Queen."

"Yeah. Excellent material."

"We think so too," said Walters. "I played it to Peel, and we want to have them on the show."

"That's brilliant! " said Bernie. "Have you given Ronnie Beck the news yet?"

"No, not yet," said Walters. "I thought you might want to do that… In fact, John and I were wondering if you'd like to produce their first session?"

Bernie agreed without hesitation.

Bernie stood on the steps of All Souls, Langham Place, looking across the road at the façade of Broadcasting House. He liked to stand there, often on his way back from lunch, watching the world go by for a minute or two.

He remembered standing there ten years previously, just before he recorded his first ever session with the Beatles. Of course, they had

290

managed to get themselves a record deal by then. This new band, Queen, hadn't even managed to do that. Yet! Hopefully, today, he could help to change all that.

He set off towards Broadcasting House. However, this time, he walked past the front door and on to the zebra crossing leading over to the Langham. BBC Radio had recently decided to replace their thirty year old audio equipment. *'And not before time,'* according to Bernie.

So, while major works were under way in the main music studios like Maida Vale, a temporary multi-track facility had been set up in Studio 1 in the Langham.

Studio 1 had been a drama studio when Bernie started at the BBC. He remembered routing programmes like *Mrs Dale's Diary*, a daily soap opera about a doctor's wife, from Langham 1 onto the Light Programme radio network during the '50s. The last time he had been in the studio, it was still full of 1940s technology. This time, he opened the door and saw a brand new Neve mixing desk.

'Wow!..' thought Bernie. *'Luxury!'*

He nodded to John Etchells, the studio manager. Bernie had never worked with him, but had heard good things about him from Jeff Griffin.

The band and the roadies were setting up their instruments while John weaved in and out, placing his mics exactly where he wanted them. Bernie thought he would leave all alone until everyone was satisfied with the setup. There would be plenty of time to talk about which songs and how they should be recorded. In the meantime, he was interested to see that only the control room had been upgraded.

The studio itself was still, basically, a drama studio. It had a *'dead'* side and a *'live'* side, which could be separated by a telescopic array of acoustic screens, and it also had a little *'dead room'* - a tiny cubicle where an actor, or someone doing sound effects, could be acoustically separated from the rest of the cast. *'Might be useful for acoustically separating a vocalist's mic from the band?'* thought Bernie. He got his paperwork and stopwatch out, and waited until all was ready.

The drummer and bass player stayed in the studio, warming up, while the lead guitarist and the singer came in to the control room to check out the proceedings. Bernie didn't really know much about them apart from what he had heard on the tape.

"Can I have the names of everyone in the band please?"

"Yeah. The drummer is Roger Taylor... The bass player is John Deacon... And I'm Brian May... Guitar," said the tall guy with the massive hair.

Bernie looked at Brian's companion. Afghan coat. Average height. Skinny. Pronounced overbite. Hair a bit straggly. Looked as if he might have been late out of bed.

"And?.."

"Freddie." Said a confident, well-enunciated voice. "Vocals and piano."

"Freddie?.." queried Bernie.

"Mercury, dear boy."

Bernie wouldn't forget that name. *'Mercury suits him,'* he thought. *'Mercurial... Impulsive... Spontaneous... I might have heard some of that in their music.'*

Bernie had a good feeling.

"How many tracks does your tape machine have?" asked Brian.

Until quite recently, the answer would have been "One." which was invariably met with an expression of utter disbelief.

This time, Bernie could answer, "Eight."

"Eight!!!" chorused Brian and Freddie.

Bernie was not surprised by the overt expression of disappointment.

"We recorded the album at Trident on 24-track." said Brian, almost in protest.

Bernie groaned inwardly.

'Here we go again.' was all he could think.

Yes, BBC Radio had upgraded the sound production equipment. The sound mixing desks were state of the art. That, at least, was true.

But when most of the commercial studios at that time were equipped with at least 16-track tape recorders, and some, like Trident, were installing the latest 24-track technology, the BBC in its infinite wisdom had decided to upgrade to... the already obsolete 8-track format.

"And why was that?" Bernie had enquired of his superiors.

"Because, Bernie, we don't want to encourage self-indulgence on BBC recording sessions."

"Pop groups can get carried away, so we are going to limit the studio upgrades to 8-tracks, which should make sessions much quicker than if they have 16 or 24 tracks to play with."

And from whose mouth had those pearls of wisdom fallen? None other than Rhys Fucking Williams. What an utter prat. Anyone who knew anything about modern recording techniques knew that more tracks made for easier, quicker sessions.

Bernie was well aware that this new band called Queen were going to find it a challenge to record their material on Langham 1's 8-track. But Bernie was nothing if not an optimist.

"I know you recorded on 24-track at Trident, and I've listened to the album, so I know that you took full advantage and recorded loads of overdubs - vocals and guitars..."

Bernie had Brian and Freddie's attention. He sensed that he might have scored a few points about listening to the album carefully.

"Now, we only have 8-track here, but I think we can make things work if we use a bit of imagination. You've already recorded the album. You'll be well rehearsed. So time is not going to be an issue. If it is, we'll overrun. Don't worry about time pressure. The mixing desk is top class, and so is the balance engineer. John will get you an excellent sound. That leaves the matter of how to get your 24-track masterpieces produced on 8-track."

"Well, there are a few tricks that we can pull on 8-track. When we've got the basic tracks down on, say 3 or 4 tracks, we can bounce multiple takes of vocals from one remaining track to the other, and build them up that way. Same goes for the guitars. And if we record each element in mono, we can save as many tracks as possible for doing this."

"When it comes to the final mix, we can spread all the mono sources around the stereo image. It won't be identical to the record. But I'm sure we can get an excellent result."

Bernie could see that what he was suggesting was getting through. Then he called John Etchells over.

"I'll leave you with John to work out how the basic tracks and then the overdubs can be planned. Let me know when you're ready to go."

With that, he sat himself in the corner and started reading a half-finished paperback he had in his briefcase. He knew that it was best for the band and the engineer to talk directly about the practicalities. They were the ones who would have to perform. He was here to make sure everyone got the best result. And this was the way he thought they would get it.

It took quite a while for Brian, Freddie and John to figure it all out. Bernie looked up once or twice to see various sheets of A4 torn up, thrown in the bin, and started afresh. In the process, it seemed that the song selection was going to be heavily influenced by the relative difficulties involved in recording them on 8-track. Eventually, it came down to,

"OK. That'll work." said Brian.

"So it's *Liar, Doing Alright, Fairy King* and *Keep Yourself Alive*." announced Freddie.

All that remained was for Bernie to confirm which band members wrote which tracks. And then they were off.

Bernie was well-pleased that *Keep Yourself Alive* was in the final selection. It was one of his favourites.

He was also well pleased that - leaving aside the underpowered multi-track tape recorder - things had definitely moved on in BBC Radio sound studios. Studio time was sufficient - if not plentiful. The studio staff were, in general, much more knowledgeable and motivated than they used to be. And the whole business of recording Radio 1 sessions was taken very seriously.

Despite these advances, in Bernie's opinion, some things still moved way too slowly. But he allowed himself the luxury of a small pat on the back for his successes in pushing for improvements over the years. No-one who knew anything about Bernie would have begrudged him that.

The session was long and complex. It overran by quite a bit, but no-one was bothered, and everyone seemed well pleased with the results. If it didn't sound exactly the same as the album, the compensation was that in a week or so, an unknown band by the name of Queen would be heard by millions for the very first time on the *John Peel Show*. After the last playback, it was time to pack up.

"Thank you very much for a great session," said Bernie. "I am sure that when the record companies come to their senses, you'll get the contract you deserve, and you will soon be heading up the charts."

Not long after that session went out on the air, the record companies revised their opinion of this strange new band called Queen. Around five months later, their first album was released on EMI - the same recording conglomerate who, ten years before, had initially turned down the Beatles - and then signed them up. Lucky for some that they got the luxury of a second chance - second time around.

The Long Goodbye

Author's note: *I wanted to quote the first nine lines of **The Pretender** by **Jackson Browne** at this point. However, I wasn't able to get permission from the publisher. This song was a personal favourite of Bernie's. It's about the compromises we all have to settle for when striving to keep body and soul together. If you can, Google it.*

*****

Top Gear, the programme which Bernie founded with such success, and which had morphed into *The John Peel Show*, was by this time a national treasure. It continued without interruption until John Peel's death in 2004. In that respect, Bernie's legacy lived on for many years.

But the truth of it was that Bernie never did get the chance to put his heart and soul into another project like *Top Gear.* His unique creation . Which offered an opportunity to showcase BBC sessions specially recorded by emerging British talent alongside the most interesting new record releases.

Bernie and his managers never really reconciled. At best, they tolerated each other. It was not a healthy situation, and it took its toll. Bernie struggled. Perhaps unwisely, he stuck it out at the BBC as a square peg in a round hole, all the time feeling trapped, because he couldn't imagine a life outside the world of radio. It was a toxic mix which led to a great deal of mental stress.

*****

That's not to say that Bernie didn't enjoy some bright spots along the way in succeeding years. One morning, Bernie caught sight of a trendily dressed young lady passing his office.

"Hey Annie!" he called out.

Annie turned back and walked in.

"Hi Bernie! How's it going?"

Annie Nightingale. Young. Pretty. Long blonde hair. All the right attributes to attract the wrong sort of attention in a male-dominated environment. Especially as she was the only female DJ on Radio 1.

In the mid-sixties, she had started off as a journalist on Fleet Street, making her mark by interviewing The Beatles, The Rolling Stones and many more besides. So, by the time she got to Radio 1 she had a deep knowledge of how things worked in the record business.

Predictably, Annie found male chauvinism just as prevalent in the world of radio as it was anywhere else. Fortunately, she had developed a thick skin to cope with the snide remarks about her gender and about the position she held as the only, and therefore *'token'* woman DJ on Radio 1.

Having experienced a great deal of toxic peer pressure himself, Bernie empathised. He had witnessed first-hand some of the crap she had to put up with, and had more than an inkling about the stuff he hadn't.

"You've drawn the short straw then."

"What are you on about Bernie?"

"They've lumbered you. I'm down to produce your Sunday afternoon request show from the beginning of the next quarter."

"Go on!" said Annie. "I'm really looking forward to it. Teddy Warrick already told me."

"Oh good! I'm glad I'm not following established Radio 1 protocol and springing the news on you straight from the rumour mill."

Annie laughed.

"Have you got time to chat?"

"Sure," said Annie. "I was listening to some new albums, but that can wait."

Annie sat down at the desk and looked over Bernie's shoulder.

"How do you get away with it Bernie?"

"What?"

"The fish tank."

"Oh that," he chortled. "That's the only thing that keeps me sane. That, and the occasional jazz cigarette."

He exhaled, slowly. "Yeah... Well, they've taken so much away from me over the years. They probably feel guilty, and have drawn a line at the fish tank. Maybe they figure that if they took that away, I'd turn suicidal. And that might give them something they couldn't deal with just by ignoring the situation, writing a bland memo or two, or firing me."

Bernie was jesting, but Annie knew the history. Everyone knew the history.

"Yes, bland is one of the more complimentary words I can think of to describe Radio 1 management," said Annie.

Bernie developed the theme,

"And when you consider how multi-layered it all is, some have observed that it's a case of the bland leading the bland? No?"

They giggled conspiratorially. Bad mouthing their bosses was an exquisite pleasure.

"Do you know that upstairs, I've heard them spouting the theory that the most effective way for a DJ to increase his popularity on air is to act the part of surrogate husband to all the women listeners," said Annie. "Isn't that pathetic?"

"They're like a stuck record." said Bernie impatiently. "Housebound housewives doing their daily chores. That is the audience which must be courted - above all others. It really is pathetic."

"I can't fathom their obsession to keep ahead of Radio 2 in audience listening figures," said Annie. "They're convinced there's safety in numbers. So long as they beat Radio 2 for listeners in the middle-of-the-road market, their future is secure."

"It's an easy sell, isn't it?" replied Bernie. "We have no idea how the BBC Board of Directors sees Radio 1. Does Radio 1 have any management objectives or targets other than maximising the audience figures? Probably not."

"But Radio 1 was supposed to provide the youth audience with a replacement for the pirate radio stations, which they tuned into in droves," Annie complained. "If they paid more attention to the younger end of the demographics... OK, they would lose some older listeners who might switch over to Radio 2. And Radio 1 listening figures would go down a bit. But if we make the younger listeners happy, wouldn't that be more in tune with why Radio 1 was set up in the first place?"

"Absolutely!" said Bernie. "The Radio 1 programmes which get the most loyal following among young people are the off-peak slots. Those which aren't expected to pull in mass audiences. But, ironically, because management aren't interested in what happens off-peak, those programmes get more licence to *'do their own thing'* which allows people like us to please the youngsters. It happened with Peel on Radio London, and again when I hired him for *Top Gear*. It's perverse. But it's the only comfort we've got. And on that very theme, how do you want to do it?"

"The Sunday afternoon show?"

Bernie nodded.

"Well... How did you do it with John Peel? I heard that programme was quite successful?"

Bernie enjoyed the sarcasm. He and Annie were going to get along just fine.

"We did it together," said Bernie. "It was as simple as that."

"Why change a winning formula?" Annie replied.

And that was that. A successful radio partnership was forged - again.

*****

Bernie and Annie's collaboration soon attracted a substantial student audience on Sunday afternoons. Which was not entirely surprising, since it was a similar time-slot to the John Peel relaunch of *Top Gear* some years before.

They and their audience had settled in to a very enjoyable groove, when, out of the blue, Radio 1 management decided to *'improve'* the schedules by moving Annie's show from Sunday afternoon to Sunday evening.

"Have you seen the slot they've put us in?"

Annie had just appeared in Bernie's office in a most agitated state.

"I have," said Bernie. "Do you know what I always find best in these situations?"

"No," said Annie.

"Take a load off your feet, and I'll get you a coffee."

By the time he came back, Annie was a bit more composed, but still clearly upset.

"Look!" said Bernie. "The received wisdom is that there will be fewer listeners during the new time slot they've put us in."

Annie shrugged.

"But we know that their received wisdom is usually received stupidity, don't we?"

The hint of a smile appeared on Annie's face.

"The thing is, we've got a new spot immediately after the *Top 40 Show* ends on Sunday evening. Now, the Top 40 pulls in a lot of listeners, but immediately after it's finished, a lot of listeners switch off, don't they?" Annie nodded.

"And why is that?" asked Bernie.

Annie shrugged again.

"Because what follows is usually a load of crap. Isn't it?"

Annie laughed.

"But what if what follows isn't a load of crap? Then maybe the listeners won't switch off?"

Bernie paused.

"It's a gift, Annie. The less likely they think we are to get to get an audience, the more they will leave us alone to do what we want. If we play our cards right, we will be able to shape the show exactly how we want it. I promise you that we will not only grow an audience, but we will grow an audience that appreciates what we are doing - and the music we are playing."

Bernie was right. Annie was delighted. And this time, Bernie did not make the same mistakes that he did on *Saturday Club* and *Top Gear*. He complied with management most of the time, sticking his neck out only when it was circumspect.

Although they did have one very close shave.

*****

A new album by The Rolling Stones had just been released. It was called *Goat's Head Soup*. Annie and Bernie immediately seized on a track called *Star Star* - an irresistibly foot-stomping boogie which, if not a complete Chuck Berry rip-off, owed more than a little to his unmistakable riffs.

They decided to feature it prominently in the next show.

A few days later, Annie was passing the time with Keith Richards at a Rolling Stones PR event. This glitzy junket took place at Blenheim Palace, the ancestral home of that avid aficionado of rhythm and blues, Winston Churchill.

"Oh, and we played *Star Star* on the show this week."

"You what!.." said Keith, choking on his fag. Then coughing the only way a nicotine addict can. Laughing through his coughs, he dragged Mick Jagger over.

"Hey Mick! Listen to this!" He looked at Annie, whose face was a blank. "Go on! Tell Mick what you just told me!"

"Er… I said to Keith that we played *Star Star* on the show this week."

Mick and Keith collapsed in heaps of laughter.

"You didn't!" said Mick, in disbelief.

Annie waited until the mirth had subsided. She knew she needed to find out why this was so funny.

"So what's the big deal then?"

"Did you listen to the words?" asked Mick.

"Yeah?"

"Did you listen to the chorus?"

She nodded.

"What did you make of the words. Can you remember how it goes?"

She thought for a while.

"Yes…" she said, slowly. "And?"

"What did you think we were singing?"

"Well… maybe I didn't quite make out properly, but it sounded a bit like *'Starbuck, Starbuck, Starbuck, Starbuck, Star.'* Is that it?"

Mick and Keith dissolved once more into paroxysms of laughter. Annie was getting a bit annoyed… And worried…

"Come on guys! What's the deal?"

Mick composed himself, "We were singing *'Starfucker, Starfucker, Starfucker, Starfucker, Star.'* "

"Yeah!" exclaimed Keith. "When we were recordin' it, we said *'there's no way anyone's ever goin' to play this one on the radio.'* "

He laughed some more.

"The crazy thing is that we've often had tracks banned when we wanted them played. This time, we recorded something especially to get it banned - and you played it."

More hysterics.

Annie was horrified.

* * * * *

Bernie was beside himself with worry.

It was some days since Annie had played *Star Star* on her Sunday request show. The BH switchboard had registered no telephone complaints, and there had been nothing in the mail from enraged vicars or the *National Viewers' and Listeners' Association* - an organisation formed by that formidable prude, Mary Whitehouse, who was a very influential and constant thorn in the flesh of the British media. But Bernie didn't kid himself. He knew that someone, somewhere would take great delight in sneaking on him.

Sure enough, the following week, he was called to the office of the Deputy Managing Director, Radio 1. The Deputy MD had a number of vaguely defined responsibilities. One of them was *'programme discipline'*. So, the incumbent was charged with the responsibility of monitoring Radio 1 output in search of the unacceptable: commercial plugs, product promotions, inappropriate political views, lewd comments, and, of course, bad language.

This was the first time that Bernie had been summoned in such a manner since he had been removed from *Top Gear*. In the meantime, there had been yet another management restructuring . The only good news was that Rhys Williams had slung his hook.

He had left the BBC for pastures new to take up a middle management position in some faceless computer company or other.

'Managing machines rather than people?' thought Bernie. *'Should be right up his street.'*

On the other hand, he wasn't sure about this new guy, Clive Nosary.

Bernie had always found him a bit of a cold fish - which was probably why his superiors had chosen him for the position.

Nervously, he made his way along the corridor. He wondered if this meeting might also be the scene of his final execution. The office of Deputy MD, Radio 1, was guarded by none other than Prunella de Ville. She was definitely a survivor. When she saw Bernie, she picked up the phone. A brief exchange took place. She hung up and told Bernie,

"You can go in now. Mr Nosary is waiting for you."

Nosary sat at his desk, unsmiling. He peered at Bernie through a pair of tortoiseshell framed glasses, silently motioning for him to take a seat, not taking his eyes off him for an instant. Rhys Williams' disdain had been annoying, but it wasn't half as sinister as Nosary's lizard-like gaze.

"You know why I have called you here?"

"Yes." said Bernie, "But I can…" He was immediately interrupted.

"We'll come to the explanations later. Although I don't see how you can wriggle out of this one."

Bernie kept his mouth shut.

"I find it quite unforgivable that any producer entrusted with safeguarding the reputation of the BBC, and the listening experience of the BBC audience, can allow a stream of the worst obscenities imaginable to be heard by millions on the radio. Not just once, but on multiple occasions."

Bernie sat motionless. Nosary looked down at a piece of paper on his desk,

"On the record in question - which you broadcast - there are twelve instances of an obscene word in each chorus. There are two choruses during the song, and there are multiple, repeated choruses on the fade out."

Nosary looked up, and glared at Bernie.

"In all, you broadcast fifty six instances of the F-word, in quick succession, live, on a Sunday evening. For God's sake!"

By this time, Bernie was getting riled. He managed to restrain himself from chiding Nosary for taking God's name in vain, especially in context with something which had happened on the Sabbath, but he couldn't resist asking,

"You've listened to the record then?"

"Of course not." asserted Nosary. "I had it analysed, forensically," he said, as if dealing with the matter of a dead rat which had just been pulled out of a sewer.

"Oh..." said Bernie. "That's a coincidence. I had it analysed too."

"What are you talking about?" said Nosary, looking completely baffled.

"I take full responsibility for everything that happened last Sunday," offered Bernie, generously.

"Of course you do." growled Nosary.

"We played a white-label, pre-release version of the record. As you know, white labels don't have any artworks, sleeve notes, printed lyrics, or anything like that."

"So?" Nosary was beginning to raise his voice.

"So the only way I could judge the content of the lyrics was to listen to them."

"That's what you're paid for. Isn't it?" snapped Nosary.

Bernie ran his hand across his brow to relieve the tension.

"I went out onto the street, and found fifty people who were willing to take the time to come into my house, one at a time, and listen to the record. Ages ranged from teens to old age pensioners. 47 out of 50 people - that's 94% - said they had no idea what the performers were singing about. The other 6% came up with the same incorrect answer - that they were singing 'Starbuck, Starbuck, Starbuck, Starbuck, Star'. And none of them guessed that the words were actually… Well, you know what they were…"

Bernie tailed off… Nosary took a long pause. He swung round in his chair and stared out of the window… Then, without looking back, he said,

"I'll deal with this later. Just get out!"

*****

For the rest of the week, life was hell. Bernie was living with the Sword of Damocles hanging over him. He found it very difficult to concentrate on his work or get a good night's sleep.

On the Friday, he had still heard nothing, so he decided to risk an official memo to Nosary, enquiring about the status of the matter.

'I might as well find out, sooner rather than later, if I'm for the chop' he thought to himself.

The following Monday, he received a curt reply:

I have decided not to take action at this time. You will continue with your current programme responsibilities. This does not mean you are exonerated. Your transgression is on file. Do not do it again!

Signed

C.Nosary
Deputy MD
Radio 1

'Bastard!' was Bernie's first reaction. *'He's kept me dangling for almost a week now... Bastard!..'*

The anger gradually subsided into relief when it finally sank in that he and Annie were off the hook. He phoned her up to give her the good news.

Having survived that close shave, Annie went on to have a long and glittering career, not just on radio but also on television, presenting the iconic BBC2 TV rock show, *The Old Grey Whistle Test.*

Then a long, long time after her work with Bernie came to an end, she eventually graduated from being the only female DJ on Radio 1 to becoming the longest serving DJ on Radio 1 as well as holding the Guinness World Record for the longest career as a female radio presenter.

What a remarkable illustration of the vagaries of life in the broadcasting business.

*****

Days, weeks and months went by. Bernie was once more in *'the zone'*. He was thankful for a quiet life.

One day, Tony King came into Bernie's office. Tony was tight with la crème de la crème of the music business. He was on affectionate, first name terms with the likes of Freddie Mercury, Elton John, David Bowie and many others, and at that time, he was John Lennon's personal manager. In many people's eyes he was the original *'Tastemaker'*. Tony always cut a very flamboyant figure. Today was no exception.

"To what do I owe the pleasure, Tony?"

"Do I have to have a reason to drop in on an old pal" he countered, good-naturedly.

"Yes." counter-countered Bernie, equally good-naturedly.

"Hands up! You got me!" gestured Tony, charmingly.

Bernie looked at him, shrugging his shoulder in enquiry.

"Did you watch the *Whistle Test* last week?"

"Yeah. John was on it."

"What did you think of the interview?"

"Great! Why?"

"No, come on Bernie! Don't be polite! What exactly did you think?"

Bernie cast his mind back to the interview. In those days stuff went out once on the telly, and that was it. No catch-up services. No video recorders. No replays. So he had to recall from memory the impression that it left on him at the time, rather than pore over the detail on a playback.

"It was just John being John," said Bernie. "The John Lennon we all know and love. Talking about his life in New York. What makes a New Yorker as opposed to an American. His green card problems. The trouble he had making the new album. How all the different Beatles get on with each other these days. The inevitable question about getting back together - or not. I think he dealt with it very well. It all sounded pretty open and honest to me."

He looked at Tony.

"But what's this all about?"

"John's convinced that he came over badly. He can't stop fretting about it. He cares about the people back home. But because he daren't leave America until he gets a green card, he can't visit anyone over here, even for a day or two."

"Can't *you* reassure him about how he came over Tony? There's no-one in the business who's closer to him than you are."

"I've tried. He's still worried about it."

Tony paused.

"Look! Would you do me a favour, and write to him. Tell him how much you enjoyed watching the interview. Say a few of the things you just said to me. It'll make him feel a lot better."

Bernie laughed.

"I haven't seen or heard from John for nearly ten years. He hasn't sent me a postcard since they stopped touring in '66. He won't have a clue who I am."

"He'll know, Bernie. Take it from me. He'll know."

*****

Bernie did what he was asked and wrote to John, by hand, sending it to the address which Tony provided. Also, as requested, he made sure not to mention that Tony had put him up to it.

A couple of weeks later, Bernie opened an airmail letter from the USA, and to his most pleasant surprise found a hand written reply from John inside.

It started off with a conventional, *'Dear Bernie, Thank you very much for the letter…'* and continued in an everyday manner, with a few typically Lennonesque schoolboy howlers thrown in here and there, such as *'…it brought a lump to my throat of which I do not know'*. And it ended, *'Signed, Winston O'Boogie.'*

Bernie found that he too had a lump in his throat.

When he next saw Tony King, Tony thanked him profusely for sending the letter and told him what had happened as a result.

"John was so happy. He said to me, *'Tony, you'll never guess who I had a letter from?'* And I said, *'Who?'* And he said, *'I got a letter from Bernie Andrews about the Old Grey Whistle Test interview.'* And then John said, *'Fancy him remembering me.'* "

313

*****

On the morning of the 9th of December, 1980, Bernie was at home having his breakfast. He switched on the radio to hear the news. The first announcement he heard was:

LAST NIGHT AT 10:52 IN THE EVENING, JOHN LENNON WAS SHOT DEAD OUTSIDE HIS HOME IN NEW YORK

Bernie froze.

*****

Some days later, Andy Peebles came into Bernie's office. Andy had been in New York to interview John Lennon.

John's new album, *Double Fantasy,* had just been released, and John was giving his first interview to the BBC since the *Whistle Test* in 1975. Among many other things, Andy particularly wanted to talk to John about *Starting Over*, as the title of that particular track seemed to reflect John's current state of mind. The interview took place just two days before John was murdered.

Bernie wasn't surprised to see Andy. He had expected to hear from him about the trip. But then Andy told him something he didn't expect.

"We just finished setting up, and John came through, looking friendly and relaxed. When he sat down, the first thing he said to me was,

"How's my mate?"

"Which mate's that?" I said.

314

"Bernie... How's my mate Bernie?"

Bernie couldn't stop a tear rolling down his cheek.

*****

When he was down, Bernie could always rely on his close friends - Jeff Griffin and Jim Waters - if he needed to get things off his chest. And since working with Annie Nightingale, he had found someone else with whom he could share his thoughts.

Annie would often invite him to her home at weekends to join her family and friends. Now and again, she would throw a party. Bernie would show up laden with promotional goodies courtesy of the latest record releases. They were always snapped up quickly.

However, it was clear to those close to him that all was not well. Increasingly, he was prone to brooding over the past. When it came down to it, he could never really forgive those who had stifled his career.

Perhaps, if he had been able to start a new life away from the BBC, things would have gone better. His dogged insistence on sticking it out weighed heavily on him. Although many of his ills were, on the face of it, self-inflicted, that didn't stop his condition from sliding gradually into severe depression. In those days, there was no support in the workplace for people like Bernie. Employees were expected to soldier on without complaint.

Early Retirement

In the end, Bernie's nerves got so bad, that he made enquiries about early retirement on compassionate grounds.

Some years before, his ex-colleague, Jimmy Grant, had successfully requested a similar arrangement, and Bernie's hope was that, given the deteriorating state of his health, he would be able to negotiate an enhanced early pension. Initially, his idea was positively received and he was told that if he persevered until his 50th birthday, in 1983, an amicable arrangement would be found.

In the meantime, efforts were made to encourage him to stay on. Perhaps some belated feelings of guilt were involved? Perhaps there was a concern that the press might get hold of a juicy story? Bernie still had lots of contacts in the media. During one exchange, Clive Nosary invited him to his office.

"Look Bernie, we'd really like you to change your mind, you know. And I'd like to ask if there's anything I can do that might convince you to reconsider."

Bernie looked Clive straight in the eye and said,

"Yes, there is."

"And what is that, Bernie?"

"You can resign."

With hindsight, that was probably not the most diplomatic way of handling things, especially since he needed Nosary on side to get the best retirement deal.

When Bernie's 50th birthday eventually came, he repeated his request for early retirement. Unfortunately, in the meantime, a new BBC Radio Head of Personnel had been transferred in from BBC Television. The reply he got this time around was quite different,

"If he wants to go, he can resign."

This would have meant having to wait ten years to collect a parsimoniously low pension. Once more Bernie felt trapped. Although he hadn't exactly helped the situation through his own erratic behaviour.

In the end, he decided to get the union on side to fight his case. Management fought him every inch of the way, but on final appeal to the Director General of the BBC himself, his appeal was upheld, and he got his wish.

The stress involved almost destroyed him.

*****

It was Saturday the thirteenth of July, 1985. Bernie and Jim had settled themselves down in front of the television. He was living in the suburbs once more. The days of Mayfair and the Beatles were a distant memory.

Bernie checked his watch. On the stroke of the hour, an aerial shot of Wembley Stadium appeared on BBC 2, and Richard Skinner announced,

"It's 12:00 noon in London. 7:00 am in Philadelphia, and around the world it's time for *Live Aid* - 16 hours of live music in aid of famine relief in Africa."

"I hope this lives up to the hype." said Jim.

"Oh ye of little faith!" retorted Bernie.

"Do you know, Bernie, they're estimating that anywhere between one and two billion people across the planet will be watching or listening in to *Live Aid* at some time today?"

"Well, I suppose if your rounding error amounts to a billion people or so, that must be considered some kind of success?" was Bernie's reply. "Of course, it's quite a bit more than the number who listened in to the two minutes' respectful silence for the War Dead at the Cenotaph in 1963. I hope the Fat Controller is duly impressed."

"Do you wish you were there? Producing this extravaganza at Wembley?"

"In principle, yes." said Bernie. "But in reality, I wouldn't be able to cope with the stress. I was always trying to get more studio time so that everyone could relax and take it easy. Until the US end from Philadelphia comes on line later in the day, Jeff Griffin and his guys will be transmitting a stream of bands playing twenty minute sets, one straight after the other. No rehearsals. No sound checks. I can't imagine how they will do it. But if anyone can, they can."

"When I started in production, the studio managers and engineers I had to deal with were mostly a shower of bloody-minded know-alls. Their self-satisfied view was that rock'n'roll was only a fad which would eventually blow over and then everyone could get back to normal: broadcasting orchestras, dance-bands and crap cover versions."

"If you look at the BBC sound crew working on *Live Aid*, between them, they have decades of experience working with the biggest rock bands in the world - sometimes under the most difficult circumstances. Jeff Griffin has been a great mentor. Chris Lycett, who's helping him with the production today, took over *In Concert* from Tony Wilson when he moved on to produce the *Friday Rock Show*. And those guys have passed on their expertise by word of mouth. There's no *BBC Academy for Recording Rock Bands*, or anything like that. Everyone in that crew is self-motivated. The rest of them - Mike Robinson, Dave Dade, Mark Farrar, John Birtwistle and Mike Walters - have learned their trade by watching and listening to their predecessors."

"The only one who I think is missing is John Etchells. After he recorded the first Queen session with me, he left the BBC to go freelance. He ended up recording albums for Queen, Bad Company and George Harrison, among others. I'm sure John would love to be at Wembley today."

"Of course the other big improvement is the equipment. Luddites like Rhys Williams no longer have a say in things they know nothing about. The BBC sound trucks here today are state of the art. The very latest SSL computer controlled sound consoles are hooked up to the most advanced 24-track tape recorders. I could have done with all that stuff when John and I recorded Queen in The Langham in 1973."

"And all the music today will be archived. There's no way that Jeff will let anything happen to the master tapes. They will all be saved. Times have changed."

Just then, the fanfare sounded for Prince Charles and Princess Diana as they took their places in the Wembley Stadium Royal Box.

"Royal fanfares, eh?" chortled Bernie. "Twenty years ago, the older generation dismissed rock music as a load of old rubbish. I hope they are all tuned in now, bowing and scraping. It's our generation of rock stars who are the royalty now."

Status Quo kicked off with *Rockin' All Over The World*, and Bernie breathed a sigh of relief. Perfect start! As he predicted, Jeff Griffin's team did a brilliant job. The afternoon progressed with few hiccups. Then Queen took the stage. Bernie and Jim sat, entranced, as Freddie & Co stole the show. After their set, Jim turned to Bernie,

"Twelve years ago, you gave those guys a break on the radio. The record companies didn't want to know until your session was broadcast on the *John Peel Show*. How do you feel now?"

"It gives me a buzz, Jim. The whole thing gives me a buzz. Not just Queen. And it's not just down to me. Jimmy Grant started it with *Saturday Club*. He took me under his wing and I moved from there on to *Top Gear*. After I was taken off it, John Peel carried on and became a national institution, and Jeff did for live concerts what I did for studio sessions. And so it went on."

"The reason that *Live Aid* is going so well is because Jeff's been working with practically all the UK bands appearing on *Live Aid* today since 1970. Then when BBC 2 realised that the Jeff's *In Concert* audio was so well produced, they started bringing their cameras along to his concerts. The whole thing morphed into the *Sight and Sound* series - BBC TV pictures transmitted simultaneously with BBC Radio stereo sound. The entire BBC production team at Wembley today got their training for *Live Aid* on *Sight and Sound*."

"That's admirable Bernie," said Jim. "It's good of you to share the credit around.

But you and I both know you did a hell of a lot to change people's attitudes to rock music at the BBC. You were the one who fought hardest for new talent to get reasonable working conditions, and to bring them to audiences who were neglected or ignored. The bands might have forgotten, and the audiences might not realise it, but they've got a lot to thank you for. In the process, you made your bosses lives a misery, and in the end, you paid for it - with your career and your health."

"Whatever." said Bernie, shrugging his shoulders. "Fancy a cup of tea?"

*****

When the Philadelphia end of *Live Aid* came on stream later in the day, Annie Nightingale popped up as the BBC's sole anchor person on the other side of the Atlantic.

"Yet another graduate from the Bernie Andrews *Academy of Rock*," Jim quipped.

"Hardly," said Bernie. "Lovely Annie. She was broadcasting long before I started working with her, and is still going strong. She's been a good friend to me, and I'm sure she'll be going for a long time yet."

*****

Early in 1994, Bernie was contacted by BBC Enterprises. They wanted to know if he had any Beatles' BBC session tapes stashed away. In fact, he had kept the original tapes of all of their *Saturday Club* appearances. He had produced all of those himself. He had also recorded lots of other Beatles sessions from a variety of BBC Radio broadcasts which had been produced by others.

"Did you give them back to the BBC then?" asked Jim.

"Yes."

"How much are you getting for them?"

"The square root of fuck all!"

"Christ, Bernie! You gave them back for nothing?"

"Yes."

"Left to their own devices, those bastards would have wiped all your Beatles recordings as a matter of course - to recycle the tapes - for what? Just to save a few bob. The only reason they survive is because *you 'disobeyed orders'* and took them home. Something you might have got sacked for if the wrong person had heard about it. Surely you could have demanded some sort of fee for looking after them?"

"The problem with being the employee of any company, Jim, is that the results of any work you do for them immediately becomes the company's property - whether that's inventing a new type of bog-roll, or producing tapes for a Beatles session. Unless your employment contract says otherwise. I had a standard employment contract with no exceptions to say that I should be entitled to any payments for returning property to them which I stole from them in the first place."

"What, not even a reward?"

"Nothing."

"Well, if it was down to me, I would have told them that I'd thrown them away."

"What good would that have done? I'd still end up with nothing."

"But what good has it done you to give them back?"

"Nothing in material terms. But the reason they were made in the first place was to give the kids a chance to hear a great new band called the Beatles. And the reason I kept them was because I thought that in the future, people would be interested in hearing them again. So, it would be kind of perverse if I just denied all knowledge and sat on them. That wouldn't do anyone any good. In any case, in those days, the Beatles were my mates and I wouldn't want to let them down."

"Can't you ask *them* for something?"

"I wouldn't know how to go about asking them. I've got Brian Epstein's phone number from 1964, and he's long dead. If I wrote to them now, some minder or other is going to filter my letter out thinking I'm a crank. It would be in the rubbish bin as soon as they read it. In any case, I really don't fancy grovelling to people who were my friends, begging for a few scraps off the table. Not my style."

Live at the BBC by The Beatles sold eight million copies during its first year of release.

*****

The millennium came and went. Bernie's BBC pension, which could never be described as generous, allowed him to keep body and soul together in a reasonably comfortable manner. But he was always looking for ways to supplement it.

He had an amazing collection of 45 rpm singles - every UK single released by every UK record company from 1958 until the day he retired. Eventually, he decided to raise some money by putting his collection on the market. Fortunately, Elton John expressed an interest, and, being Elton, paid a very generous amount in exchange.

Bernie was delighted. He kept the proceeds in his holiday fund - for special treats.

He had already given the BBC his Beatles tapes for nothing, and they had made a fortune out of them, so eventually, they asked if he had any other BBC archive material sitting in his vault.

He said he had, and gave them the details (including the never-transmitted version of the Animals' *House of the Rising Sun*). They made an offer for the job lot based on a *'warehousing fee'*. Bernie decided, *'Why not?'* He could do with a few more treats, like a holiday in Spain and getting his roof fixed. On the day they were due to do the deal, the BBC phoned up and said that, on reflection, Bernie's collection was only worth half of what they had originally offered. Bernie's retort was,

"Fuck off!"

Instead, Bernie gave his tapes to John Beecher, a record promoter he had known since his early days. By this time, John was running a specialist record company, and was confident that he could help Bernie exploit his amazing collection of tapes.

In the course of helping him out, John, his wife Sandi, and Bernie became close friends. John would often call and tell him what had become of his recordings, and Bernie found himself being adopted by John's family. It was a happy outcome for Bernie. On one occasion, John and Sandi even took Bernie with them on a holiday to Spain.

Bernie was growing old and unwell. He was suffering from a nervous disease which caused an uncontrollable tremor when he stood for too long. During these episodes, Bernie, cantankerous at the best of times, became even more so.

When they were flying out to Spain, John and Sandi arranged for a wheelchair so that Bernie didn't have to stand up for too long. On arriving at the door of the plane, Bernie got out of the chair. Unfortunately, there was a delay, and Bernie remained standing for some considerable period. On seeing this, Sandi observed, encouragingly,

"You see, Bernie! You can do it!"

For her pains, she received the death stare from Bernie.

*****

By his own admission, Bernie knew he could be a pain in the arse. But for John and Sandi Beecher, the bright parts far outshone the dark.

Then, one day in 2010, John called by to see how Bernie was doing. He was getting frail, and his medication caused him to stammer. Sometimes he would muddle his words or even misremember things. It wasn't dementia, because when the inconsistencies were pointed out to him, he would more often than not agree that he had mixed up his thoughts and words.

Perhaps, for this reason, Bernie was keen to talk about the past. Perhaps he wanted to prove to himself that he wasn't *'going gaga?'*.

"How long have we known each other John?"

"Oh, I don't know. Since the early 60s?"

"Yeah… I remember you knocking on my door when I started as a producer."

John nodded.

"You seemed ever so surprised when I invited you in... Even more surprised when I was interested in hearing the records you were plugging."

"Well, yes... In those days, if I knocked on a BBC producer's door and stuck my head round the door, they would more often than not tell me to *'fuck off!'* I even got escorted off the premises a couple of times for not having an appointment."

Bernie laughed.

"Some of the bastards would look at me, pick up the record I had left for them, and take great delight in dropping it into the waste-paper basket. And there was one guy who took the record out of its sleeve and threw it at me like a Frisbee. Nearly took me head off."

Bernie laughed again, and then coughed a bit when the laughter became too much.

"Yes, those guys were proper BBC producers. Respect!"

John changed the subject.

"What happened to Jim Waters then? He hasn't been around for a while."

Bernie looked sad. He paused, thoughtfully.

"He won't talk to me any more."

"Why not?"

"We fell out."

"What about?"

"I don't want to talk about it."

And that was that. John knew that Jim had been a close friend for the greater part of Bernie's life. John knew it was a tragedy. But they never spoke of Jim again.

"I really feel my age now," said Bernie.

John nodded.

"I might even sell up and go to Spain. At least the winters are bearable over there."

John nodded again.

"I don't think I can get through another winter here."

He didn't.

Bernie died on June the 11th, 2010.

*****

Author's note: *I wanted to close with more words from **The Pretender** by **Jackson Browne**. The song has an appropriate Gospel feel to it. However, I couldn't get clearance from the publisher. The 12th to 15th lines begin, 'I've been aware…' and end, '…greater awakening'. And then I wanted to quote the last few words from the start of the final refrain. They start, 'Are you there?…' and end '…only to surrender.' If you can, Google them. They're quite poignant, and always make me think of Bernie.*

Radio producer who helped music's biggest names record their first BBC sessions - by Annie Nightingale

I Produced Their First Session was the title of the book that Bernie Andrews never got around to writing. Mention any popular music name of distinction from the 1960s and 70s and Bernie, who has died aged 76, would say, "I did their first session", meaning he had produced their first – and crucial – BBC radio recording. Bernie would often work into the small hours to produce the best performance possible, and he allowed the musicians to overrun their strictly allotted studio time. He then sensibly, and with great foresight, took the master tapes home and hid them from the sort of BBC bureaucracy that became infamous for "wiping" tapes for the sake of economy.

The Beatles, the Rolling Stones, Jimi Hendrix, David Bowie, T Rex, Fairport Convention and many others had Bernie to thank. He often booked double sessions so that the young and mostly impecunious musicians could make better use of precious BBC recording time. According to Bernie's friend and fellow producer Jeff Griffin, the Rolling Stones had failed their first BBC radio audition, but Bernie foiled the corporation by booking them as a backing band for Bo Diddley. He then recorded some of the band's own numbers and sent the results to the Audition Unit as a "trial broadcast". This time the Stones passed the test – a necessary box for them, at that moment, to tick.

Bernie grew up in Eltham, south-east London. After doing his national service in the RAF, and working as a Post Office telephone engineer, he joined the BBC in 1957 as a technical operator. He became a producer, having proven that he had a huge empathy and understanding of music and broadcasters.

Before Radio 1 was launched in 1967, Bernie produced Saturday Club on the Light Programme, one of the few shows on the network to feature pop music. Bernie's frequent booking of the Beatles in their early days was a significant step for them, which they did not forget. For Saturday Club's fifth anniversary show, in 1963, Bernie lined up the Beatles, the Everly Brothers and Kenny Ball's Jazzmen, among many others, and overspent the budget on performers from the permitted £310 to a scandalous £483, 12 shillings and sixpence. Bernie also entertained the Beatles in their early days at his flat in Shepherds Market in Mayfair, west London, and they kept in touch with him, sending him letters and tour postcards throughout their career.

Bernie effectively launched the BBC career of John Peel. He championed John's early Top Gear broadcasts, and fought to keep him as a presenter when not all of the BBC management was keen to do so. Bernie was John's first producer, nurturing his abilities as a DJ and broadcaster, before John's long-running partnership with John Walters began.

Bernie was a sort of guerrilla figure within the BBC. He became my producer in the early 70s, after Radio 1 had deliberately broken up the partnership between Bernie and John Peel. Why? The BBC seemed not to approve of too close a partnership between producer and presenter. I had only recently been allowed on to the previously all-male Radio 1.

Sexism was still rife, and Bernie helped enormously to build my confidence and my abilities. He kept an aquarium full of goldfish in his office to calm him and counteract his frequent angry run-ins with the management. He also partook of the odd jazz cigarette, smoked surreptitiously under his desk, with the windows wide open.

Bernie built up a huge record library, at one time owning a collection of every 45rpm pop record released in Britain since 1958.

He lived for music. He worked non-stop. I used to refer laughingly to his nine-to-five existence – 9pm to 5am. He would call me at home at all hours, not that I minded, to discuss the finer points of a programme running order, or to agonise over which record we were going to drop because of time constraints.

We were always getting into trouble for playing songs with dubious lyrics. When the Rolling Stones released Goats Head Soup in 1973, I listened to the album in Bernie's office and then played some tracks on a live Radio 1 show the same night. One was called Star Star. Its chorus, absolutely not obvious unless you had it pointed out, repeated the words "star fucker" several times. When this came to light, it was Bernie as producer who was carpeted.

Bernie prepared his defence thus: he took the LP back to his then home, in Wraysbury, Middlesex, and invited passers-by – total strangers – into his house, saying: "Please can you have a listen to this song and tell me if you can hear any, well, 'rude' words in the lyrics?" Not one of his "focus group" could detect any offending words in Mick Jagger's vocal. But Bernie stood to be fired over this incident, and it took several weeks, and a lot of anguish on his part, before he was exonerated.

Bernie was dedicated to his calling as a producer and extremely conscientious. During the spell of my request show on Radio 1, in pre-email days, he would scrutinise every letter and card that had been sent in. If he was suspicious that a record was being requested rather too much, he would track down the requestee, phone them, and then give them a good grilling to ensure this was not a record company employee trying to get a free plug. But eventually the rebelliousness of his personality to the more corporate aspects of the BBC proved incompatible. Bernie took early retirement in 1984 and lived in Spain and in Dorset.

John Peel, myself and other Radio 1 broadcasters fortunate enough to have worked with Bernie are indebted to him. He built our careers with the most dedicated altruism. He had a Goonish sense of humour and was a celebrated eccentric. He took lightbulbs back to John Lewis's department store if he considered they had not fulfilled their life span. He once insisted on helping a man with a white stick across Oxford Street. The man eventually convinced Bernie that he had 20:20 vision, did not wish to cross Oxford Street and was just trying to carry home a new broom handle.

On one occasion, when a group of guests arrived at Bernie's home, they included a poised and beautiful woman who told him she was a singer. He sat her down and gave her advice about her future career. He had not recognised her as the already highly successful Marianne Faithfull.

There is an apocryphal story, recounted by himself, of Bernie producing a session with Stevie Wonder. The cue light in a BBC studio signifying "ready to record" is traditionally green. Bernie is reputed to have said to Wonder, blind almost since birth, "When you're ready, Stevie, on the green."

Bernie is survived by his brothers John and David.

Bernard Oliver Andrews
radio producer
born 17 August 1933
died 11 June 2010

*****

Printed in Great Britain
by Amazon

46646123R00192